Holt MUSIC

TEXAS TEACHER'S EDITION Grade 8

Eunice Boardman Meske
Professor of Music and Education
University of Wisconsin—Madison
Madison, Wisconsin

Barbara Andress
Professor of Music Education
Arizona State University
Tempe, Arizona

Mary P. Pautz
Assistant Professor of Music
  Education
University of Wisconsin—Milwaukee
Milwaukee, Wisconsin

Fred Willman
Associate Professor of Music and
  Education
University of Missouri—St. Louis
St. Louis, Missouri

Special Texas Edition Contributor
Jack Noble White
Texas Boys Choir
Forth Worth, Texas

Holt Music

The Program To Count On When Performance Counts

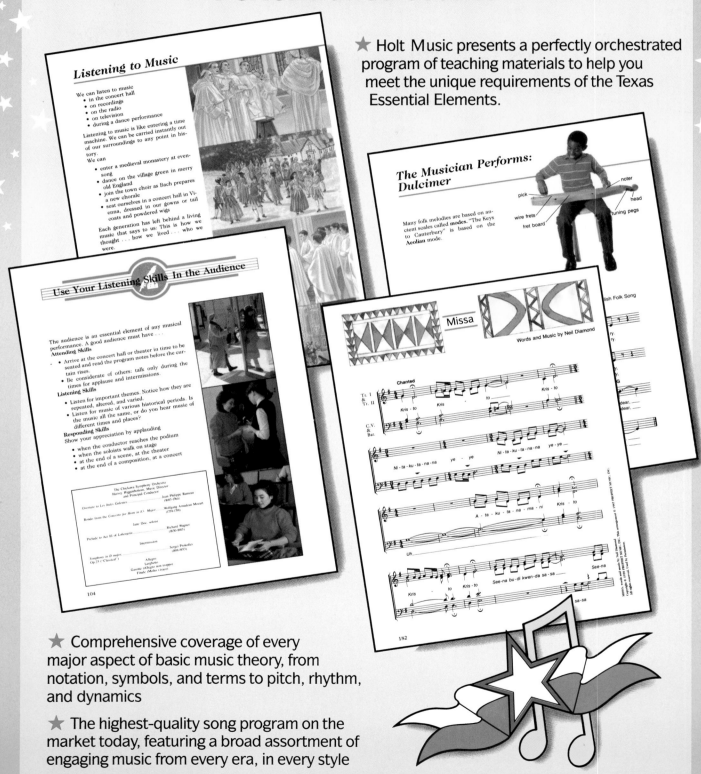

★ Holt Music presents a perfectly orchestrated program of teaching materials to help you meet the unique requirements of the Texas Essential Elements.

★ Comprehensive coverage of every major aspect of basic music theory, from notation, symbols, and terms to pitch, rhythm, and dynamics

★ The highest-quality song program on the market today, featuring a broad assortment of engaging music from every era, in every style

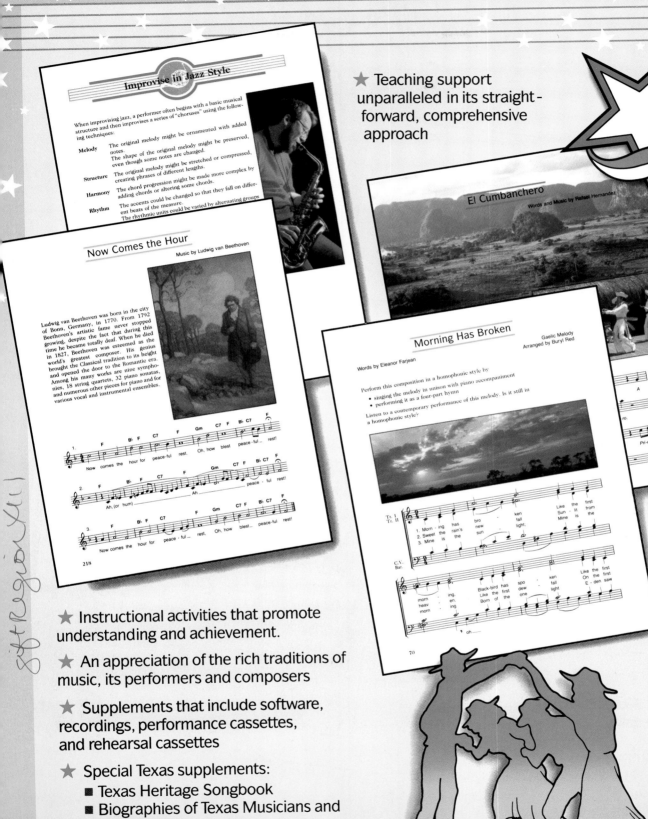

★ Teaching support unparalleled in its straight-forward, comprehensive approach

Improvise in Jazz Style

When improvising jazz, a performer often begins with a basic musical structure and then improvises a series of "choruses" using the following techniques:

Melody — The original melody might be ornamented with added notes.
The shape of the original melody might be preserved, even though some notes are changed.

Structure — The original melody might be stretched or compressed, creating phrases of different lengths.

Harmony — The chord progression might be made more complex by adding chords or altering some chords.

Rhythm — The accents could be changed so that they fall on different beats of the measure.
The rhythmic units could be varied by alternating groups.

El Cumbanchero

Words and Music by Rafael Hernandez

Now Comes the Hour

Music by Ludwig van Beethoven

Ludwig van Beethoven was born in the city of Bonn, Germany, in 1770. From 1792 Beethoven's artistic fame never stopped growing, despite the fact that during this time he became totally deaf. When he died in 1827, Beethoven was esteemed as the world's greatest composer. His genius brought the Classical tradition to its height and opened the door to the Romantic era. Among his many works are nine symphonies, 18 string quartets, 32 piano sonatas, and numerous other pieces for piano and for various vocal and instrumental ensembles.

218

Morning Has Broken

Gaelic Melody
Arranged by Buryl Red

Words by Eleanor Farjean

Perform this composition in a homophonic style by
• singing the melody in unison with piano accompaniment
• performing it as a four-part hymn

Listen to a contemporary performance of this melody. Is it still in a homophonic style?

70

★ Instructional activities that promote understanding and achievement.

★ An appreciation of the rich traditions of music, its performers and composers

★ Supplements that include software, recordings, performance cassettes, and rehearsal cassettes

★ Special Texas supplements:
■ Texas Heritage Songbook
■ Biographies of Texas Musicians and Composers
■ Unit Tests designed for the Texas Essential Elements
■ Music Evaluations correlated to the Texas Essential Elements

Exciting Songs And Activities

Quality songs from every era form the basis for developing true understanding of music theory.

Pages and pages of fun-to-do activities help students develop their vocal and instrumental skills.

A clear and effective note-reading program gives thorough attention to musical literacy — understanding the great staff, key and time signatures, and more. Top quality recordings develop and clarify these concepts.

Listening lessons help students to recognize the unique sounds of a variety of instruments. Many of them also ask students to apply critical thinking skills in analyzing music, comparing and contrasting, and choosing alternatives.

Activities are exciting, involving, and fun for individual students, small groups, or the entire class.

LISTENING

Prelude to Act III from *Lohengrin*

by Richard Wagner

Richard Wagner (1813–1883) was one of the most important composers of the Romantic era. Wagner devoted most of his life to composing operas. He regarded opera as a total art work encompassing music, drama, and visual art. Wagner's opera *Lohengrin* is representative of certain aspects of music from the Romantic era. The large symphony orchestra of the late nineteenth century. The prominent use of brass and percussion instruments, the chromatic melodic lines set in very high registers, and the dramatic climaxes add to the emotional quality of this truly romantic music.

1. The prelude opens with the vigorous "Festival Theme," played *fortissimo* by the entire orchestra and punctuated by crashes of cymbals. Notice the **chromatic** nature of the melody. The "Festival Theme" is stated twice.

The **tone color** of the French horns makes the introduction of the "March Theme" especially imposing.

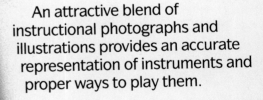

The Musician Performs: Guitar

Learn how to "pick" folk tunes on the guitar.

Playing Position
Hold the guitar comfortably and securely. Rest your left foot on a foot rest or a small coffee can. Place the guitar so that there are four points of contact with the body:
1. Underneath the right forearm
2. Against the chest
3. Inside the right knee
4. On the left knee

If you are holding the guitar correctly, your right hand will fall directly in front of you.

Your body should be vertically aligned, and your shoulders level. Slant the guitar so that the head is slightly higher than your shoulders.

Hand Positions
• Place the thumb on the back of the guitar neck to provide balance and support for fingers pressing down on the strings.
• Press strings with fingertips to avoid touching adjacent strings.
• Fingers on the left hand are numbered in this order:

124

An attractive blend of instructional photographs and illustrations provides an accurate representation of instruments and proper ways to play them.

Teacher's Edition

Coming Through With More For You

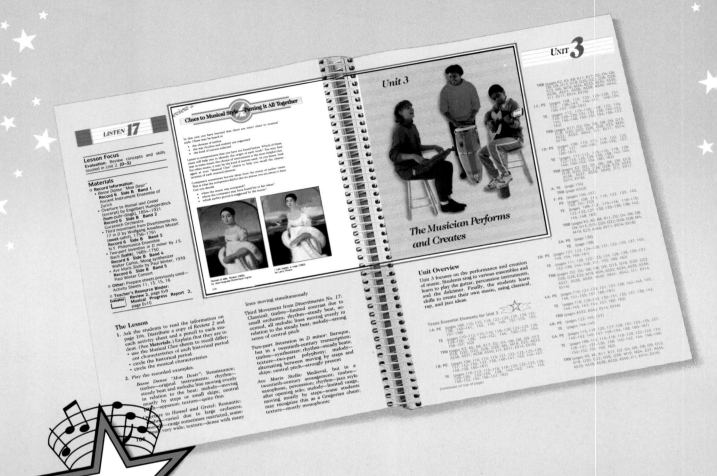

Unit Openers make lesson planning easy by identifying — with page references — the Texas Essential Elements taught in the units.

In the first lesson of each lesson group, a special logo highlights Essential Elements to be taught.

Lesson Focus pinpoints the concept about to be covered. The program offers a full introduction to music theory.

Materials include recordings with first-quality selections from every major musical period.

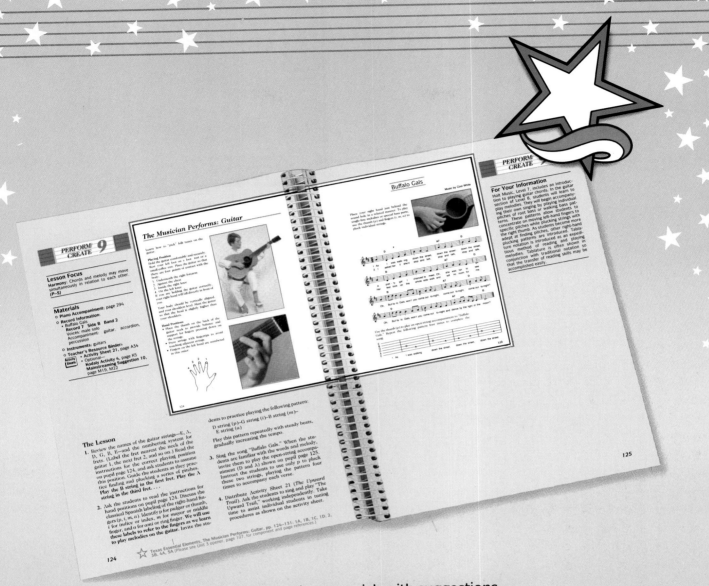

Lesson plans are rich with suggestions for individual, small-group, and large-group performances. Activities provide both instrumental and vocal applications.

Hands-on experience enables students to become familiar with the characteristics and sounds of a wide variety of instruments.

Opportunities abound for students to truly develop their singing ability — with step-by-step teaching help in guiding their breathing, diction, and tone production.

Optional activities enable students to further enrich their musical skills as performers and as audience.

Supplementary Materials

Tailor-Made For Texas Needs

Texas Heritage Songbook

You'll find a wealth of music to spark enthusiasm and pride in every student in your class. The collection includes a host of contemporary and traditional songs that truly reflect the diversity of the Lone Star State.

The Teacher's Resource Binder, Texas Edition

The Texas TRB features eleven supplemental booklets, including these special Texas components:

★ **Tests for the Texas Essential Elements** a complete set of tests designed to meet the objectives of the Texas Essential Elements

★ **Correlated Music Evaluations** Checkpoints, Reviews, and Musical Progress Reports correlated to the Texas Essential Elements

★ **Biographies of Texas Musicians and Composers** four biographies of celebrated Texas composers and musicians

The Lesson Cycle

HOLT MUSIC helps music educators fulfill their teaching goals by providing teaching strategies that correspond to those steps contained in the Lesson Cycle.* The result is quality planning, teaching, and learning.

[A] Planning and Focus on Objective — to solicit student attention; to generate and motivate learner interest

[B] Explanation/Check Understanding — information presented through a variety of formats

[C] Guided Practice to Check Mastery — an opportunity for students and teacher to evaluate together how well the lesson has been comprehended so far

[D] Independent Practice — an opportunity for students to evaluate independently how well they have comprehended the lesson

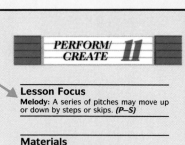

PERFORM/CREATE 11

Lesson Focus
Melody: A series of pitches may move up or down by steps or skips. *(P–S)*

Materials
○ **Piano Accompaniments:** pages 298, 299
○ **Record Information:**
  • Can the Circle Be Unbroken?
    Record 7 Side B Band 5
    Voices: mixed voices
    Accompaniment: guitar, piano, percussion
  • The Cruel War
    Record 7 Side B Band 6
    Voices: female solo
    Accompaniment: guitar, harp
○ **Instruments:** guitars
○ **Teacher's Resource Binder:**
  Activity Sheets • **Activity Sheet 23,** page A36
  • **Activity Sheet 24,** page A37
  • Optional—
    Orff Activities 4, 13, pages O8, O28

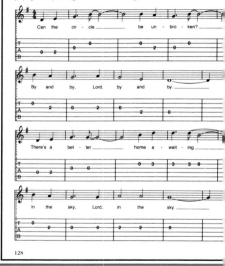

Can the Circle Be Unbroken?

Adapted and Arranged by [

Use the rest stroke.

The rest stroke is performed by pulling your finger toward you across one string and coming to rest on the next. Follow the tablature to learn this melody. Use the rest stroke. Alternate fingers *i* and *m* when playing. Make your fingers "walk" on the strings.

Can the cir - cle be un - bro - ken?

By and by, Lord, by and by.

There's a bet - ter home a - wait - ing

In the sky, Lord, in the sky.

128

The Lesson
1. Play the recording for "Can the Circle Be Unbroken?" and "The Cruel War." Learn to sing these songs. When the students are very familiar with these melodies, they may begin learning to play them on the guitar.

2. Ask the students to open their books to page 128. Demonstrate the "rest stroke" technique. Use fingers *i* and *m*. Make these fingers "walk" slowly on the high E string four times. After each "step," the finger should rest on the B string. Repeat this on the B string with fingers coming to rest on the G string. Invite the students to continue to practice the "rest stroke" by repeating this sequence on the D and A strings.

3. Ask the students to read and play the tablature for "Can the Circle Be Unbroken?" Use the rest stroke technique.

128

4. Before continuing, instruct the stude practice alternating fingers *i* and *m* aga lowing the notation on page 129.

5. Ask the students to read and play the ture for "The Cruel War." Alternate si and playing this melody until all three v have been completed. All the students play, or individual guitarists may be sel to play the melody as an instrumenta between verses.

6. Extend the students' repertoire by distrib Activity Sheet 23 (*Aura Lee*). Encourag students to learn to play this song on own. They will find this melody challe because the ring finger is used to play the fret. They will need to stretch their finge ther to reach this fret.

7. Invite the students to transcribe a song

* The Lesson Cycle, from MODEL FOR EFFECTIVE TEACHING AND SUPERVISION by Jim Boyd. Copyright 1985, Jim Boyd.

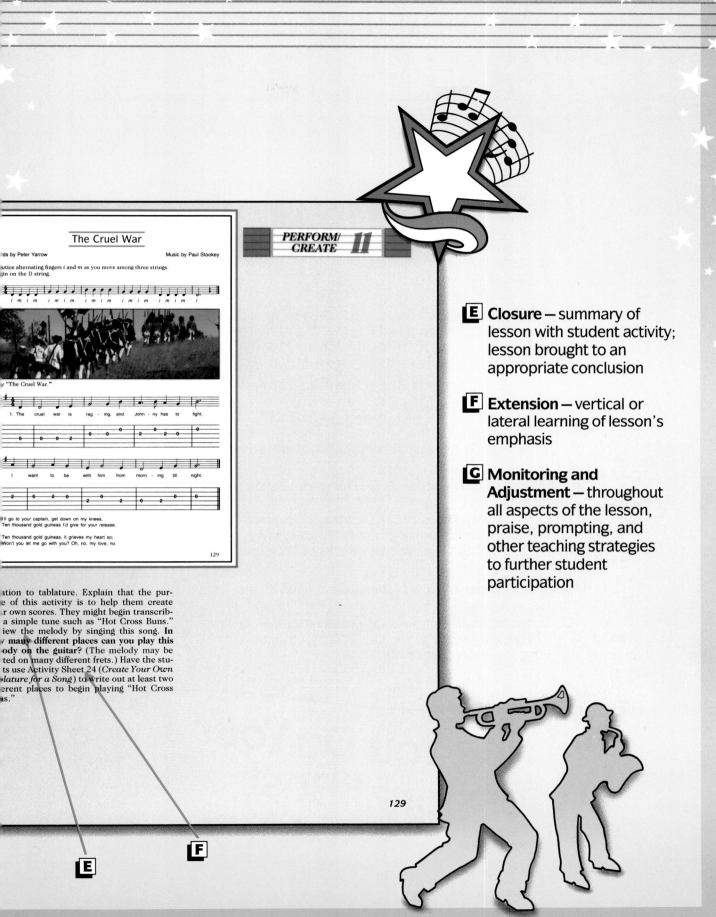

The Cruel War

...rds by Peter Yarrow

Music by Paul Stookey

...ctice alternating fingers *i* and *m* as you move among three strings.
...gin on the D string.

i m i m   i m i m   i m i m   i m i m   i m i m   i

..."The Cruel War."

1. The cruel war is rag - ing, and John - ny has to fight,
   I want to be with him from morn - ing till night.

...'ll go to your captain, get down on my knees,
Ten thousand gold guineas I'd give for your release.

Ten thousand gold guineas, it grieves my heart so;
...Won't you let me go with you? Oh, no, my love, no.

129

...ation to tablature. Explain that the pur-
...e of this activity is to help them create
...r own scores. They might begin transcrib-
... a simple tune such as "Hot Cross Buns."
...iew the melody by singing this song. **In**
...v many different places can you play this
...ody on the guitar? (The melody may be
...ted on many different frets.) Have the stu-
...ts use Activity Sheet 24 (*Create Your Own*
...lature for a Song) to write out at least two
...erent places to begin playing "Hot Cross
...s."

PERFORM/ CREATE **11**

E **Closure** — summary of lesson with student activity; lesson brought to an appropriate conclusion

F **Extension** — vertical or lateral learning of lesson's emphasis

G **Monitoring and Adjustment** — throughout all aspects of the lesson, praise, prompting, and other teaching strategies to further student participation

F

E

129

Texas Essential Elements For Music

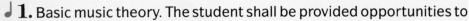

♩**1.** Basic music theory. The student shall be provided opportunities to
   a. know and use the great staff
   b. know and use pitch and rhythmic notation
   c. know and use musical symbols and terms
   d. know and use common keys and time signatures
   e. recognize intervals
   f. use dynamics

♩**2.** Singing techniques. The student shall be provided opportunities to develop and use the singing voice, including basic principles of proper breathing, diction, and tone production.

♩**3.** Study of instruments. The student shall be provided opportunities to
   a. learn about the history and development of musical instruments
   b. recognize the instruments by sight and sound

♩**4.** Music history and literature. The student shall be provided opportunities to
   a. hear and discuss works from all major musical periods, including the music of contemporary life
   b. learn about the lives and works of selected composers

♩**5.** Performance activities. The student shall be provided opportunities to
   a. participate in individual, small ensemble, or large-group performances of vocal or instrumental music
   b. practice audience etiquette

Helping You Do Your Professional Best

Texas Essential Elements Planning Guide

Unit	Lesson Groups	Essential Elements	PE Pages	TE Pages	TRB Pages
1	The Many Roles (pp. 6–30)	1A	7–9; 11–13; 20–21	8; 11; 15; 17; 19; 20–21; 24	K2; K5; K8; E2; M4; AS8; AS16; AS19; I2; I3; I24; EV2
		1B	7–9; 11–13; 20–21	8; 11; 15; 17; 19–21; 23–24	K2; K5; K8; E2; M4; M6; AS5; AS6; AS7; AS8; AS16; AS19; I2; I3; I24; EV2
		1C	7–13; 16; 19–23	8; 11; 15–16; 19; 21; 23–24	M11; I2; I3; I24; EV2
		1D	7; 11; 20–21; 23	8; 11; 15; 19–21; 24	M6; M9; AS6; AS8; AS16; AS19; I2; I3; I24; EV2
		1F	10; 19		
		2	7–9; 20	8; 11; 14–15; 17–20; 24	K5; M4; M9; AS5; AS7
		3B	21; 23	21; 23–24	M4; M9; AS16; AS19; I2; I3; I24
		4A	7; 10–13; 23	8; 11; 14; 16; 23–24; 28	AS20
		4B		10; 14; 28	
		5A	7–9; 19; 20; 22	8; 11; 14–15; 17–21; 24	K5; E5; M4; M9; AS5; AS8; AS16; AS18; I2; I3; I24
		5B			E13
1	Planning and Producing a Musical Event (pp. 31–50)	1A	33–37	33; 40–41; 51	I7
		1B	33–37	33; 40–41; 51	I7; EV6
		1C	32–33; 48	40–41; 48	M11; AS21; I7; EV5; EV6
		1D	33–34	33; 40–41; 51	I7; EV6
		1F			EV5; EV6
		2	34–38	33; 39–41; 51	
		3B	33	33; 40–41; 49	AS21; I7
		4A	33; 48–49	32–33; 39–41; 48; 50	M11; AS21; EV6
		4B	49	49	B1; AS21
		5A	32–38	33; 39–41; 51	I7
		5B	39–49		E2; EV5; EV6
2	Listening Skills (pp. 52–73)	1A	58–60; 68; 70–71	59; 69–70	K17; E15; M14; I7
		1B	58–61; 66–68; 70–71	56–57; 59; 61–66; 70; 73	K17; E15; M14; AS23; AS24; AS28; I7
		1C	56–63; 66–68; 70–71	52; 56–61; 63; 65–66; 69–73	K17; E15; M14; AS22; AS23; AS24; AS28; AS29; I7; EV7; EV9
		1D	58–59; 68; 70	59; 61; 70; 73	K17; E15; M14; I7
		1E	62	63–64	
		1F	56; 59–61	52; 57; 59–61; 73	E15; AS23
		2	61; 70	60; 70–73	K17; E15; M14
		3A	56–57; 64	56–57; 59	
		3B	56–59; 70	56–59; 73	E15; M14; AS22; I7; EV7
		4A	52; 56–71	52–53; 56–66; 69–73	K17; E15; AS22; AS23; AS24; AS25; AS26; AS27; AS28; AS29; EV7; EV9
		4B	53–55; 58–59; 61; 64–65; 69; 72–73	52; 59; 69–70; 73	B5; B3; B7; E15
		5A	70–71	61; 70–73	E15; M14; I7
2	Music and Drama (pp. 74–106)	1A		93–95	
		1B		93–95; 106–107	AS30
		1C	81	74–76; 93–95; 106–107	AS30; AS31

		1D		93–95	
		1E		106–107	
		1F		106–107	
		2		83; 93–95	
		3A	75		E15
		3B	75	75–76	E15; AS31
		4A	74–76; 81–82; 106	74–76; 82–84; 93–94; 106–107	AS30; AS31
		4B	82; 93	75–76; 83–84; 93–94	B9
		5A	81	83; 93–95	
		5B	104; 105	104–105	
3	The Musician Sings (pp. 108–123)	1A	108; 110; 115; 119; 122–123	110–112; 115–116; 118–120; 122–123	K2; K5; O6; O13; O18; O20; O22; M4; M19; AS33; I11
		1B	108; 110; 115; 119; 121–123	110–112; 115–116; 118–120; 122–123	K2; K5; K11; O6; O13; O18; O20; O22; M4; M19; AS33; I11
		1C	108; 115; 123	112; 115–116; 118; 122	O6; O13; O18; O20; O22; AS32; AS33; I11
		1D	108; 110; 115; 119; 122	111–112; 115–116; 118; 120; 122–123	K2; O6; O13; O18; O20; O22; AS33; I11
		2	108; 115; 119; 122	108–112; 115–116; 118–119; 122–123	K2; K5; K11; O6; O13; O18; O20; O22; M4; M19
		3B	121; 123	111; 120; 122–123	O6; O13; O18; O20; O22; M19; AS32; I11
		4A	119; 121–123	118; 120–122	AS32
		4B	122		
		5A	115; 119	108–112; 115–116; 118–120; 122–123	K5; K11; O6; O13; O18; O20; O22; M19;I11
3	The Musician Performs: Guitar (pp. 124–131)	1A	125; 129; 131	126; 129–130	K5; K8; O8; O26; O28; AS36; AS37; AS38; EV11
		1B	125–129; 131	126; 129–130	K5; K8; K11; O8; O26; O28; AS34; AS35; AS36; AS37; AS38; EV11
		1C	125–128; 131	124; 126; 128–129; 131	O8; O26; O28; EV11
		1D	125; 129; 131	126; 129–130	O8; O26; O28; AS36; AS37; AS38; EV11
		2		127–130	K5; K8; K11; O8; O26; O28; EV11
		3B	124–129; 131	124; 126; 128; 130–131	O8; O26; O28; M19; AS34; AS35; AS36; AS37; AS38
		4A	131	130–131	
		5A	125; 127–129; 131	124; 126–131	K5; K8; K11; O8; O26; O28; M19; AS34; AS35; AS36; AS38
3	The Musician Performs: Percussion (pp. 132–137)	1A			K8
		1B	132–135; 137	132–135	K8; AS39
		1C	132	132	
		2	135	135–136	K8
		3A	136		
		3B	132–135; 137	132–136	AS39

Unit		Lesson Groups	Essential Elements	PE Pages	TE Pages	TRB Pages
			4A	137	135; 137	
			5A	133–135; 137	132–136	K8; AS39
3		**The Musician Performs: Dulcimer** (pp. 138–143)	1A	138; 140–141; 143	138; 142	K17; O2; O4; O9; E23; AS40
			1B	138; 140–141; 143	138; 140–142	K17; O2; O4; O9; E23; M24; AS40
			1C	138–143	138; 140–142	K17; O2; O4; O9; E23; M24
			1D		138; 142	O2; O4; O9; E23; AS40
			2		138; 142	K17; O2; O4; O9; E23
			3A		139	
			3B	139–143	138; 140–142	O2; O4; O9; E23; M24; AS40; AS41
			4A	138; 142–143	138; 142	
			4B			
			5A	140–142	138; 140–142	K17; O2; O4; O9; E23; M24; AS40
3		**The Musician Composes, Improvises, and Arranges** (pp. 144–162)	1A	145; 149; 151–153; 155; 157–158	144; 150–152; 154; 156–157; 162	EV14; EV16
			1B	145–147; 149–158; 160–161	144; 146; 150–152; 154; 156–157; 162	K11; M24; AS42; EV14; EV16
			1C	144–147; 149–154; 156–157; 159–161	144; 146–148; 150–152; 154; 156–157; 162	AS42; EV14; EV16
			1D	145–146; 149–155; 157; 160–161	144; 146; 150–152; 154; 160; 162	EV14; EV16
			1E		154	AS42
			1F	156–157		
			2	145; 149; 151–152	144; 148; 162	K11; EV14; EV16
			3B	145; 149; 154; 160–161	144–146; 151; 155; 160; 162	AS42; EV14; EV16
			4A	145; 149; 151–155; 157; 160–161	144–145; 147; 154; 157; 160; 162	AS42; EV14; EV16
			4B	145; 157	144–145	B13
			5A	145–147; 149–154; 158; 160–161	144; 146–148; 150–152; 155; 160; 162	K11; EV14; EV16
4		**The Choral Sound** (pp. 163–219)	1A	164–167; 169–177; 190–192; 215	164; 166–168; 170; 174; 176; 178; 182; 184; 188; 190; 192–193; 195; 199–202; 207–208; 212; 215–216; 219	K14; K17; O11; O24; O30; M4; I15; I20; EV17; EV20, EV22
			1B	164–167; 169–177; 190–192; 215	164; 166–168; 170; 174; 176; 178; 182; 184; 188; 190; 192–193; 195; 199–202; 207–209; 212; 215–216; 219	K11; K14; K17; O11; O24; O30; M4; AS46; AS47; AS48; I15; I20; EV17; EV20; EV22
			1C	170–177; 190–192; 215	164; 166; 168–170; 174; 176; 178; 182; 184; 189–190; 192–193; 195; 199–203; 207–208; 212; 215–216; 219	O11; O24; O30; AS46; AS47; AS48; I15; I20; EV17; EV20; EV22

Unit	Lesson Groups	Essential Elements	PE Pages	TE Pages	TRB Pages
		1D	164–167; 169–177; 190–192; 215	164; 166–167; 170; 174; 176; 178; 182; 184; 188; 190; 192–193; 195; 199–202; 207–208; 212; 215–216; 219	K14; O11; O24; O30; AS47; I15; I20; EV17; EV20; EV22
		1E		168	
		1F		179; 184–185; 193; 202–203; 208; 212	K14; AS47; EV20; EV22
		2	164–167; 169–177; 190–192; 215	164; 166–170; 174–176; 182–185; 188; 190; 192–193; 195–196; 199–203; 207–208; 212–213; 215–217; 219	K11; K14; K17; O11; O24; O30; M4; AS48; EV17; EV20; EV22
		3B		196; 199; 201; 208; 215–217; 219	O11; O24; O30; I15; I20; EV20
		4A	174–177; 192	169–171; 174; 184; 189–190; 199; 208	AS46; AS47; AS49
		4B	218		
		5A	164–167; 169–177; 190–192; 215	164; 166–170; 174–176; 178–179; 182–185; 188; 190; 192–193; 195–196; 199–203; 207–208; 212–213; 215–217; 218–219	K11; K17; O11; O24; O30; AS48; I15; I20; EV17; EV20; EV22

MUSIC

TEACHER'S EDITION Grade 8

Eunice Boardman Meske
Professor of Music and Education
University of Wisconsin—Madison
Madison, Wisconsin

Barbara Andress
Professor of Music Education
Arizona State University
Tempe, Arizona

Mary P. Pautz
Assistant Professor of Music
    Education
University of Wisconsin—Milwaukee
Milwaukee, Wisconsin

Fred Willman
Associate Professor of Music and
    Education
University of Missouri—St. Louis
St. Louis, Missouri

Holt, Rinehart and Winston, Publishers
New York, Toronto, Mexico City, London, Sydney, Tokyo

Copyright © 1988
by Holt, Rinehart and Winston, Publishers
All Rights Reserved
Printed in the United States of America

Acknowledgments for previously copyrighted material
and credits for photographs and art begin on page 392.
ISBN 0-03-005328-5
7890 032 987654321

HOLT MUSIC

It's the leader of the band!

CONSIDER THE ADVANTAGES . . .

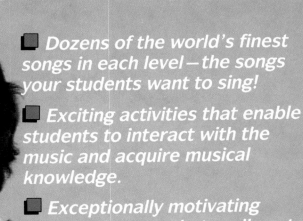

■ Dozens of the world's finest songs in each level—the songs your students want to sing!

■ Exciting activities that enable students to interact with the music and acquire musical knowledge.

■ Exceptionally motivating listening lessons that really get students involved in learning.

■ Flexibly organized Teacher's Editions, rich with background information and no-nonsense teaching strategies.

■ A wealth of supplementary materials that enhance, extend, and enrich.

Music That Motivates

Every song in HOLT MUSIC builds on the natural enthusiasm that students have for singing, dancing—expressing themselves in creative ways! You'll find hundreds and hundreds of authentic songs that students really *want* to sing—songs with built-in appeal.

Choose from a rich variety of songs: contemporary, traditional, American and European folk, classical, holiday music, and more.

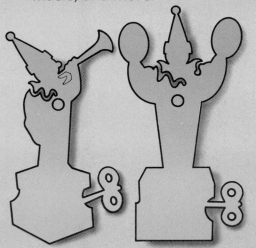

Just look at some of these favorites:

Fame
Matilda
Grab Another Hand
Amen
Wadeleeacha
Laredo
When You and I Were Young
  Maggie Blues
Come Join in the Chorus
Muddy Water
Can the Circle Be Unbroken?

Lively, colorful photographs and illustrations provide the perfect visual accompaniment.

Music to Learn From

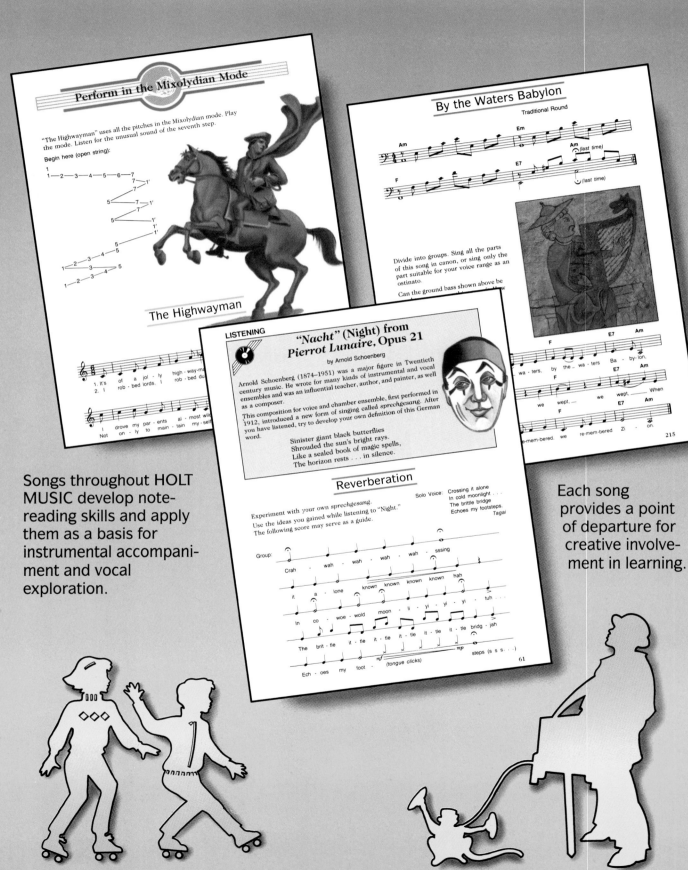

Songs throughout HOLT MUSIC develop note-reading skills and apply them as a basis for instrumental accompaniment and vocal exploration.

Each song provides a point of departure for creative involvement in learning.

Special graphic aids reinforce note—reading skills and enhance the students' understanding of rhythm, melody, and harmony.

Music to Interact With

Engaging activities help students understand, relate to, and interact with music right from the start. These activities are more than entertaining—they're truly *instructive*, designed to strengthen and enhance musical understanding.

The Composer and the Lyricist

A musical performance begins with an idea. It might be some words jotted down by a lyricist . . . or a few notes of a melody that a composer devises.

The lyricist communicates ideas by choosing

- words that evoke images
- rhyming words for phrase endings
- words that create a natural rhythmic flow

The composer will express the text by

- following the natural rhythm of the words

Convert Your Telephone Number Into Music

Using a similar method to the one used for "The Earth's Magnetic Field," you can compose a piece of music using your telephone number and the computer. Each of the digits in your telephone number can be converted into a pitch. If you were to make this conversion without a computer, you might do it this way:

Assign one of the following pitches to each digit of your telephone number:

Talking Drums

Hundreds of years before Western cultures developed rapid communication systems, some Africans sent messages from village to village over many miles using talking drums. This was possible because many African languages are tonal.

In a tonal language, the meaning of a word depends on the pitch at which each syllable is spoken.

For example, the Lokele people of northern Zaire use the word *lisaka* (lee-sah-kah) to mean three different things:

Higher sound		This means "puddle" or "marsh."
Lower sound	li-sa-ka	
	ka	This means "promise."
Higher sound	li-sa-	
Lower sound		
	sa-ka	This means "poison."
Higher sound	li-	
Lower sound		

You can see how very important it is to speak the higher and lower sounds in the correct place!

Drum language uses these higher and lower sounds to communicate messages. The combination of higher and lower sounds makes it possible to actually communicate messages using talking drums.

136

The Choreographer

Many musical performances take on an added dimension when the choreographer creates movements to accompany the music.

The choreographer

- devises interesting movements
- plans a sequence of movements that fits the form of the music
- rehearses the movements with the choir

Create movements for "Let the Rafters Ring." Write down your plan. Rehearse the choreography.

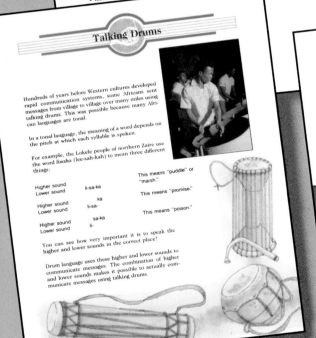

22

Irresistible activities inspire singing, clapping, making up melodies and rhymes, and more—the true exhilaration of musical expression. Many activities involve poetry or related arts.

Short instrumental experiences begin at Kindergarten, employing readily available instruments.

Music Worth Listening To

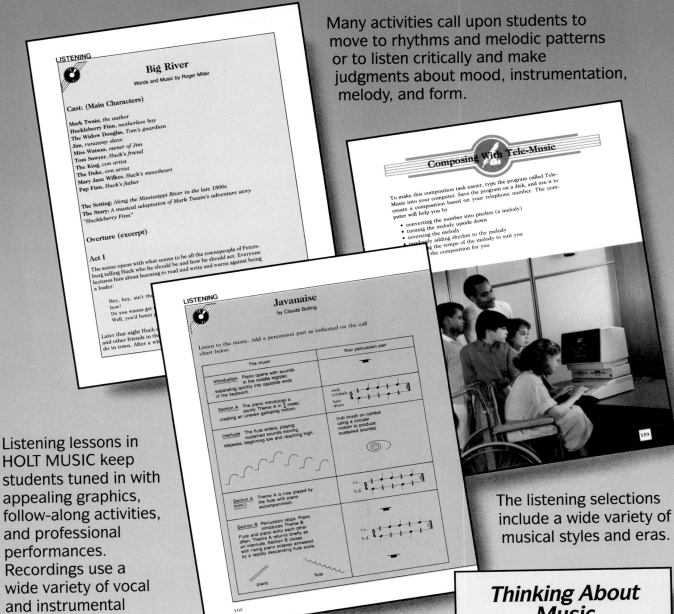

Many activities call upon students to move to rhythms and melodic patterns or to listen critically and make judgments about mood, instrumentation, melody, and form.

Listening lessons in HOLT MUSIC keep students tuned in with appealing graphics, follow-along activities, and professional performances. Recordings use a wide variety of vocal and instrumental sounds to heighten awareness of form, mood, melody, and musical styles.

The focus is on active participation to make music exciting, involving, and fun!

The listening selections include a wide variety of musical styles and eras.

Thinking About Music

Both activities and listening lessons supply ample opportunities to develop and reinforce thinking skills. Exercises are designed to improve students' ability to think, through analysis and evaluation, comparison and contrast, choosing alternatives, and more.

Music That's Realistic to Teach!

Whatever your musical background, you'll find all the backup help you need in HOLT MUSIC Teacher's Editions: concrete information, strategies you can rely on, and solid, flexible lesson plans with many optional suggestions. Every page is designed to bring musical understanding and appreciation within reach of all your students.

Each lesson begins with a clear objective and a complete list of program materials, including a detailed summary of recordings and the voices and instruments used.

A special logo signals when activity sheets are available for the lesson.

Each lesson begins with a motivating activity that leads naturally into the lesson content.

Step-by-step teaching instructions ensure that the lesson objective is met. Commentary and questions to the student are highlighted in boldface type.

 MUSICIANSHIP **13**

Lesson Focus
Expression: The expressiveness of music is affected by the way timbre, tempo, and texture contribute to the musical whole *(D–S)*

For Your Information
Prior to this lesson, you might collect clippings from magazines that contain record reviews (such as *Ovation, Stereo Review,* and *Downbeat*).

 The Critic

A musical performance may seem to end with the final curtain, but for the performers there is one more important moment: when they open the morning papers to read the review prepared by the critic.

Music Notes *by Anne Welsbacher*

The Farnsworth Falls Youth Symphony, consisting of senior high school students, gave an even and solid performance of Smetana's "The Moldau" and Borodin's *Symphony No. 2 in B minor*. The first piece, conducted by Sheila Halpern, opened well, with a flute solo that flowed smoothly and was strong without being overbearing. Although the wood-wind section had some difficulty with pitch—especially the English horn, which was often flat—the piece as a whole was played well, with knowledge of the material evident, particularly in the string section. Conductor Halpern paced the composition well, with particularly fine control over the final climactic tempo. The piece by Borodin was the better performed of the two; conductor John Ricardo kept the majesty intact and a steady, strong rhythm prevailed throughout. The string section gave a particularly fine rendition of the opening measures of the composition; the strings were perfectly on pitch and set a tempo from which the orchestra as an ensemble never wavered. Both pieces were well balanced; the winds never covered the strings, and the accompaniment was delicate while providing a solid foundation for the main theme.

Analyze these two newspaper reviews.

Make a list of the aspects of the performance that the reviewer discusses.

Collect reviews of musical performances from a newspaper or magazine. Do your samples touch on the same topics as the reviews shown here?

Attend a local concert or performance of a musical, and write a review.

Oklahoma! by Rodgers and Hammerstein was duced with vitality and warmth by the Farnsw State University Theater last weekend. The mu takes place in Oklahoma, shortly before it bec a state of the Union, and deals with two se sweethearts, their families and friends. Pat Bro as Laurie, played her role with honesty and v She gave her character personality, singing her songs with the same good timing and high qu that she shows when she speaks. Barbara Ma as the comic character Ado Annie, had tremenc energy, and Carol Shapiro, as the kind, no-sense Aunt Eller, gave strength to the musical. good were Brad Davis as Curly and Greg Mu as Will. Tom Sonno, as the "heavy," Jud, succee in creating the moody character, and his "In Room" was chilling and effective. The orche directed by Elspeth Esterhazy, was professi and talented; the effective lighting was by Jo Corelli; the fine costumes by John Franklin; an well-paced direction by Cindy Stewart.

48

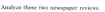

The Lesson

1. Ask the students to open their books to page 48 and read the reviews prepared by a high school student. **What skills does a critic need?** (knowledge of the music being performed, an understanding of what constitutes a good performance, and an ability to express oneself clearly in writing)

2. Discuss aspects of a performance that could be critiqued:
   - overall quality
   - conductor's technique
   - performer's technique
   - expressiveness of the performance

3. **Do all critics agree?** (No, critics each have their own opinions and are responding to what they hear. Often two critics at the same concert will review it quite differently.) **Are the opinions of critics always correct?** (No. S acknowledged masterpieces of great com ers such as Beethoven, Wagner, Debussy, Stravinsky were harshly criticized at pren performances.)

4. Ask the students to bring concert and re reviews from newspapers and magazines. these on a bulletin board. Compare review rock concerts and records with reviews of and classical performances, and discuss s larities and differences among the reviews

5. Plan to attend a concert as a class. Assi critique as a homework assignment.

OPTIONAL

Freedom of choice is truly yours—the Junior High texts are designed for maximum flexibility. Each book is divided into four self–contained units. Units 1 and 2 allow students to explore ways of participating in music, as well as music of different traditions and times. Units 3 and 4 provide a wealth of materials for instrumental and choral performances.

The lesson closes with an activity in which the students apply what they have learned.

Optional steps are labeled with a logo.

''For Your Information'' provides a quick, convenient reference for background information about lesson contents.

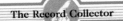

The Record Collector

e big performance is over. The reviews have been written; the per-
mers have continued their tour to another town. You can still re-
ember the music . . . sort of. With a recording, you can have the
rformance, or one like it, at your fingertips.

e Record Collector

- sometimes goes shopping for a specific recording by a specific performer
- sometimes browses through the bins of the local record shop to discover recordings of all kinds of music
- sometimes goes to the public library to compare two perfor- mances of the same composition before purchasing a recording of one performance
- always takes good care of records (and tapes) to preserve their quality

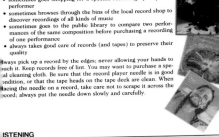

lways pick up a record by the edges; never allowing your hands to
ouch it. Keep records free of lint. You may want to purchase a spe-
al cleaning cloth. Be sure that the record player needle is in good
ondition, or that the tape heads on the tape deck are clean. When
acing the needle on a record, take care not to scrape it across the
ecord; always put the needle down slowly and carefully.

ISTENING

The Great Gate of Kiev
by Modest Mussorgsky

Modest Mussorgsky (1839–1881) was a Russian composer of the romantic era. Among his best-known works are "A Night on Bald Mountain" and the opera *Boris Godunov.*

Listen to four different recordings of this music. How would you prepare information about each version for use by a record collector?

49

MUSICIANSHIP 14

Lesson Focus
Expression: The expressiveness of music is affected by the way timbre, tempo, and texture contribute to the musical whole. **(D–S)**

Materials
○ **Record Information:**
- The Great Gate of Kiev, from *Pictures at an Exhibition* by Modest Mussorgsky (moo-**sorg**-skee), 1839–1881
  Record 2 Side A Bands a–d
  Band a: Paul Schenly, piano
  Band b: Kazuhito Yamashita, guitar
  Band c: New York Philharmonic Leonard Bernstein, conductor
  Band d: Tomita, synthesizer

○ **Other:** a pencil for each student
○ **Teacher's Resource Binder:**
  | Activity Sheets | • **Activity Sheet 10**, page A21 |
  - Optional— **Mainstreaming Suggestion 6,** page M11

The Lesson

. Write the following on the chalkboard: "The Record Collector: who, what, when, where, why." Ask the students to brainstorm regard- ing the recording artists involved, the musical selections, and so on; list their comments on the chalkboard. (Some students may be very sophisticated in their knowledge of recordings while others may be unaware of the variety, having limited their browsing and purchases to current popular recordings.)

. Read and discuss the information on page 49. Set the following scenario. **Someone has asked you to pick up a recording of *Pictures at an Exhibition.* You stop at the record store and discover that there are four ver- sions of the same piece. Will all the record- ings be the same?** Play the opening section for

each recorded version of "The Great Gate of Kiev." Modest Mussorgsky originally com- posed *Pictures at an Exhibition* for solo piano. The four recordings of the excerpt, "The Great Gate of Kiev," employ the original instrumentation (piano) and three variants; the orchestral transcription is traditional, and the guitar and synthesizer versions are con- temporary arrangements.

3. Distribute Activity Sheet 10 (The Great Gate of Kiev). Ask the students to prepare informa- tion that would assist a record collector; they are to complete the activity sheet as they lis- ten to the four versions of "The Great Gate of Kiev." Provide them with the title, composer, and performers. (See **Materials.** The other an- swers follow: Type of music—Classical; Instrumentation—1. piano, 2. guitar, 3. or- chestra, 4. synthesizer; answers will vary for "Special features" and "Preference scale.")

49

Music That's Manageable

The **Teacher's Resource Binder** makes classroom management uncommonly convenient. Blackline masters help teachers structure the course to match individual preferences.

Teachers who use the **Kodaly** approach will find creative teaching ideas and fun-filled student charts— all correlated to HOLT MUSIC.

The **Orff** activities will delight your class with chants, games, and lively instrumental arrangements.

The **Biography** series brings music personalities to life.

A complete set of **Evaluations** provides a comprehensive testing program for HOLT MUSIC.

Students who are especially interested in music or who are academically gifted will find plenty of challenges in the **Enrichment** ideas.

Students will love working with the call charts, games, puzzles, costume patterns, and other idea-packed **Activity Sheets.** These blackline masters are designed to supplement, extend, and enrich the basic lesson plans.

Mainstreaming activities ensure that involvement in music learning is an important part of every child's day.

Instrumental Accompaniments provide simple arrangements of songs in the series for student instrumental performance.

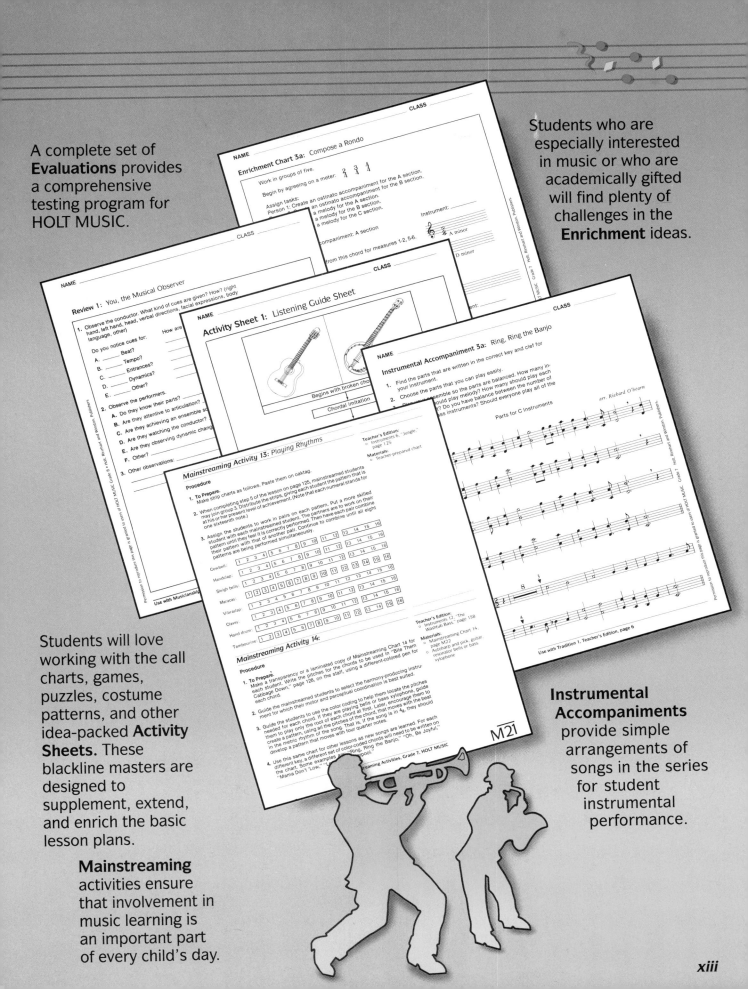

Music to Play

Recordings

A set of first-quality recordings serves a dual purpose: to give students a model for performance and to provide a valuable instrumental and vocal resource. Dual-track stereo allows separation of recorded voice and accompaniment.

A sturdy carrying case includes an index cross-referenced to lessons in the Teacher's Edition.

Song and listening selections appear in lesson order.

Extra Feature!

Each record package includes two performance cassettes. These cassettes contain instrumental tracks of songs from the program. They are specially edited to produce optimum sound for public performance.

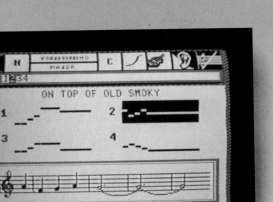

Supplementary Items

Software uses songs from HOLT MUSIC to encourage active experimentation. Students can rearrange phrases, shift tempo, or alter rhythm and print out the new musical scores to save and share with classmates. There are three separate programs: grades K–2, 3–5, and 6–8.

The _Holiday Song Book_ includes lyrics and piano accompaniments for an additional 50 songs celebrating a year's worth of holidays— Mother's Day, Columbus Day, the Fourth of July, and more.

COMPONENTS CHART	K	1	2	3	4	5	6	7	8
Pupil Book		✓	✓	✓	✓	✓	✓	✓	✓
Jumbo Book	✓	✓							
Teacher's Edition	✓	✓	✓	✓	✓	✓	✓	✓	✓
Recordings	✓	✓	✓	✓	✓	✓	✓	✓	✓
Teacher's Resource Binder	✓	✓	✓	✓	✓	✓	✓	✓	✓
Holiday Song Book	✓	✓	✓	✓	✓	✓	✓	✓	✓
Computer Software	✓	✓	✓	✓	✓	✓	✓	✓	✓
Performance Cassettes	✓	✓	✓	✓	✓	✓	✓	✓	✓

HOLT MUSIC offers you a total package for your classroom needs. A list of components is given in the chart at the left.

TABLE OF CONTENTS

UNIT 1 Musicianship ... 5

UNIT 2 The Listening Experience...51

UNIT 4 The Choral Sound ... 163

Meet the Authors

Eunice Boardman Meske is Director of the School of Music and Professor of Music and Education at the University of Wisconsin, Madison. She works with university students in a ''lab school'' where she and her students teach grades K-8. Meske holds a Ph.D. from the University of Illinois.

EUNICE BOARDMAN MESKE

BARBARA ANDRESS

Barbara Andress is Professor in the School of Music at Arizona State University, Tempe. She received a B.A. and M.A. in education from Arizona State University. Andress has taught general music and instrumental music and for over twenty years was a district music supervisor.

Mary Pautz is Assistant Professor of Music Education at the University of Wisconsin, Milwaukee. In addition to teaching music education methods, she also teaches elementary music classes as part of a practicum for music majors. Pautz is a doctoral candidate at the University of Wisconsin, Madison.

MARY PAUTZ

FRED WILLMAN

Fred Willman is Associate Professor of Music Education at the University of Missouri, St. Louis. Willman holds a Ph.D. from the University of North Dakota, Grand Forks. He has worked extensively in the development of computer software for use in music education.

Consultants

Nancy Archer
Forest Park Elementary School
Fort Wayne, Indiana

Joan Z. Fyfe
Jericho Public Schools
Jericho, New York

Jeanne Hook
Albuquerque Public Schools
Albuquerque, New Mexico

Danette Littleton
University of Tennessee at Chattanooga
Chattanooga, Tennessee

Barbara Reeder Lundquist
University of Washington
Seattle, Washington

Ollie MacFarland
Detroit Public Schools
Detroit, Michigan

Faith Norwood
Harnett County School District
North Carolina

Linda K. Price
Richardson Independent School District
Richardson, Texas

Buryl Red
Composer and Arranger
New York, New York

Dawn L. Reynolds
District of Columbia Public Schools
Washington, D.C.

Morris Stevens
A.N. McCallum High School
Austin, Texas

Jack Noble White
Texas Boys Choir
Fort Worth, Texas

Contributing Writers

Hilary Apfelstadt
University of North Carolina
at Greensboro
Greensboro, North Carolina

Pat and Tom Cuthbertson
Professional Writers
Santa Cruz, California

Louise Huberty
(*Special Kodaly Consultant*)
Milwaukee Public Schools
Milwaukee, Wisconsin

Susan Kenney
Brigham Young University
Salt Lake City, Utah

Janet Montgomery
Ithaca College
Ithaca, New York

Richard O'Hearn
Western Michigan University
Kalamazoo, Michigan

Diane Persellin
Trinity University
San Antonio, Texas

Arvida Steen
(*Special Orff Consultant*)
The Blake School
Minneapolis, Minnesota

Field Test Sites

While HOLT MUSIC was being developed, parts of the program were field tested by 25 teachers in 18 states. These teachers played a crucial role in the program's development. Their comments, suggestions, and classroom experiences helped HOLT MUSIC become the workable, exciting program it is. Our grateful appreciation goes to the following teachers who used our materials in their classrooms.

ARKANSAS
Judy Harkrader
Vilonia Elementary School
Vilonia

COLORADO
Nancylee Summerville
Hutchinson Elementary School
Lakewood

Robert Horsky
Goldrick Elementary School
Denver

Joan Tally
Eiber Elementary School
Lakewood

Germaine Johnson
University of Northern Colorado
  Laboratory School
Greeley

GEORGIA
Angela Tonsmeire
Cartersville Elementary School
Cartersville

Nancy Clayton
Norman Park Elementary School
Norman Park

INDIANA
Nancy Archer
Forest Park Elementary School
Fort Wayne

Elizabeth Staples
School #92
Indianapolis

Pat Gillooly
School #90
Indianapolis

KANSAS
Shelli Kadel
El Paso Elementary School
Derby

KENTUCKY
Patricia Weihe
Wright Elementary School
Shelbyville

MASSACHUSETTS
Marya Rusinak
Kennedy School
Brockton

MISSISSIPPI
Dottie Dudley
Crestwood Elementary School
Meridian

Mira Frances Hays
Forest Seperate School District
Forest

MISSOURI
Elizabeth Hutcherson
Parker Road Elementary School
Florissant

NEW JERSEY
Lorna Milbauer
North Cliff School
Englewood Cliffs

NEW YORK
Ruthetta S. Smikle
Hillary Park Academy
Buffalo

NORTH CAROLINA
Julie Young
Burgaw Elementary School
Burgaw

OKLAHOMA
Cindy Newell
Washington Irving Elementary School
Durent

OREGON
Larry Verdoorn
Hall Elementary School
Gresham

PENNSYLVANIA
Marianne Zimmerman
Steele School
Harrisburg

TENNESSEE
Sarah Davis
Powell Elementary School
Powell

WEST VIRGINIA
Eva Ledbetter
Cross Lanes Elementary School
Cross Lanes

WISCONSIN
Jill Kuespert Anderson
Lannon Elementary School
Lannon

A Guide To Holt Music

The HOLT MUSIC program can help you provide rich and enjoyable experiences for all of your students. The information given below will help you get acquainted with the Pupil Book, the Teacher's Edition, the Teacher's Resource Binder, and the Recordings.

Organization Of The Program

Levels 7 and 8 of HOLT MUSIC are divided into four self-contained units for maximum flexibility. Each unit contains two tools for tracking the students' musical growth: a **Checkpoint** and an **Evaluation**. The Checkpoint allows the teacher to monitor the students' comprehension of material presented early in the unit. The Evaluation is a final unit test.

Types Of Lessons In The Book

☐ **Song lessons**—Most lessons in the program are song-based. Song lessons are identified by a colored band above and below the title. Usually both the music and the words are in the Pupil Book. However, in certain lessons only the words appear in the Pupil Book, and it is expected that students will learn the song by listening. The lessons are designed so that students will grow in note-reading skills as they progress through the grades. For this reason it is strongly recommended that the lessons in each unit be followed in page order.

☐ **Listening lessons**—These lessons are built around a recording of a classical, folk, or contemporary work. Listening lessons featured in the Pupil Book are identified by a logo. Complete titles, composers, and performer credits are listed in the "Materials" section of the Teacher's Edition.

Many of the listening lessons have a chart or an illustration designed to help guide the children through the listening experience. In some lessons the recording includes "call numbers"—spoken numbers recorded over the music. The call numbers correspond to the numbers on the chart and help to focus attention on important features as the music continues.

☐ **Activities**—Many activity-based lessons are included in HOLT MUSIC. The type of activity in the Pupil Book is identified by a special logo: a quill pen and an ink bottle for creative activities, a French horn for performance activities, and a human figure for activities involving movement.

The activity is always structured in some way; for example, a poem, a story, or a picture in the Pupil Book might serve as a focal point for creative exploration, or the students could be invited to explore certain sounds on instruments.

Using The Recordings

The recordings are essential teaching aids for HOLT MUSIC. The song recordings may be used in various ways: to help students learn words and melody if songs are beyond their current reading level; and to provide examples of appropriate tempo, diction, expression, and vocal tone quality. For teaching flexibility, song recordings have voices on one channel and instruments on the other. By turning the balance control completely to the right, you will hear instruments only. The grooves between all selections are locked.

Special Helps For The Teacher

☐ The **Scope and Sequence Chart,** pages xxviii–3, summarizes concepts, terms, and skills covered in each grade level.

☐ The **Teacher's Glossary,** page 388, gives definitions of musical terms used in the text.

☐ A discography, **Suggested Recordings for Student Listening,** lists representative listening selections from each historical era. The recordings may be acquired through local retail outlets or libraries. These recordings may be used to augment the classroom listening program in HOLT MUSIC or they may be suggested to individual students who are interested in pursuing musical study on their own.

☐ Complete **Classified and Alphabetical Indexes,** starting on page 394, provide a convenient way to locate songs, poems, listening lessons, and particular skills and concepts.

☐ Step-by-step **lesson plans** are provided for each page of the Pupil Book. The **Lesson Focus** indicates the concept to be studied and gives, in abbreviated form, an indication of the primary behavior and mode stressed. **P–I,** for example, means "perform" in the "ikonic mode." (See "The Generative Approach to Music Learning," page xxvi.)

☐ The **Teacher's Resource Binder** includes Activity Sheets, Biographies, Evaluations, and suggestions for Instrumental Accompaniments, Enrichment, Kodaly, Mainstreaming, and Orff. All binder materials are cross-referenced to lessons in the Teacher's Edition. This enables you to adapt or expand individual lessons to fit your special needs.

☐ **Instrumental accompaniments**—Most songs contain chord names for autoharp or guitar accompaniment, and many lesson plans include accompaniments for students to perform on classroom instruments. Piano accompaniments, provided in the back of the Teacher's Edition, are cross-referenced to each lesson plan. The piano score includes markers showing where a new line begins in the Pupil Book. The symbol $\overset{2}{\overline{v}}$ above the score, for example, indicates that the second line of music in the Pupil Book begins at this point.

To the Classroom Teacher

The classroom teacher's role in music education varies from school to school. Whatever the situation in your district, the classroom teacher is vital to the success of the total music program.

Many teachers approach music with mixed feelings: enthusiasm, apprehension, curiosity, or insecurity. These attitudes are influenced by the musical knowledge the teacher possesses, the memory of music in his or her own school experience, and by heavy demands on the teacher's time.

HOLT MUSIC welcomes the classroom teacher's participation. The suggestions that follow are provided with the hope that they will alleviate fears and encourage the teacher to enjoy and learn music with the students.

1 "I Don't Know How To Teach Music!"

Every classroom teacher can teach music with HOLT MUSIC—if he or she is willing to learn with the students and read through the lessons in the Teacher's Edition. The "generative" approach used in HOLT MUSIC can help the teacher learn along with the students.

Music presents a special challenge because of the need to occasionally demonstrate by singing, moving, or playing. HOLT MUSIC helps the teacher as much as possible with

■ comprehensive, easily understood lesson plans
■ quality demonstration recordings
■ a teaching sequence that works
■ appealing songs, listening lessons, and poetry
■ activities that are fun for students to do

2 "There Isn't Time To Teach Music!"

The pressure for students to achieve in all curricular areas is intense. However, music can be interspersed throughout the school day. Sing a song to begin or end the day; create an instrumental accompaniment to enrich a story; share the music from the culture being highlighted in social studies.

The Curriculum Correlation section in the Teacher's Resource Binder provides many suggestions for integrating music into your day. To expand class time for music, set up music centers where small groups may work on their own.

However, a scheduled time devoted to music is just as important as time scheduled for other subjects. Just as reading throughout the day does not take the place of reading class, neither should the use of music throughout the day be considered sufficient. To achieve an understanding of music there must be a sequential course of study.

3 "I Don't Have Time To Hunt For Materials!"

The authors of HOLT MUSIC have gathered and organized all materials for you. You will find

■ Complete lesson plans that include a lesson focus, an introduction, a development and a conclusion. Usually a lesson can be completed in 20 to 30 minutes.
■ Integration of all types of activities—listening lessons, dances, creative experiences, and songs—within a lesson.
■ Boldfaced dialogue in the lesson plans that may help you in presenting the lesson, especially if you are not familiar with musical concepts and terms.

4 "The Kids Will Laugh If I Sing!"

Students may need encouragement at first. However, young people will eventually sing if a positive atmosphere is created. Common teaching errors that hinder singing include

■ expecting students to sing before they are ready (A new song must be heard several times before the students sing it.)
■ expecting students to sing too loud

The students may laugh the first time they hear you sing. You are not alone: They are even more likely to laugh at a music specialist who has a trained voice! If you can laugh with the class and proceed with the song, the laughter is soon forgotten and the music enjoyed. Or if you prefer, you can rely on the recordings. By adjusting the balance on the stereo, the voice only may be heard; this is especially helpful in teaching a new song.

5 "What Will I Do With the Boys?"

There is nothing inherent in the genes of boys that causes them to have an aversion to music! Often they will be the most enthusiastic supporters. Expect all students to enjoy music; expect everyone to learn. You will find that an activity-based, hands-on experience in music will spark enthusiasm in both boys and girls. They will never tire of opportunities to play bells and autoharps, to use props such as streamers, wands, and balloons, or to work with the activity sheets provided in the Teacher's Resource Binder.

6 "I Can't Play the Piano!"

While playing the piano is helpful, it is not essential for teaching music. Instead, you can play the recordings or use autoharp accompaniments.

7 "I Remember How I Hated Music When I Was In School!"

Teachers who have had pleasant experiences with music are likely to approach music teaching with enthusiasm. Others, unfortunately, may have less pleasant memories. What was it in the experience that caused the bad feelings? You can prevent another generation from having unpleasant experiences by avoiding those stressful practices you recall.

The Generative Approach To Music Learning

HOLT MUSIC'S generative approach is based on the recognition that

Learning begins with a "need to know." Real learning occurs only to the extent that the student willingly makes a commitment to the act of learning. Learning based on intrinsic "need to know" goals, which the learner personally indentifies, is more permanent than learning based on extrinsic goals such as rewards or adult approval.

Learning leads to more learning. Once the student is personally committed to learning, each achievement is "generative"; it provides the foundation and the impetus for further learning.

Learning is future-oriented. The student who becomes enthralled with the learning process continues to seek opportunities to learn as long as each experience leads toward personal independence and self-actualization. Music learning thus approached allows the learner to become

☐ more deeply involved in the aesthetic experience

☐ aware of music as an avenue of one's own personal expression

☐ musically independent

The Generative Instructional Theory

The Generative Instructional Theory recognizes that music learning, whether formal or informal, involves four components. These components include

1. The musical concept to be learned. Musical understanding emerges gradually as the learner develops musical concepts, that is, principles or ways of categorizing musical sounds.

Concepts stressed in the generative approach include

☐ those related to musical elements
  - pitch (melody and harmony)
  - duration (rhythm and tempo) ■ dynamics
  - articulation ■ timbre (qualities of sound)

☐ those that reflect the way musical elements are organized into a complete musical statement that has ■ form ■ texture ■ an expressive nature ■ a cultural context (time and place)

The Scope and Sequence chart beginning on page xxviii gives the concepts covered in HOLT MUSIC.

2. A musical example that embodies the concept to be learned. Examples are selected for their musical value reflecting

  - diverse musical heritages
  - diverse times and places
  - many forms of human emotion
  - many different combinations of voices and instruments

3. A musical behavior through which the learner interacts with music, gradually developing essential musical concepts by

  - performing music through singing and playing

  - describing music through moving, visualizing, and verbalizing
  - creating music through improvisation or composition

4. A conceptual mode that enables the learner to communicate understanding and move through three stages of conceptualization:

☐ **The enactive mode:** The learner begins to associate concept with example through observation, manipulation, and experimentation. Understanding is "acted-out" as the student interacts directly and nonverbally with the musical sound.

☐ **The ikonic mode:** The learner internalizes musical sound images that can be recalled even when the musical sound is absent. The learner demonstrates understanding through pictorial representations that "look like" the music sounds or with simple verbal imagery such as up-down, longer-shorter, or smooth-jerky.

☐ **The symbolic mode:** The learner builds on previous enactive and ikonic experiences until verbal and musical symbols gradually become associated with the sound.

The Lesson Focus

Lesson plans in HOLT MUSIC are built on the recognition that these four components must be present in order for learning to take place. The **Lesson Focus** for each plan identifies the concept, the behavior, and the conceptual mode. An example follows.

Lesson Focus
Melody: A series of pitches may move up, down, or remain the same. *(P–I)*

  - The **behavior** is identified at the end of the concept statement by the first letter.
    P Perform (singing/playing)
    D Describe (move/verbalize/visualize)
    C Create (improvise/compose)
  - The **conceptual mode** at which it is expected that most students will be functioning in this lesson is identified by the second capital letter.
    E Enactive *I* Ikonic *S* Symbolic

Thus in the example given above, the designation *(P–I)* at the end of the concept statement indicates that the behavior stressed in the lesson is **Perform** and that the students will be primarily using the **Ikonic** mode in that lesson.

The Generative Approach To Music Reading

Lessons that help develop music-reading skills are an integral part of any learning sequence that leads toward musical independence. The generative approach to music reading used in HOLT MUSIC

☐ is based on a cyclic process that takes the learner through three stages corresponding to the three modes of conceptualization (See chart.)

□ provides a lesson sequence that recognizes that a learner may be functioning at different stages of the cycle simultaneously—for example, a student might be reading simple rhythms from notation (symbolic stage) while associating melodies with ikons (ikonic stage) and learning harmonies aurally (enactive stage).

□ presents each new skill in relation to the musical whole, rather than through pattern drill alone.

□ distinguishes between sight-reading (playing an instrument from notation) and sight-singing.

Reading Rhythm

The generative approach to reading rhythm

□ recognizes that reading of rhythm depends on the perception of durational relationships

□ is based on a two-dimensional approach
  ■ sensing durations within the melodic rhythm in relation to the underlying beat, and
  ■ sensing durations in the melodic rhythm in relation to the shortest sound within that rhythm

The **additive approach** described in Step 2 is used because

□ it is the rhythmic relationship to which the young person seems to respond most readily

□ it allows the student to solve rhythmic problems by using addition rather than division

□ it is the basis for rhythmic organization used in the music of many non-Western cultures, as well as in much of the popular music of today.

Reading Melody

The generative approach to reading melody

□ begins with melodies based on major or minor modes because these are most familiar to the contemporary American child

□ uses the body scale (see below) to help the beginning student internalize pitch relationships

□ stresses the hearing and performing of melodies in relation to the underlying harmony

□ makes use of scale numbers to describe tonal relationships because numbers

  ■ provide the learner with a way of internalizing and recalling melodic pitches in relation to a tonal center
  ■ build on a numerical concept that most children have when this stage is introduced
  ■ allow for meaningful transfer to the reading of staff notation
  ■ are commonly used to describe chord structure, thus helping the student to understand the relation of melody to harmony

---

Lessons that develop reading skills take the student through the three conceptual modes.

ENACTIVE MODE The student performs the rhythm of a melody and metric grouping by imitating what is heard.

IKONIC MODE The student associates rhythms with ikons that represent duration in relation to

■ the shortest sound   ■ the beat and accent

As the student associates these ikons with sound patterns, vocabulary is introduced to describe

■ sounds that make up the melodic rhythm (short, long, lo-ong)

short short long   short short long   lo-ong

■ sounds in relation to the beat (shorter than, longer than)

shorter same longer   lo-ong

■ the accent (moves in twos, moves in threes)

moves in twos   moves in threes

SYMBOLIC MODE The process is completed as the child transfers the ability to read ikons to reading traditional music notation.

ENACTIVE MODE The student performs in response to melodies heard. During this stage the body scale is introduced, providing the child with another means of sensing and responding to pitch relationships.

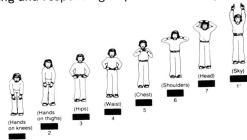

(Hands on knees) 1   (Hands on thighs) 2   (Hips) 3   (Waist) 4   (Chest) 5   (Shoulders) 6   (Head) 7   (Sky) 1'

IKONIC MODE The child first associates melodies with ikons that represent the up-down, step-skip relationship of pitches. Later, pitches are labeled with scale numbers to show their relationship to the tonal center.

1   2   3   1   1

SYMBOLIC MODE The student transfers the ability to read a new melody from scale numbers to staff notation.

1 2 3   1 5, 1

Scope and Sequence

As students grow in their understanding of musical concepts, they acquire skills for manipulating their own musical environments. Page numbers following each concept statement guide the teacher to lessons in HOLT MUSIC, Level 8, that focus on that concept. Boldfaced numbers represent lessons where that concept is dealt with as a primary focus of the lesson. Other numbers indicate

Concepts	Ikon	Musical Symbol
RHYTHM ■ Music may be comparatively fast or slow, depending on the speed of the underlying pulse. ■ Music may become faster or slower by changing the speed of the underlying pulse. *Pages:* 10, 58, 116, 124 ■ Music may move in relation to the underlying steady beat or shortest pulse. *Pages:* **16–18**, 62, 120, 124, **146–147**, **150** ■ A series of beats may be organized into regular or irregular groupings by stressing certain beats. *Pages:* **19**, **62–63**, **132**, **133**, **134**, **135**, **160**, **182–183**, **200–201**, 202 ■ Individual sounds and silences within a rhythmic line may be longer than, shorter than, or the same as other sounds within the line. *Pages:* 170, 188 ■ Individual sounds and silences within a rhythmic line may be longer than, shorter than, or the same as the underlying steady beat or shortest pulse. *Pages:* 95, 118, 120, 132, **170**, 200, 202 ■ Accented sounds within a rhythmic line may sound with, before, or after the accented underlying beat. *Pages:* 62–63, 118, 136, 151, 160, 199		
MELODY ■ A series of pitches may move up, down, or remain the same. *Pages:* 7, 66, 67, 93, 136, 168 ■ A series of pitches may move up or down by steps or skips. *Pages:* 7, 66, 67, 76, 94–95, **128–129**, **130–131**, 168, **188–189**, 200 ■ Each pitch within a melody moves in relation to a home tone. *Pages:* 14, 66, 67, 76, 108, 110, 122, 151–152, 166, 193 ■ A series of pitches bounded by the octave ''belong together,'' forming a tonal set. *Pages:* 14, 58, 72, 108, **138–139**, **140–141**, 142, 166, 184, 218 ■ A melody may be relatively high or low. *Pages:* 66, 67, **108–109** ■ Individual pitches, when compared to each other, may be higher, lower, or the same. *Pages:* 135, 136		
TIMBRE ■ The quality of a sound is determined by the sound source. *Pages:* 20, 56, 58, 75, 120 ■ The quality of a sound is affected by the material, shape, and size of the source. *Pages:* **56–57**, 134, 146 ■ The quality of a sound is affected by the way the sound is produced. *Pages:* 20, 56, 60, 61, 110, 115, 116, 126, 133, 134, 138, 146, 160, 164, 169, 174, 176, 190, 212 ■ The total sound is affected by the number and qualities of sounds occurring at the same time. *Pages:* 20, 110, 134, 135, 145, 167, 178		
DYNAMICS ■ Music may be comparatively loud or soft. *Pages:* 20, 58, 72, 94, 184, 193 ■ Music may become louder or softer. *Pages:* 10, 20, 58, 72, 184, 193		

lessons where the concept is dealt with, but not as the primary focus.

The skills list gives a sampling of representative behaviors for Level 8. Page numbers listed give only one example of a lesson where that skill is developed. For a comprehensive listing of skills, refer to the Classified Index of Activities and Skills, page 397.

Verbal Symbols (Terms)	Skills/Behaviors	
beat tempo meter triplet syncopation clave (pattern) fermata	**Perform**	Play a clave pattern on a percussion instrument. *132* Play percussion instruments and sing in an African-style ensemble. *134—135*
	Describe	Tap the short sound while chanting the words of a song in rhythm. *THROUGHOUT* Conduct in $\frac{2}{4}$, $\frac{3}{4}$, and $\frac{4}{4}$, using appropriate beat patterns. *19* Determine beat groupings in $\frac{5}{4}$ meter. *160* Tap a steady pulse with accents to indicate changing meter. *182*
	Create	Develop a rhythmic ostinato and "scratch" sounds to accompany a rap. *146—147* Write lyrics for a "talking" blues. *150*
skip-step half step-whole step phrase contours: undulating, arched, terraced, irregular range motion central pitch modes: Aeolian, Ionian, Mixolydian intervals: unison, second, third, fourth, fifth, sixth, seventh, octave blues notes definite pitch-indefinite pitch	**Perform**	Play songs in various modes on the dulcimer. *140—143* Sightread the melody of a song by breaking it down into rhythmic and melodic components. *188*
	Describe	Determine own singing range by singing a song in different keys. *108* Transcribe a song from traditional notation to guitar tablature. *128—129* Identify the arrangement of whole and half steps in the Ionian and Mixolydian modes. *139—141* Read song tablature while playing the dulcimer. *142—143*
voice parts: treble, baritone, changing voice; soprano, alto, tenor, bass instruments and ensembles: orchestra; recorder, Baroque flute, crumhorn, shawm, hunting horn, vielle, harpsichord; modern flute, trumpet, French horn, grand piano; synthesizer; dulcimer (fret), conga drum, talking drums vibrato *sprechgesang* drone	**Perform**	Sing with awareness of vocal resonance and enunciation. *115—116* Use the rest stroke technique when playing guitar. *128* Play the conga drum, using a variety of playing positions to produce different sounds. *133* Sing with a bright sound or a dark sound. *174*
	Describe	Show awareness of voice placement. *110*
	Create	Develop a vocal-instrumental rendition of a poem, using *sprechgesang*. *61*
dynamic contrast *crescendo* *decrescendo*	**Perform**	Sing with sensitivity to dynamics. *THROUGHOUT*
	Describe	Determine by listening how dynamics are used in a song. *184*

	Concepts	Ikon	Musical Symbol
ARTICULATION	■ A series of sounds may move from one to the next in either a smoothly connected or a detached manner. *Pages:* 10, 61, 68, 72, 94, 169, **176**, 182, 184, 200 ■ The quality of a sound is affected by the way the sound begins, continues, and ends. *Pages:* 72, 164		
HARMONY	■ Chords and melody may move simultaneously in relation to each other. *Pages:* 7, **20**, 40, 112, **118–119**, 122, **124**, 130, **151–152**, **166–167**, 188, **192**, **215**, **216–217** ■ A series of simultaneous sounds may alternate between activity and rest. ■ Two or more pitches may be sounded simultaneously. *Pages:* 78, **126–127**, 151, 168, **196** ■ Two or more musical lines may occur simultaneously. *Pages:* **14–15**, 19, 40, **112, 115, 116**, 118, 120, **122–123**, 130, 141, **144–145**, **164, 168, 207**, 216, **218**		
TEXTURE	■ Musical quality is affected by the distance between the musical lines. *Page:* 168 ■ Musical quality is affected by the number of or degree of contrast between musical lines occurring simultaneously. *Pages:* 20, **21**, 40, 41, 62–63, **68–69, 70–71, 72–73, 110–111**, 116, 118, 120, 200		
FORM	■ A musical whole begins, continues, and ends. *Pages:* 122–123, 160–161 ■ A musical whole is a combination of smaller segments. *Pages:* 40, 58, 72, 76, 112, **120, 121**, 122–123, 142, 144–145, 160 ■ A musical whole may be made up of same, varied, or contrasting segments. *Pages:* 40, 58, 72, 108–109, 122, 130, 132, 142, 154, 160, 195, 196, 200, 203, 215, 218 ■ A series of sounds may form a distinct musical idea within the musical whole. *Pages:* 40, 41, 75, 122–123, 160–161 ■ A musical whole may include an introduction, interludes, and an ending segment. *Pages:* 122–123, 160–161		
EXPRESSION	■ Musical elements are combined into a whole to express a musical or extramusical idea. *Pages:* 6–9, 22, 32–38, 39, 47, 58–59, 61, 74, 75–81, 82–92, 93–103, 104–105, 136, 150, 154, **190**, 208, 212 ■ The expressiveness of music is affected by the way timbre, dynamics, articulation, rhythm, melody, harmony, form, tempo, and texture contribute to the musical whole. *Pages:* **10–13**, 14, 16, **48**, 49, 52, 72, 82, 94, 118, 142, **148, 156–157**, 164, 167, 169, 170, 174, **178–179, 184–185**, 190, 192, **193, 195, 199, 202–203**, 207, **208–209, 212–213**		
TIME & PLACE	■ The way musical elements are combined into a whole reflects the origin of the music. *Pages:* **23–27, 28–31**, 39, **52–55**, 58, **60**, 66, 74, 82, 118, 138, 146–147, **154–155, 169**, 170, **174–175**, 188 ■ A particular use of timbre, dynamics, articulation, rhythm, melody, harmony, and form reflects the origin of the musical whole. *Pages:* 39–41, **56–57**, 58, 62, **64–65, 66–67**, 72, 74, 76, 77, 78, 118, 130, 132, 136, 196, 199		

Verbal Symbols (Terms)	Skills/Behaviors
accent *legato* attack *staccato* decay sustain	**Perform** Sing with adequate breath control and support to maintain a *legato* sound. *176* **Describe** Determine whether a song should be sung *legato* or *staccato*. *176*
key major mode minor mode chord root (of chord) third (of chord) fifth (of chord) lowered seventh chord sequence ground bass walking bass modulation chromatic	**Perform** Play melody and walking bass accompaniment on the guitar, using correct playing position. *124–131* Sing five-note chords by adding one note at a time. *196* **Describe** Recognize a common chord sequence underlying different melodies. *112* Determine whether a song is in a major or minor key by listening. *184* Recognize the interval relationship between parts of a song. *168* **Create** Improvise a vocal melody over a ground bass. *144–145* Improvise vocal echo patterns over the sustained notes of a melody. *148–149* Compose jazz riffs based on chord tones. *151–153*
unison-ensemble parallel motion soloist-chorus contrary motion thick-thin homophony polyphony monophony	**Perform** Sing in unison and in two to four parts. *THROUGHOUT* **Describe** Develop definitions for different types of texture by examining musical notation. *68* Identify textural features of recorded selections. *68–72* Compare voice parts in a song arrangement. *THROUGHOUT*
verse-refrain prelude overture coda canon round ostinato rondo arrangement madrigal opera Broadway musical	**Perform** Sing a three-part round. *215* **Describe** Compare the different themes of a listening selection with voice parts of a song arrangement. *120–121* Discuss the form of an **AB** song. *203* Recognize a canon by listening. *196*
musical style	**Perform** Rehearse and conduct a choir. *16–19* **Describe** Discuss how choreography relates to and enhances music. *22* Identify where and how certain types of music are used in a Medieval music drama. *75–76* Analyze the way lyrics and compositional techniques help to create a mood. *208* **Create** Plan, rehearse, and videotape a musical program as a member of a production team. *28–31* Play high-low drum sounds to express spoken phrases. *136–137*
musical roles: composer, lyricist, conductor, instrumentalist, vocalist, arranger, choreographer, producer, critic styles: folk, country, Dixieland, gospel, jazz (improvisation, riffs, scat singing), blues, soft-shoe, Latin-American, Afro-Cuban, calypso, rap (scratch music) eras: Medieval, Renaissance, Baroque, Classical, Romantic, Twentieth century pavane minuet waltz Charleston barbershop quartet	**Perform** Sing a madrigal with appropriate dynamics, articulation, tempo, and accompaniment. *72–73* **Describe** Identify stylistic features of song arrangements. *23–24* Associate different instrumental timbres with appropriate time periods. *56–57* Interpret written rhythm to conform with barbershop style. *174* **Create** Prepare an arrangement of a song. *23–27* Improvise in a jazz style. *154–155*

To the Student

Many people think that only a person who wants to become a professional performer can enjoy the study of music. Actually, people of many interests and abilities can find great gratification in music. When considering how to learn about and be involved in music, you have many options. This book will help you to explore a number of these options.

Maybe you've thought about participating in a musical production. In Unit 1, you can learn about various ways you might be involved in a performance, such as composing and writing lyrics, singing and acting, preparing props and operating a video camera, or reviewing the performance. After you've learned how to put a musical production together, listen to the Broadway musical *Big River* and think about all the people who contributed to this performance.

Maybe you've listened to a piece of music and thought, What am I hearing? How am I supposed to listen to this music? Knowing how to listen can greatly increase your enjoyment of all kinds of music. In Unit 2, you can develop or refine your listening skills by learning about music from long ago and nearer to the present. On these pages, you can also focus on the parts of music—instrumental and vocal sounds, rhythm, melody, and texture. Then listen to three works from the world of musical theater—*The Play of Daniel*, *Madama Butterfly*, and *The Tender Land*. Has your musical ear changed? Are you hearing the music in a different manner?

Perhaps you've decided that you would like to focus on performing or creating music. Are you interested in vocal performance or in performing instrumental music? Or do you want to create new musical sounds? In Unit 3, learn about your singing voice: Find your vocal range and sing in different ensembles with your classmates. Continue in the unit, and learn to play guitar, percussion instruments, and dulcimer. Then apply your performance skills and make your own music, using classical, rap, and jazz ideas and such musical tools as the computer.

For many people, choral singing is their most important connection to the world of music. Unit 4 provides many opportunities to develop your choral skills toward a lifetime of singing enjoyment.

No matter where you focus your musical energies, you are certain to find some aspect of music that will be right for you. This book should help you to identify areas of musical involvement that you might investigate throughout your life.

4

Unit 1

Musicianship

Unit Overview

Unit 1 presents various musical roles and career possibilities through such activities as composing and writing lyrics, singing and acting, preparing props and operating a video camera, collecting recordings, and reviewing musical performances. After the students have learned how a musical production is put together, they have the opportunities to stage their own productions and listen to a Broadway musical.

MUSICIANSHIP 1

Lesson Focus

Expression: Musical elements are combined into a whole to express a musical or extramusical idea. *(D–S)*

Materials

○ **Piano Accompaniment:** page 222

○ **Record Information:**
- My Lord
  Record 1 Side A Band 1
  Voices: mixed choir
  Accompaniment: electric organ, electric guitar, electric bass, piano, percussion

○ **Instruments:** guitar and/or double bass

○ **Teacher's Resource Binder:**
- Optional—
  Instrumental Accompaniment 8,
  page 124

The Many Roles

> # WANTED:
>
> | | |
> |---|---|
> | COMPOSER | LYRICIST |
> | CONDUCTOR | VOCALISTS |
> | INSTRUMENTALISTS | CHOREOGRAPHER |
> | ARRANGER | CRITICS |
> | PRODUCER | PRODUCTION STAFF |
> | TELEVISION CREW | |
> | | |

Have you ever stopped to think about how many people are involved in bringing a musical performance to life? Can you imagine how many different roles requiring musical skills must be filled?

Whether the final production is a single song or a full-length musical, many people have assisted in some way, taking on many different musical and nonmusical roles in order to ensure success.

Think about a recent performance you have attended, heard on a recording, or seen on television. Make a list of different musical jobs that had to be performed before the production could be heard. Then scan this unit and compare your list with the roles discussed here.

Consider the musical skills and knowledge required for each role. Which of these roles would you feel qualified to perform? In which would you like to become more involved?

6

The Lesson

1. Explain to the students that the purpose of this unit is to introduce them to a variety of roles related to music and that they will have an opportunity to participate in musical activities that they may experience later in life as amateurs or professionals. Read page 6 aloud with the students, and discuss the tasks needed to prepare and produce a concert. List these tasks on the chalkboard; then list the personnel needed to accomplish the tasks: lyricist, composer, conductor, instrumentalist, vocalist, choreographer, recording engineer.

2. Help the students to consider which skills might be needed for each role. Then ask the students to evaluate their own skills and interests. **Consider which roles you might be able to fill.**

3. Ask the students to listen to the recording of "My Lord." Discuss the skills and personnel needed to produce the recording of this song; refer to the list on the chalkboard.

4. Determine each student's vocal range. (See **For Your Information**.) Then invite the students to examine the parts for the arrangement of "My Lord" (shown on pages 7–9). Ask them to find the voice part for their range, and examine that part to note where skips, steps, and repeated notes occur (Tr. I: repeated notes, skips, and steps; C.V. and Bar.: mostly steps and repeated notes; Tr. II: mostly skips and repeated notes). Work with each voice part separately. Give the starting pitch for that part and play a chordal accompaniment. Encourage each group to read its part independently. When each group has learned its part, ask all the groups to sing their parts together.

Texas Essential Elements, The Many Roles, pp. 6–30: 1A, 1B, 1C, 1D, 1F, 2, 3B, 4A, 4B, 5A, 5B (Please see Unit 1 opener, page 4, for component and page references.)

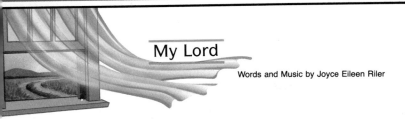

My Lord

Words and Music by Joyce Eileen Riler

Listen to a recording of "My Lord." What personnel were required to produce this recording? What tasks had to be accomplished? Learn your part of the arrangement shown on pages 7–9; then combine all the parts for a performance.

Refrain

Tr. II

(melody) My Lord's gon-na come in the morn - in', My Lord's gon-na

stay through the night, My Lord's gon-na watch o - ver me, and

ev - ery-thing's gon-na be all right, __ all right. __

Divide into groups. Add the harmony parts to this refrain.

C.V.
Bar.

My Lord's gon - na come, _____ My Lord's gon - na come, _____

My Lord, _____ ev-ery-thing's gon-na be all right, __ all right. __

7

For Your Information

Use the following procedure to organize the students quickly into vocal parts for singing. Assume that the girls can sing either Tr. I or Tr. II and ask them not to sing at this time. Ask all the boys to sing "Go Tell Aunt Rhody" (page 144) several times in the key of C major. Start the group, then walk among them. Boys who are singing the melody an octave lower are Baritones. Ask the Baritones to stop singing. Change the key to G major and ask the remaining boys to sing. Walk among the group, listening for the unchanged voices (those singing an octave higher or those who cannot sing this low). These boys are Tr. I or II. The remaining boys will be singing fairly comfortably in the range around middle C. These students have changing voices. Organize the class into four groups for part singing: Tr. 1 and II (girls and boys who sing in this range can be placed in either group at this time), C.V., and Bar.

5. Ask the students to learn all three verses and perform the song in the sequence listed on page 8.

6. Invite a guitarist (or double bass player) to provide an accompaniment using the chord symbols for "My Lord." (The double bass player might improvise a bass line using the chord symbols as a guide.)

Tr. I

My Lord, _____ My Lord, _____ My Lord, My Lord,

ev - ery-thing's gon - na be all right, _ all right. _

Perform the song in this sequence: unison refrain; three-part refrain;
alternate verses with three-part refrain; coda.

Verse

Tr. II
C.V.

1. Shad-rach, Me-shach, A - bed - ne - go __ in the
2. Mo - ses led the __ chil-dren of Is - ra - el
3. Lit - tle Da - vid __ flung a stone __ and

fier - y fur - nace were tossed. ____ Ev - ery - bod - y
down to the Red __ Sea shore, ____ Phar - oah and __ his
made Go - li - ath fall. _____ Man, you should __ have

thought their end ____ was near. ____ But __
ar - my close _____ be - hind. _____ Then the
seen his ar - my run. _____ Then the

they had faith ____ that the Lord a - bove ____ would
wa - ters part - ed, let Mo - ses through, __ but
chil-dren of Is - ra - el gave a shout ____ and

8

come and save the day, _____ And I could swear I
Phar - oah's ar-my was drowned, _____ And from the shore came
fol - lowed them a - way, _____ And ev - ery - bod - y

1. & 2. D7 *cresc.* F **3.** D7 *cresc.* F

heard those fel-lows say, say,
Mo - ses' thank-ful sound,
heard their he - ro

Coda *mf* B♭   E♭7

Tr. I — My Lord, My Lord,

Tr. II — My Lord's gon-na watch o - ver me, and

C.V.
Bar. — My Lord, _____

mf B♭   *sub. p* E♭ B♭

ev - ery-thing's gon - na be all right!

ev - ery-thing's gon - na be all right!

ev - ery-thing's gon - na be all right!

9

Lesson Focus

Expression: The expressiveness of music is affected by the way dynamics, rhythm, melody, and harmony contribute to the musical whole. *(P—S)*

Materials

○ **Piano Accompaniment:** page 227
○ **Record Information:**
  • You'll Never Walk Alone
    Record 1   Side A   Band 2
    Voices: mixed choir
    Accompaniment: piano, harp, percussion
○ **Other:** a pencil for each student
○ **Teacher's Resource Binder:**
  Activity Sheets • **Activity Sheet 1**, page A4

The Composer and the Lyricist

A musical performance begins with an idea. It might be some words jotted down by a lyricist . . . or a few notes of a melody that a composer devises.

The lyricist communicates ideas by choosing

  • words that evoke images
  • rhyming words for phrase endings
  • words that create a natural rhythmic flow

The composer will express the text by

  • following the natural rhythm of the words
  • stressing important words by accenting them or by stretching them out over one or many notes
  • choosing certain pitches to enhance the expressiveness or structure of the text
  • selecting dynamics that create focal points and climaxes in the music
  • composing a particular style of accompaniment to enhance the mood of the words

All of these elements are present in the song "You'll Never Walk Alone."

Can you discover how the composer and lyricist used these elements to make the music expressive?

10

The Lesson

1. Many students may already be familiar with "You'll Never Walk Alone" (pages 11-13). Many Broadway musicals are written by a team consisting of a lyricist and a composer. Explain that Richard Rodgers and Oscar Hammerstein made up one of the most well-known Broadway musical teams. Ask the students to read the information on pupil page 10. Guide the students to understand that the composer and the lyricist must work together to produce the final product. Explain that both the music and the text must express ideas in a way that will be understood by the listener.

2. Ask the students to follow the music to "You'll Never Walk Alone" as they listen to the recording. Encourage them to think about what the composer and lyricist are communicating and how they have accomplished this. Discuss the text. Guide the students to realize that the text is somewhat dramatic and that the song builds to a climactic point at the end.

3. Distribute a copy of Activity Sheet 1 (*You'll Never Walk Alone*) and a pencil to each student. Ask the students to indicate on the sheet how the song progresses toward its strong conclusion. Each element should be considered and described on the activity sheet.

4. Discuss the students' findings. (See *For Your Information.*) Have the students listen to the recording again to confirm their answers.

5. Assign the vocal parts, and help the students learn the song. When the students can accurately sing the vocal parts, have them sing the song with the piano or recorded accompaniment. Ask the students to sing *legato* and expressively.

You'll Never Walk Alone

Words by Oscar Hammerstein II

Music by Richard Rodgers

11

MUSICIANSHIP 2

For Your Information

Answers for the activity sheet follow:

Text: Somewhat dramatic; toward the end of the song words are repeated for emphasis.

Dynamics: begin softly, gradually becoming louder

Rhythm: Notes gradually become longer (more stretched out).

Phrase length: All phrases are four measures long; each phrase comes to a climactic point, creating an "arch" shape.

Melodic range: moving gradually from low to high to emphasize the final climactic point of the song

Accompaniment: light, arpeggiated (broken chords) throughout

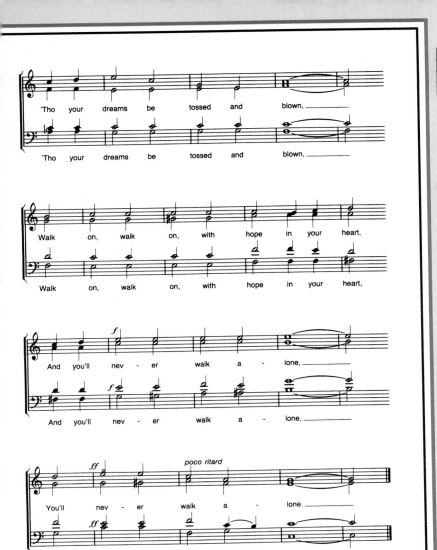

13

13

Lesson Focus

Harmony: Two or more musical lines may occur simultaneously. *(P–S)*

Materials

○ **Piano Accompaniment:** page 232

○ **Record Information:**
  • Good Night, Ladies
    Record 1 Side A Band 3a
    Voices: male solo
    Accompaniment: small show orchestra
    Band 3b: Pick a Little, Talk a Little
    Voices: treble voices
    Band 3c: Good Night Ladies/Pick a Little, Talk a Little
    Voices: mixed voices

○ **Other:** overhead projector

○ **Teacher's Resource Binder:**

  Activity Sheets • **Activity Sheet 2,** page A5
  • Optional—
    Mainstreaming Suggestion 1, page M4

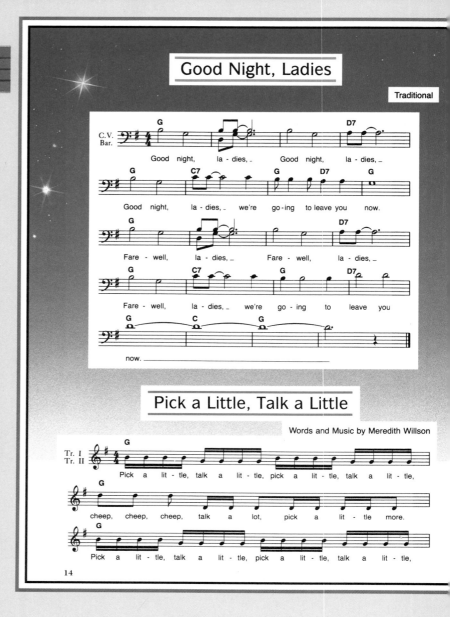

The Lesson

1. Ask the students to open their books to page 14. Teach the students the familiar tune "Good Night, Ladies" by listening to the recording and following the music.

2. Discuss with the students that one of the goals of the composer and lyricist is to produce music with both unifying and contrasting elements. Wilson (as composer and lyricist) probably felt this concern when he wrote "Pick a Little, Talk a Little" and arranged "Good Night, Ladies." The problem was how to make these songs equally effective when sung separately and together. Ask the students to examine the scores on pages 14–15. **What unifies the two songs?** If necessary, direct their attention to the chord symbols in each song. (The harmony—the chord sequence is the same in each song.) **How did the composer-lyricist create the contrasts?**

("Good Night, Ladies" has many long sounds in the melody and sustained vowel sounds in the words. "Pick a Little, Talk a Little" has many short sounds in the melody and lots of consonants that require rapid enunciation.)

3. Ask the students to look at "Pick a Little, Talk a Little" again. **Which words generally move with the shortest sounds?** (sixteenth notes for "pick a little, talk a little") **Which words move with longer sounds?** (eighth notes for "cheep," "lot," "more") In a moderate tempo, tap even sixteenth notes ($\frac{4}{4}$ meter) and ask the students to chant the words in rhythm.

4. After the students have become familiar with the words and rhythm of "Pick a Little, Talk a Little" increase the tempo. Encourage the students to exaggerate consonants such as *p, t,* and *ch.*

14

MUSICIANSHIP **3**

For Your Information

The songs "Pick a Little, Talk a Little" and "Good Night, Ladies" are sung as partner songs in the musical *The Music Man* (lyrics and music by Meredith Willson).

D7 cheep, cheep, cheep, talk a lot, pick a lit - tle more.

G Pick a lit - tle, talk a lit - tle, pick a lit - tle, talk a lit - tle,

C7 cheep, cheep, cheep, talk a lot, pick a lit - tle more.

1. G / D7 Pick a lit - tle, talk a lit - tle, pick a lit - tle, talk a lit - tle,

G cheep, cheep, cheep, cheep, cheep, cheep, cheep, cheep!

2. G Pick a lit - tle, talk a lit - tle, pick a lit - tle, talk a lit - tle,

D7 pick a lit - tle, talk a lit - tle, pick a lit - tle, talk a lit - tle,

G cheep, cheep, cheep, cheep, cheep, cheep, cheep, cheep,

C cheep, cheep, cheep, cheep, cheep, cheep, cheep,

G cheep, cheep, cheep, cheep, cheep, cheep, cheep!

Pick a lit - tle, talk a lit - tle, cheep!

15

5. **How many pitches are used in this song?** (six) Point out that the three most commonly used pitches are derived from a G major chord. Tune up this G major chord by singing the *arpeggio* G–B–D–B–G–D,–G up and down several times. Then challenge the students to sing "Pick a Little, Talk a Little" independently.

6. When the students have learned the song, divide the class into two groups. Tr. I and II can sing "Pick a Little, Talk a Little" while the C.V. and Bar. sing "Good Night, Ladies."

7. Return to the song "Good Night, Ladies" at another time. Distribute Activity Sheet 2 (*Good Night, Ladies—Harmony*) and ask the students to sing the harmony parts for the song. Divide into four groups, with Tr. I singing the melody and, for the harmony parts, Tr. II (begins on the fifth), C.V. (on the third), and Bar. (on the root). **Could the harmony parts be** combined with "Pick a Little, Talk a Little" to create a new arrangement? (yes)

15

MUSICIANSHIP 4

Lesson Focus

Rhythm: Music may move in relation to the underlying shortest pulse. *(P–I)*

Materials

○ **Piano Accompaniment:** page 238
○ **Record Information:**
  • Let the Rafters Ring
    Record 1 Side A Band 4
    Voices: mixed choir
    Accompaniment: 12-string guitar, rhythm guitar, double bass, piano, percussion
○ **Other:** overhead projector
○ **Teacher's Resource Binder:**
  Activity Sheets
  • **Activity Sheet 3,** page A6 (Prepare a transparency.)
  • **Activity Sheet 4,** page A7 (Prepare a transparency.)
  • **Activity Sheet 5,** pages A8–A15
  • Optional—
    Kodaly Activity 5, page K8

The Lesson

1. Review the roles of the composer and lyricist (page 10); then ask the students to turn to page 16. Direct the students' attention to the song credit; they will notice that the composer and the lyricist are the same person. Ask the students to listen to the recording of "Let the Rafters Ring," paying special attention to the melody (Part 2 for Section A and Part 1 for Section B). **Do the lyrics begin with words that can be sung in an interesting rhythm?** (yes) **Does the rhythm follow the natural flow of the words?** (yes) **How does the composer contrast Sections A and B?** (Section B has a different melody that is *legato*; it begins with a skip from low to high rather than the high-to-low skip that begins Section A; and it has many even notes, whereas Section A has mostly dotted rhythms.)

2. Display the transparency prepared from Activity Sheet 3 (*Let the Rafters Ring—Rhythm*) on the overhead projector. Direct half of the class to tap an even pattern of sixteenth notes while the other half taps the rhythm of Part 1 of "Let the Rafters Ring." Reverse part assignments and repeat the exercise.

3. Challenge each student to combine these patterns, tapping sixteenth notes with one hand and the rhythm of the song with the other.

4. Display the transparency prepared from Activity Sheet 4 (*Let the Rafters Ring—Melody*) on the overhead projector, directing the students to use numbers to read and sing the melody. (Bar. and some C.V. will sing an octave lower than the other voices.)

5. Ask the students to combine the information gained in Steps 3 and 4 to read and sing Part 1 from the score on pages 16–18.

For Your Information

The next five lessons (Musicianship 4–8) will deal with various activities based on the song "Let the Rafters Ring." Voicing options for "Let the Rafters Ring": Any voice may sing any part. C.V. and Bar. sing an octave lower than notated. One voicing option follows:

Section A: Part 1—C.V. and Tr. II
Part 2—Tr. I and Bar.

Section B: (Measures 10–14 and 22–26)
Part 1—Tr. I and Tr. II
Part 2—C.V. and Bar.

6. Play the melody for Part 2 on the piano, assisting Tr. I and Bar. (8ve lower) as they sing Section A and C.V. and Bar. as they sing Section B to the end. Assign all vocal parts (See **For Your Information**.), and invite the students to perform the entire song.

7. **OPTIONAL** Return to "Let the Rafters Ring" after the students have had experience as conductors (Musicianship 5) and instrumentalists (Musicianship 7). Appoint a conductor, providing him or her with Activity Sheet 5 (*Conductor's Score—Let the Rafters Ring*). Provide class time for the conductor to study this score and practice appropriate cues for an instrumental and vocal performance of "Let the Rafters Ring."

The Conductor

A musical performance begins to come alive when the conductor rehearses the performers.

Before the rehearsal, the conductor

- studies the score and considers what might contribute to an expressive performance
- makes decisions about tempo, articulation, dynamics, and phrasing
- prepares the score by adding conducting cues and indicating the performers' entrances and expression markings

During the rehearsal, the conductor directs the performers by

- giving the basic beat pattern with the right hand

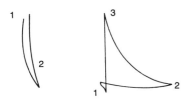
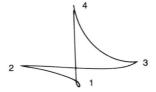

- providing cues for entrances with the left hand

- altering the motions of both hands to communicate expressive ideas

Refer to the score for "Let the Rafters Ring" on pages 16–18. Study the expression markings and the cues shown in red. Practice the basic $\frac{4}{4}$ conducting pattern. Take turns conducting and rehearsing the performers.

19

MUSICIANSHIP 5

Lesson Focus
Rhythm: A series of beats may be organized into regular or irregular groupings by stressing certain beats. *(P–S)*

Materials
○ **Piano Accompaniments:** pages 288, 296, 316, 238
○ **Record Information:**
  - Hand Me Down My Walkin' Cane
    Record 7   Side A   Band 2
    Voices: mixed voices
    Accompaniment: banjo, acoustic guitar, double bass
  - Down in the Valley
    Record 7   Side B   Band 3
    Voices: treble voices
    Accompaniment: fiddle, guitar, harmonica
  - Aura Lee
    Record 9   Side A   Band 6a
    Voices: mixed voices
    Accompaniment: acoustic guitar
  - Let the Rafters Ring
    (Record 1   Side A   Band 4)
○ **Other:** transparent food wrap
○ **Teacher's Resource Binder:**
  - Optional—
    Mainstreaming Suggestion 3, page M6

The Lesson

1. Ask the students to open their books to page 19 and read the text. Discuss the tasks of a conductor.

2. Invite the students to practice the basic conducting patterns shown on page 19. Instruct them to use only their right hand. Play the following recorded selections as the students practice the appropriate conducting patterns for "Hand Me Down My Walkin' Cane" in $\frac{2}{4}$ meter (page 117); "Down in the Valley" in $\frac{3}{4}$ meter (page 127); and "Aura Lee" in $\frac{4}{4}$ meter (page 169).

3. Discuss the function of cueing. Ask the students to practice cueing entrances with the left hand while continuing to conduct basic patterns with the right hand.

4. Examine the vocal score of "Let the Rafters Ring" (pages 16–18). Discuss the cues indicated. In a slow tempo, have the students sing the vocal parts while practicing the basic conducting pattern and indicated cues. When appropriate, play the recording of the song while all conduct from the score.

5. Give several students the opportunity to conduct "Let the Rafters Ring" while the class sings the song. Remind the conductors that they must be familiar with both vocal parts if they are to know when the choir is making any errors.

6. *OPTIONAL* Ask the students to select a song from Unit 4. They can add conducting cues by putting transparent food wrap over the book pages and notating cues directly on the wrap. Each student should study the song and then be prepared to rehearse and conduct the choir.

19

MUSICIANSHIP 6

Lesson Focus

Harmony: Chords and melody may move simultaneously in relation to each other. *(D–S)*

Materials

○ **Piano Accompaniment:** page 238
○ **Record Information:**
   • Let the Rafters Ring
     (Record 1   Side A   Band 4)
○ **Teacher's Resource Binder:**
   • Optional—
     Enrichment Activity 1, page E2
     Mainstreaming Suggestion 4, page M9

The Vocalist

A musical performance often includes vocalists as well as instrumentalists. The vocalists may perform as soloists or as members of an ensemble.

Select the part most appropriate for your range.

Warm up your voice and sing together.

Choose soloists to create improvised melodies. Perform these melodies with the ensemble as they sing "Sing Away . . ."

20

The Lesson

1. Help the students to be aware of their role as a vocalist in an ensemble. Discuss the importance of a balanced sound in a choral ensemble:

    • All voices should have a good quality.
    • All voices need to be singing in their proper range.
    • Each group has the responsibility to control its volume to achieve an overall blend.

    Review the vocal range of each group by examining the ranges listed on page 20. Discuss that it is often possible for voices to sing in more than one group (most Tr. I and II singers can perform either part). Use the vocal warm-up "Sing-a-way . . ." to practice achieving a good ensemble sound.

2. Discuss the role of the vocal soloist. Explain that the soloist can sing alone or with a back-up group of choral or instrumental perform-

    ers. **How do the soloist and choral ensemble interact when they are performing together?** Conclude that both the soloist and the ensemble are striving for an expressive performance. The soloist will probably be the dominant voice, with the ensemble's support.

3. Invite one or more soloists to improvise melodies (using the syllables "doo-dee-dah") as the rest of the class performs "Sing-a-way . . ." in parts. Students will find improvising on "Sing-a-way . . ." to be relatively easy as the chord sequence is simple and repetitious. The soloists may feel more at ease if allowed to practice their improvisations while everyone is singing. When appropriate, plan an arrangement of "Sing-a-way . . .," deciding when each soloist will sing.

4. Return to "Let the Rafters Ring" (pages 16–18), and perform the song again.

OPTIONAL

20

The Instrumentalist

A musical performance usually includes instrumental performers. They may perform all the parts of the music or provide an accompaniment for the vocalists.

The instrumentalist

- plays the part appropriate for his or her instrument
- practices that part in order to learn the music and play it accurately
- rehearses with the conductor to prepare for the performance

Instrumental parts for "Let the Rafters Ring"

21

MUSICIANSHIP 7

Lesson Focus

Texture: Musical quality is affected by the number of musical lines occurring simultaneously. *(P–S)*

Materials

○ **Piano Accompaniment:** page 238

○ **Record Information:**
- Let the Rafters Ring
  (Record 1 Side A Band 4)

○ **Instruments:** cello, double bass, or diatonic bass xylophone; resonator bells (or glockenspiels); guitar; autoharp; piano; tambourines

○ **Other:** Activity Sheet 5 as prepared for Musicianship 5 (page 19)

○ **Teacher's Resource Binder:**

Activity Sheets
- **Activity Sheet 6,** pages A16–17
- Optional—
  Instrumental Accompaniment 1, page 12

The Lesson

1. Read page 21. Discuss the role of the instrumentalist. Ask the students to examine the instrumental parts for "Let the Rafters Ring."

2. Play the recording, and distribute all available tambourines. Encourage all students to read and play the tambourine part either by clapping hands or by using tambourines.

3. Ask the students to examine the cello or double bass part. Explain that the part may also be played by a diatonic bass xylophone, if the performer rests on the C♯ in Measure 14.

4. Direct the students' attention to the bell part, and point out that the performer will begin playing after 34 measures of rest. (Resonator bells or glockenspiels may be substituted here.)

5. Distribute Activity Sheet 6 (*Piano, Guitar, and Autoharp Parts*) to students capable of reading these parts independently.

6. Divide into groups and ask each student not playing piano, guitar, or autoharp to select a part from page 21. Ask each instrumental group to appoint one member of the group to be its conductor. Tambourine players should be encouraged to create new rhythms in addition to the given part.

7. When the students have learned their parts, assemble the entire class. Appoint one student class conductor. Provide the class conductor with a copy of Activity Sheet 5 (see **Materials**). The conductor should rehearse the instrumental group and write cues on the score to assist in the performance of "Let the Rafters Ring."

21

MUSICIANSHIP 8

Lesson Focus

Expression: Musical elements are combined into a whole to express a musical or extramusical idea. *(P–E)*

Materials

○ **Piano Accompaniments:** pages 288, 238

○ **Record Information:**
  • Hand Me Down My Walkin' Cane
    (Record 7   Side A   Band 2)
  • Let the Rafters Ring
    (Record 1   Side A   Band 4)

○ **Teacher's Resource Binder:**
  | Activity Sheets | • **Activity Sheet 7**, page A18 |

For Your Information

Students may initially resist participating in a choreography activity because of shyness, fear of appearing clumsy, or peer pressure. Encourage a class discussion of these problems. Share similar experiences, if applicable.

The Choreographer

Many musical performances take on an added dimension when the choreographer creates movements to accompany the music.

The choreographer

• devises interesting movements
• plans a sequence of movements that fits the form of the music
• rehearses the movements with the choir

Create movements for "Let the Rafters Ring." Write down your plan. Rehearse the choreography.

22

The Lesson

1. Direct the students' attention to page 22. Ask if any students have been involved in a program that used choreography or have ever attended a performance that used choreography. Invite these students to describe their experiences and demonstrate any movements they may know.

2. Hand out copies of Activity Sheet 7 (*Group Movements*). Allow the students time to read the activity sheet and experiment with the suggested movements.

3. Divide the class into small groups. Choose a song such as "Hand Me Down My Walkin' Cane" (page 117) that has a strong rhythmic feeling and a text that suggests movement. Play the recording. Ask each group to choreograph the song.

4. Invite each group to perform for the class. Discuss the choreography; point out unique features among the groups and movements that the groups may have in common. Ask the students to discuss how each choreography relates to the music, how the music was enhanced, and the precision of the performance.

5. Ask the groups to choreograph "Let the Rafters Ring." Use the recording. Invite them to experiment with several movement ideas to create their choreography.

6. *OPTIONAL* If appropriate, ask the students to attend a high school swing choir concert. Students may be given "extra credit" for written or oral reports on either the overall effectiveness of the choir's performance or the relationship of their movements to the music.

The Arranger

A musical performance may include newly composed songs or arrangements of melodies composed by someone else.

The arranger

- selects an interesting melody
- chooses a musical style
- creates instrumental and vocal parts
- notates a part for each performer

Examine the rhythmic ideas shown below. Listen to the recording of each arrangement and follow the vocal scores beginning on the next page. Can you identify the significant features of each arrangement?

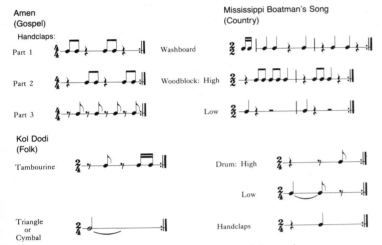

After you have listened to the various arrangements and discussed the different characteristics of each style, prepare your own arrangement of one of the three songs.

23

Lesson Focus

Time and Place: The way musical elements are combined into a whole reflects the origin of the music. **(D–S)**

Materials

○ **Piano Accompaniments:** pages 247, 242, 244

○ **Record Information:**

- *Kol Dodi*
  Record 1   Side A   Band 5
  Voices: mixed voices
  Accompaniment: clarinet, trumpet, trombone, tuba, violin, cimbalom, mandolin, accordion, double bass, percussion

- *Mississippi Boatman's Song*
  Record 1   Side A   Band 6
  Voices: mixed voices
  Accompaniment: ocarina, banjo, piano, double bass, washboard, percussion

- *Amen*
  Record 1   Side A   Band 7
  Voices: mixed voices
  Accompaniment: electric organ, electric guitar, piano, electric bass, percussion

(continued on next page)

The Lesson

1. Discuss the role of an arranger. Direct the students' attention to the information given at the top of page 23. Ask the students to follow the percussion parts shown on page 23 as you play the recording of "Kol Dodi." **Why do you think these rhythms are appropriate for a folk style arrangement?** (Answers may vary. Guide the students to discover that the rhythms and percussion parts are dancelike and syncopated, suggesting a folk dance from another country.)

2. **How might an arrangement of "Mississippi Boatman's Song" (page 25) differ from *Kol Dodi*?** (Guide the students to consider that instruments such as washboard, guitar, and fiddle might be used in "Mississippi Boatman's Song." The boatmen may have used the song as a dance. Call and response may have been used: A leader or a small group of people would sing first, then the others would respond.) Listen to the recording of "Mississippi Boatman's Song." **Did the arranger use any of the ideas you expected?** (Answers may vary.)

3. Follow the procedure used in Step 2 for "Amen" (pages 26–27). (Help the students discover that the syncopated rhythms and bass line convey a feeling of rhythmic excitement despite the somewhat slow tempo.)

4. Discuss the stylistic differences among the three songs. Divide the class into three groups. Have each group learn one of the three songs from this lesson. Add the percussion parts shown on page 23, and perform each song for the class.

Materials *(continued)*

○ **Instruments:** guitar; percussion such as tambourine, cymbals, washboard, and woodblocks, triangle, high and low-pitched drums

○ **Other:** a pencil for each student

○ **Teacher's Resource Binder:**

Activity Sheets
• **Activity Sheet 8**, page A19
Checkpoint 1, page Ev2

Evaluation
• Optional—
Instrumental Accompaniment 2, page I3
Kodaly Activity 1, page K2
Mainstreaming Suggestion 5, page M11

Kol Dodi

Israeli Folk Song

Kol do - di, kol do - di, kol do - di, hi - në ze ba.

M'- da - lëg al he - ha - rim, ___ m'- ka - pëts al ___ ha - g'va - ot. ha - g'va - ot.

24

5. Ask each group to create a "new" arrangement for its song. Each arrangement should include percussion parts. The students may wish to modify the tempo, original percussion parts, or the vocal harmony parts of "Mississippi Boatman's Song" and "Amen." Encourage each group to notate its arrangement, if possible, using Activity Sheet 8 (*Manuscript Paper*). Ask each group to perform its new arrangement and discuss the arrangement's style and unique qualities with the class.

Mississippi Boatman's Song

Traditional

C.V.:
Oh, the boat-man dance, the boat-man sing, The
The oy-ster boat should keep to shore, The
boat-man good for ev-ery-thing. When the boat-man
fish-ing smack should ven-ture more. The schoo-ner sails becomes on shore, He spends his mo-ney and he works for more.
fore the wind, The steam-boat leaves a streak be-hind.

Tr. I: Yo - ho! The boat-man row Up and down the riv-er in his old ba-teau.
Tr. II: Yo - ho! The boat-man row Up and down the riv-er in his old ba-teau.
C.V.: Yo - ho! The boat-man row Up and down the riv-er in his old ba-teau.
Bar.: Yo - ho! The boat-man row Up and down the riv-er in his old ba-teau.

25

For Your Information

The Hebrew Text for *Kol Dodi* is pronounced as follows:

Kohl doe-**dee**, hih-**nay** zay bah.
May-dah-**layg** ahl hay-hah-**reem**,
May-kah-**pets** ahl hah-g'vah-**oht**.

The translation for *Kol Dodi* follows:

I hear the voice of my beloved;
He comes leaping up the mountains,
Climbing the hills.

Amen

Spiritual

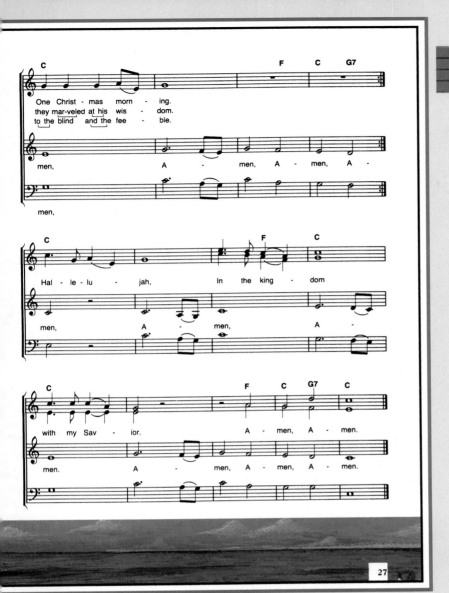

Lesson Focus

Time and Place: The way musical elements are combined into a whole reflects the origin of the music. *(P–S)*

Materials

○ **Other:** videotape recorder, microphone, video camera (with zoom lens and mounted on a tripod, if possible), monitor; headphones; pencils

○ **Teacher's Resource Binder:**

Activity Sheets
- **Activity Sheet 9**, page A20
- Optional—
  Enrichment Activities 3, 4, pages E5–E14

The Television Studio

Television is an important medium for recording and broadcasting

- live concerts
- operas and musicals
- solo recitals
- commentaries about music
- improvised performances
- programs about music
- commercials that use music

How can you use television equipment to assemble a broadcast program that includes a musical performance?

28

The Lesson

1. Discuss the basic TV studio equipment shown in the illustrations on pages 28–30. (See **For Your Information.**)

2. Divide the class into production teams consisting of a producer or director, a camera operator, and a videotape operator. Each group will plan a production that will result in a videotape. The students may tape any of the following:

   - a live concert
   - an opera or a musical (see pages 32–38 for a possible example)
   - a solo recital or chamber music concert
   - a commentary about or description of a favorite piece of music or an improvised musical performance
   - a program about some other aspect of music

   - a biography of a musician that might include a performance of his or her composition(s)
   - a commercial that uses music

   Ask each production team to decide on a program and begin planning the production using Activity Sheet 9 (*Story Board/Script/Cues*). Use the sample on page 31 as a guide. The plan should include the sequence of events that will occur within a production; begin with an introductory sequence; include a series of segments that develop the focus of the production; and conclude with a section that creates a feeling of closure. For each of the segments, the students should include a sketch of what might be seen on the screen by the viewer, a description of the audio that will accompany that segment, and comments that will aid the production team in carrying out its plan. Encourage the students to be sure that this initial production is reasonably short and simple.

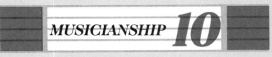

The Production Staff

Personnel	Function	Personnel	Function
Executive Producer	• Is in charge of one or several programs	Stage Manager	• Manages all activities on studio floor • Directs performers on the floor, relaying director's cues to the performers and supervising the floor personnel
Producer	• Takes charge of one production • Is responsible for all personnel working on the production • Also, sometimes serves as writer and/or director	Stage Hands	• Assemble sets • Display cue cards • Operate other prompting devices • Operate microphone booms
Associate Producer	• Assists producer in all production matters	Studio or Remote Supervisors	• Oversee all technical operations
Field Producer	• Assists producer by taking charge of operations away from the studio	Technical Director	• Acts as engineering crew chief
Production Assistant	• Assists producer and director	Camera Operators	• Operate the cameras
Director	• Is in charge of directing performers and technical crews • Transforms a script into an effective video and audio message	Lighting Director	• Controls the lighting of the production
		Video Operators	• Adjust camera controls
		Audio Engineer	• Is in charge of all audio operations
		Videotape Operator	• Runs the videotape machine and does videotape editing

29

For Your Information

Before taping a production, necessary resources such as visuals, musicians, a narrator, chairs, music stands, video recorder, microphone, camera, headphones, and monitor should be secured. If you are uncertain about connecting and operating videotape equipment, confer with the audiovisual specialist in your building. It might be useful to present (or have the audiovisual specialist present) a brief introduction on the operation of the AV equipment for each of the student operators or for the entire class.

3. Once the plan has been completed, each member of the production team should determine what he or she will do to implement the plan. The producer or director should be in charge of coordinating the production. The camera operator should assume responsibility for operating the camera, and the videotape operator should be responsible for placing microphones and recording the program.

4. Rehearse the production before taping, until each segment flows smoothly into the next. The camera or videotape operators may check out their equipment and set appropriate recording levels during the rehearsal. When the production is rehearsed, tape it, following the directions on the activity sheet.

5. Share the tape of each production with the entire class. Invite constructive comments and suggestions for improvements. Encourage students to consider the following:

• Did the focus of the production come through clearly?
• Was music used effectively?
• Did each segment flow smoothly into the next?
• Were the camera shots effective?
• Did the microphone placement allow each person to be heard clearly?
• Was the presentation interesting?

OPTIONAL

6. The class may want to choose one of the programs and expand it or may choose to write a new, more extensive program. In either case, the project should use a larger production staff (see the chart on page 29) and incorporate musicians from the class.

The Television System

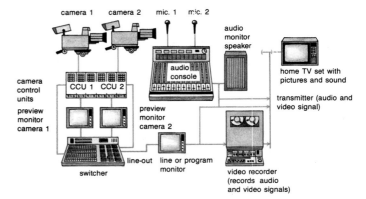

camera 1   camera 2   mic. 1   mic. 2

audio monitor speaker

home TV set with pictures and sound

audio console

camera control units

CCU 1   CCU 2

preview monitor camera 1

preview monitor camera 2

transmitter (audio and video signal)

line-out   line or program monitor

switcher

video recorder (records audio and video signals)

A television system may include very complex equipment, as shown in the diagram above, or it may be quite simple, as shown below. Most school and home equipment will be limited to one camera, one microphone (or a microphone built into the camera), a video recorder, and a monitor or TV set.

Connect your equipment as shown below. A set of headphones should be connected to the headphone or speaker output jack of the recorder.

microphone   camera   headphones   TV set or monitor

video recorder

30

Planning and Producing
A Musical Event

Program *String Quartet*
page *1* of 5

Video	Audio	Comments
GLENDALE MIDDLE SCHOOL PRESENTS SONG and DANCE —ROBERT WASHBURN	**String Quartet:** (Begin playing at measure 94) (Music ends)	Close camera shot on title card
	Announcer: Welcome to another mini-concert by the Glendale Middle School String Quartet.	Close-up shot of announcer
	Announcer: Today the focus of our concert is 20th century string music, more specifically the music of Robert Washburn.	Begin with shot of announcer; cut to shot of quartet (include all players)
	Announcer: Featured today is first violinist, Darryl White...	Zoom from quartet to first violinist
	Announcer: Second violinist, Sandra Chen...	Pan to second violinist

31

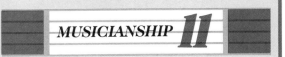

MUSICIANSHIP 11

Lesson Focus

Expression: Musical elements are combined into a whole to express a musical or extramusical idea. *(P–E)*

Materials

○ **Piano Accompaniment:** page 248
○ **Record Information:**
  • Fame
  Record 1   Side A   Band 8
  Voices: mixed choir
  Accompaniment: saxophone, trumpet, trombone, synthesizer, electric guitar, electric bass, percussion
○ **Instruments:** assorted band and orchestral instruments; assorted small percussion (unpitched) instruments; drum set; piano; xylophones; double bass; two sets of resonator bells and mallets
○ **Teacher's Resource Binder:**
  • Optional—
  Instrumental Accompaniment 3, page I7
  Enrichment Activity 2, page E2

NOW CASTING!

What Every Singer Should Know About Acting	
Needed:	
Producer	Chorus and Dancers
Director	Instrumentalists (Pit Orchestra)
Conductor	Costumer
Choreographer	Stage Designer
Singers-Actors:	Rehearsal Pianist
Instructor	Props Manager
Susan	Light and Sound Technicians
George	Publicity Manager

Think about the skills you will need for each role. Decide which on-stage or backstage jobs you might apply for. What criteria should be used in casting these roles?

The Producer
A producer is always available to help and to make sure that all the parts of the production flow smoothly.

The Director
The director may wish to have the actors speak the parts for the first run-through, planning when they are to enter, where they should move, and so on.

The Conductor(s)
The conductors work with the members of the chorus and the orchestra. They prepare the song and accompaniment and an overture and a finale.

The Vocal Performers
The vocal performers should be able to
  • read music
  • sing in a style appropriate to the role
  • perform expressively
  • act the role believably

Prepare for the tryouts. Read the script. Choose one of the roles. Plan how you will perform the role. Think about the melodies you might improvise for your lines.

32

The Lesson

1. Organize students to produce the musical drama "What Every Singer Should Know About Acting." Explore the roles and procedures outlined on pages 32–33. As a class, read through the drama; then listen to the recording of the song "Fame." After the class has become familiar with "What Every Singer Should Know About Acting," choose a producer, a director, a conductor, and a choreographer. Allow the remaining students time to read the script silently and think about how they can be a part of the production. Discuss their ideas and then hold auditions. Help the producer, director, and conductor cast roles, appoint production personnel, and designate musicians (for the chorus and orchestra).

2. Divide the class into groups according to their production roles. Discuss some of the ways they might approach their individual tasks.

Chorus:
• Appoint a rehearsal conductor.
• Listen to the recording of "Fame."
• Learn to sing "Fame."
• Use resonator bells to identify the pitches for the humming accompaniment to the solo *recitatives.*
• Create a harmony part using the chord sequence on page 33.
• Create choreography for the first scene.

Orchestra: Instrumentalists will work with the conductor to prepare an accompaniment for the song "Fame."

Orchestra Conductor:
• Discuss with orchestra members how they can create a bridge between the song and the humming part of the chorus.
• Make decisions as to when the orchestra will or will not be playing.
• Assign instrumental parts. (Be prepared to transpose the instrumental parts if needed.)

The Orchestra
Instrumentalists in the orchestra should be able to

- read music
- play an instrument
- improvise or compose a part following a harmonic sequence
- perform expressively
- listen carefully and balance with the rest of the orchestra

Examine this chord sequence. It can be used to accompany "Fame" as sung by the vocal performers (see page 34); repeat this sequence four times and end with the F minor chord.

repeat ad lib.

What instruments will you use to play the root of each chord? Which instruments will play the remaining pitches? Could someone play a variation of the melody of "Fame" and create an overture? Or new variation for a finale?

Stage Personnel
The stage personnel help to determine production needs, acquire props, and prepare for staging the show.

The Rehearsal
The director and the conductor must work together to plan a smooth transition from the overture to the dramatic action to the closing instrumental finale.

The cast works in groups to prepare the many parts of the production; then the full ensemble premieres the performance.

For Your Information
The students will have an opportunity to perform songs and improvise *recitatives* (sung dialogue) during the course of this lesson. The improvised *recitatives* will be a challenge for most students. Begin by instructing students to speak the lines, adding vocal inflections to exaggerate the words. Ultimately, students should sing the words, improvising pitches and articulations to express the text dramatically.

- Assign percussion parts; include a drum set, if available, and other classroom percussion instruments.

Cast Members:
- Appoint a drama coach to help the "Instructor" learn to read his or her lines clearly and expressively.
- "Susan" and "George" may need help in improvising their *recitatives*.

Stage Personnel:
- Determine production needs.
- Acquire props.
- Prepare for staging the show.

3. When all students have practiced their parts, instruct the producer and director to coordinate and rehearse the production. Refine the production, and perform the musical drama.

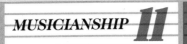

Story by Harvey Rudoff

A fine arts high school in a large metropolitan city. A group of students are in rehearsal, dancing and singing. Their instructor interrupts.

Fame

Lyrics by Dean Pitchford

Music by Michael Gore

34

Instructor: *(speaking)* Singers are expected to be able to act. Acting lessons are expensive and time-consuming. Many young singers can't afford them. Yet it will do them no good to learn to sing the music if they can't act out the story. What is needed is a jiffy course in acting that contains the basic principles of stagecraft in simple, easily understood terms. Briefly, that is what I propose to do.

We will begin our first lesson by tackling the art of sitting down. *(writes "Sitting Down" on the board to emphasize the point)*

Try sitting down. Go ahead—that's terrible! You need a lot of practice before attempting that before an audience; because sitting down takes place mostly behind you. You can't watch yourself do it. So ask somebody to observe you while you practice, and ask for criticism.

(Attention is focused on new scene: Susan practicing sitting.)

Chorus: *(sustains these pitches throughout the improvised recitative)*

Tr. I
Tr. II
C.V. } (8ve
Bar. } lower)

(sustain through recitative)

Hm ———

Susan:	Oh, George, come here a minute.
George:	Okay, what do you want?
Susan:	Watch this.
George:	Watch what?
Susan:	This—look. *(sits down)* How was that?
George:	How was what?
Susan:	For heaven's sake, George, I sat down.
George:	Oh.
Susan:	Well?
George:	I guess it was okay.
Susan:	Just "okay"? Is that all you can say?
George:	Well—
Susan:	Look, George, I'll do it again. Now this time, watch. *(sits down again)*
George:	Oh, that's good. That's very good.
Susan:	Thanks, George. *(practices sitting some more)*
George:	Say, that's my lunch you're sitting on!
Susan:	Wha— gee, I'm sorry, George. *(hands him his lunch)*
George:	Thanks.
Susan:	Are you mad, George?
George:	I had a hard-boiled egg and a jelly sandwich in there.

35

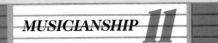

Susan:	I'm sorry, George.
George:	And a tomato.
Susan:	I said I was sorry.
George:	How would you like it if I sat on your lunch?
Susan:	I—
George:	I never did anything to you, did I?
Susan:	Please, George.
George:	If I had known you were going to do that, I wouldn't have put the slice of pie in it.
Susan:	Pie?
George:	I would have put a hard roll in, or an apple, or something that wouldn't squash.
Susan:	Look, George, it was an accident. I didn't mean to sit on your lunch. I was practicing sitting, that's all. I didn't know your lunch was there. Won't you please forgive me, George?
George:	I don't know . . . .
Susan:	I have to practice sitting, George. I want to be an actor, I mean an actress . . . .
George:	An actor? Like Marlon Brando?
Susan:	. . . or someone like Meryl Streep.
George:	I met Marlon Brando once.
Susan:	Really?
George:	He's not the kind of guy that would sit on someone's lunch.
Susan:	Look, George . . . .

(Song returns, sung partway through, with singers humming an accompaniment.)

36

(sustain through recitative)

Hm _____

(Scene briefly shifts back to the instructor.)

Instructor: *(writes on board, "How to Stand Up")* Standing up is not as difficult as sitting down, but to be on the safe side, call someone over and have that person watch you do it.

(Scene changes again to Susan and George.)

Susan: Say, George, come over here and watch me.
George: I'm not talking to you. You sat on my lunch.
Susan: Gosh, are you still thinking about that? That was last week.
George: Well . . . .
Susan: Come on, George, be a good sport and watch me.
George: Well, okay.
Susan: How do I look? *(stands up)*
George: Fine—except the way you're standing.
Susan: What's wrong with how I'm standing?
George: Oh, never mind. It's nothing.
Susan: I want to know, George. Tell me.
George: Forget it. I'd better not.
Susan: Please tell me. How else will I become a good actor?
George: Well, if you must know—you're standing on my lunch.

37

(Chorus sings first three phrases of "Fame" as scene shifts back to the classroom)

Instructor: *(writes on board, "Today's Lesson: How to Cry")* In order to cry, you must think of something really sad. Think of the dent you put in the front fender of your dad's car.

It is true that some actors conceal half an onion in a pocket as they go onstage. When they have to cry, they take a whiff of it and burst into tears. The trouble is that any onion strong enough to make you cry can also be smelled by the people in the first six rows of the theater. It is embarrassing to see them cry before you do. In short, you must have a good reason to cry. It is better not to fake it. Now take that young man over there. See him? Listen to those sobs! His face is buried in his hands, and his shoulders are heaving in absolute grief. I can see the tears dropping to the floor, can't you? That young man must certainly have something to cry about. Why, isn't that George? Oh, for Pete's sake, George!

(Curtain descends as the chorus sings the complete song "Fame.")

38

LISTENING

Big River

Words and Music by Roger Miller

Cast: (Main Characters)

Mark Twain, *the author*
Huckleberry Finn, *motherless boy*
The Widow Douglas, *Tom's guardian*
Jim, *runaway slave*
Miss Watson, *owner of Jim*
Tom Sawyer, *Huck's friend*
The King, *con artist*
The Duke, *con artist*
Mary Jane Wilkes, *Huck's sweetheart*
Pap Finn, *Huck's father*

The Setting: *Along the Mississippi River in the late 1800s*
The Story: *A musical adaptation of Mark Twain's adventure story "Huckleberry Finn"*

Overture (excerpt)

Act I

The scene opens with what seems to be all the townspeople of Petersburg telling Huck who he should be and how he should act. Everyone lectures him about learning to read and write and warns against being a loafer:

> Hey, hey, ain't the situation concernin' education aggravatin'? And how!
> Do you wanna get to heaven?
> Well, you'd better get your lessons or you won't know how . . .

Later that night Huck sneaks out of his bedroom to join Tom Sawyer and other friends in the cave. They brag about all the mischief they'll do in town. After a while Huck returns home.

39

Lesson Focus

Expression: Musical elements are combined into a whole to express a musical or extramusical idea. *(P–S)*

Materials

○ **Piano Accompaniments:** pages 250–258
○ **Record Information:**
  • *Big River*
    by Roger Miller, 1936–
    Record 1 Side B Bands 1–7
    Original Broadway Cast
    Linda Twine, conductor
○ **Teacher's Resource Binder:**
  • Optional—
    Biography 1, pages B1–B2

The Lesson

1. Guide the students to listen actively and perform parts of the Broadway musical *Big River* (pages 39–47). You might appoint one narrator or ask several students to read parts of the narration aloud. Play the recording of each song several times to help the students learn these songs.

2. Start by asking the students to open their books to page 39. Discuss the setting for the musical: along the Mississippi River. Review the characters in the cast. Many students will be familiar with the story, which is a musical adaptation of Mark Twain's *The Adventures of Huckleberry Finn.* The action opens with the actor who portrays the author, Mark Twain, warning the audience: "Persons attempting to find a motive to this narrative will be prosecuted; persons attempting to find a moral in it will be banished; persons attempting to find a plot in it will be shot by order of the author, Mark Twain."

3. Listen to the recording and discuss the following selections from *Big River.*

The Music: The music in this drama represents many different styles of American music. Students will hear styles such as country, Dixieland, and gospel.

The Overture (excerpt) (Band 1): The overture creates an atmosphere for the musical and introduces some of the songs. The use of the harmonica, guitar, and fiddle gives the overture a "country" sound.

Waitin' for the Light to Shine (Band 2): Listen to the recording to acquaint students with the melody (page 40). Tr. I and Tr. II can sing the song as written, with Tr. I singing the upper part and Tr. II singing the lower part where harmony is indicated. C.V. should sing the

For Your Information

You might present *Big River* to the students in two ways. One way is to approach the musical as a listening lesson, with students reading the narrative and following the score as recorded selections are played. A second, more active approach is to encourage the students to learn to sing the songs and perform them with the recorded selections (see Step 3). The musical could be performed by reading the libretto aloud and singing the songs or could be staged for others to enjoy.

Later that night Huck's Pap shows up in Huck's bedroom and drags his son off to a cabin in the woods. He threatens and yells at Huck. When his Pap is asleep, Huck sees the chance to escape. He runs away to hide on Jackson's Island. While on the island he reflects on his character, singing a plaintive song.

Waitin' for the Light to Shine

I have lived in the dark-ness for so long, I'm wait-ing for the light to shine. Far be-yond _ ho-ri-zons, I have seen be-yond the things I've been, _ be-yond the dreams I've dreamed, _ are the things I've done, In fact each and ev-ery one are the way that I was taught to run. I am wait-ing for the light to shine, _ I am wait-ing for the light to shine. I have lived in the dark-ness for so long, I'm wait-ing for the light to shine.

40

Tr. II part, but they will be out of range at Measures 2 and 3 and should adjust by singing an octave lower. Bar. should sing the Tr. 1 part an octave lower throughout.

Muddy Water (Band 3): Jim begins this song (page 42) and is soon joined by Huck. The song has a hard-driving rhythm, suggesting, perhaps, the urgency of Jim's escape. Jim sings the refrain, which is followed by Verse 1; Huck joins in at the repeat of the refrain; Verse 2 is sung by Jim alone; the refrain is repeated again, with a tambourine part added. The refrain is repeated twice and then modulates up a whole step. The song ends with a slow, embellished coda typical of gospel style.

Help the students learn "Muddy Water." Tr. I and Tr. II can sing the song as notated. C.V. will have some range problems (high C's throughout) and will have to drop out or sing

an octave lower as needed. Bar. can sing the melody an octave lower than written. The accompaniment is dronelike (using mostly repeated pitches).

Invite interested students to improvise a harmony part by following the chord symbols. Begin by singing a single-pitch harmony line. **Sing middle C for both the C and F chords and move down a half step to B for the G7 chord.**

Then divide the students into three groups and create a three-part harmony from the chord symbols for "Muddy Water." Start by assigning each pitch of the C major chord to a separate group and proceed in the manner shown in the following example.

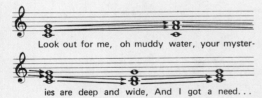

Look out for me, oh muddy water, your myster-

ies are deep and wide, And I got a need...

When the Sun Goes Down in the South (Band 4): This song is set in a Dixieland style and is performed by King, Duke, and Huck. Play the recording several times to acquaint students with the music. Ask them to sing the lyrics (page 44) with the recording.

You Oughta Be Here with Me (Band 5): This selection (page 45) is an example of country music. The acoustic guitar begins playing in $\frac{3}{4}$ meter with steady strums. This waltzlike pattern continues throughout the song. Simple harmonies are supplied by violin (fiddle) and harmonica. The light accompaniment allows

the listener's attention to focus on the singer rather than on the instrumental parts. After repeated listenings, ask the students to sing along with the recording.

Leavin's Not the Only Way to Go (Band 6): Tr. I and Tr. II can sing the melody as notated (pages 46–47): Bar. sings an octave lower. C.V. should sing the first phrase an octave lower and the second phrase as notated and should continue to alternate in this way throughout the song.

Muddy Water (Reprise) (Band 7): The finale to this musical is a reprise (return) of the song "Muddy Water." If necessary, refer the students to the music (page 42). Ask them to sing along with this reprise, and encourage them to improvise harmonies.

Huck's reflective mood doesn't last long. The free-spirited Huck bounces back by showing his "I don't care" attitude:

> I, Huckleberry, me
> Hereby declare myself to be
> Nothing ever other than
> Exactly what I am . . .

Huck soon finds that he is not alone on Jackson's Island. Miss Watson's slave Jim, who has run away to keep from being sold downriver to New Orleans, is also there. Huck makes a decision to team up with Jim and help him to get to the free states. With just minutes to spare, they evade a posse by shoving a raft onto the river. Then they head away for freedom.

Muddy Water

42

43

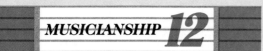

The road to freedom is hazardous. Huck and Jim narrowly escape capture and a collision with a steamboat. When all finally seems quiet, they are interrupted by a couple of con artists, King and Duke, who are trying to escape an angry mob. King and Duke commandeer the raft with Huck and Jim still on it. Once they are safely away from the mob, they begin to sing about how they duped the townsfolk. Huck is drawn into their talk and joins their singing.

When the Sun Goes Down in the South

Verse 1:
When the sun goes down in the south
And the moon comes up in the east,
Well, step right up and see the wonder of the ages.
It's a guaranteed visual feast.

Refrain:
When the darkness falls on the town
And the north star's startin' to rise
Oh, you can't imagine a menagerie air
Created by a couple of guys.

Verse 2:
Well, anybody wonderin' what they're going to see
Is gonna have to ante up a dollar for the ticket.
Anybody wonderin' what's goin' on
Is gonna find out when they chase us through the thicket.

(repeat Refrain)

Verse 3:
When the sun goes down in the south
And the hayseeds stand in line.
Well, step right up and see the duo
Bod'ly do the doo wah diddy on the clothes line.

Act II

The second act begins with King, Duke, and Huck going ashore at Bricktown, Arkansas to con the townsfolk while Jim remains with the raft. They are delighted when an unsuspecting "young fool" brags about a fortune left by a death in the Wilkes family. King and Duke present themselves as the rightful heirs to the fortune, depriving the beautiful and innocent Mary Jane Wilkes of her estate. Huck, smitten with Mary Jane, steals the money back. When Huck is trying to return the money to Mary Jane's home, she appears unexpectedly. Mary Jane sings an ironic love song to her dear departed father. Huck listens as he hides nearby.

44

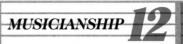

You Oughta Be Here with Me

If you think it's lonesome where you are tonight,
Then you oughta be here with me.
If you think there's heartaches where you are tonight,
Then you oughta be here with me.
'Cause with you I'm whole, without you I'm cold.
If teardrops are fallin; where you are tonight,
Then you oughta be here with me.
Is loneliness callin' where you are tonight?
Then you oughta be here with me.
'Cause with you I'm whole, without you I'm cold.
So if you think about me where you are tonight,
Then you oughta be here with me.

Upon finding out what Huck has done for her, Mary Jane asks him to
stay awhile and become her friend. He is deeply moved but also realizes his responsibility to Jim. The conflict of indecision is reflected in
the song Huck, Mary Jane, and Jim sing. (*Two scenes are shown, one
depicting Mary Jane and Huck in town and the other showing Jim
at the river.*)

45

Leavin's Not the Only Way to Go

Did the morn-ing come too ear - ly? Was the
lay and let your feel - ings grow ac -

night not long e - nough? Does a tear of hes - i - ta - tion fall___ on
cus-tomed to the dark ___ And by morn-ing's light you just ___ might solve ___ the

ev - ery-thing you touch? Well, it might be just a les - son for the
prob-lems of the heart. And it all might be a les - son for the

has - ty heart to know. ___ May-be leav-in's not the on - ly way to go. ___
has - ty heart to know. ___ May-be leav-in's not the on - ly way ___ to go. ___

1.   2.
___ 2. May-be ___ Peo-ple reach new ___ un-der-stand-ings all ___ the

time. They take a sec-ond look, may-be change their mind. Peo-ple

reach new ___ un - der-stand - ings ev - ery day. ____ Tell me not to

46

reach, I'll just go a - way.— Did the morn-ing come too ear - ly? Was the

night not long e - nough?— Does a tear of hes - i - ta - tion fall — on

ev-ery-thing— you touch? Well, it might be just a les - son for the

has - ty heart to know,— May-be leav-in's not the on - ly way— to go.

— And a heart with-out — a home— is such a

lone-ly row to hoe. May-be leav-in's not the on - ly way— to go. ——

Huck returns to the raft, only to find that Duke has been tarred and feathered and Jim is gone. Duke admits he has sold Jim. Huck feels guilty and writes to Miss Watson, telling her where she can find Jim. Feeling even more depressed, he tears up the letter, determined to free Jim by himself. In a surprising turn to the plot, Tom Sawyer shows up and decides to help Huck free Jim from his captors. Huck and Tom succeed in freeing Jim. Jim gets ready to go up North to make money and free his family. Huck decides to go out West to get away from any attempts to "civilize" him. Huck and Jim sing a reprise of "Muddy Water," and Tom and Huck part with Jim as he heads up the river.

Huck ends up alone once more, thinking of their journey. "It was like the fortune Jim predicted long ago," he says, "considerable trouble and considerable joy."

47

Lesson Focus

Expression: The expressiveness of music is affected by the way timbre, tempo, and texture contribute to the musical whole *(D–S)*

For Your Information

Prior to this lesson, you might collect clippings from magazines that contain record reviews (such as *Ovation, Stereo Review,* and *Downbeat*).

The Critic

A musical performance may seem to end with the final curtain, but for the performers there is one more important moment: when they open the morning papers to read the review prepared by the critic.

Music Notes *by Anne Welsbacher*

The Farnsworth Falls Youth Symphony, consisting of senior high school students, gave an even and solid performance of Smetana's "The Moldau" and Borodin's *Symphony No. 2 in B minor.* The first piece, conducted by Sheila Halpern, opened well, with a flute solo that flowed smoothly and was strong without being overbearing. Although the woodwind section had some difficulty with pitch—especially the English horn, which was often flat—the piece as a whole was played well, with knowledge of the material evident, particularly in the string section. Conductor Halpern paced the composition well, with particularly fine control over the final climactic tempo. The piece by Borodin was the better performed of the two; conductor John Ricardo kept the majesty intact and a steady, strong rhythm prevailed throughout. The string section gave a particularly fine rendition of the opening measures of the composition; the strings were perfectly on pitch and set a tempo from which the orchestra as an ensemble never wavered. Both pieces were well balanced; the winds never covered the strings, and the accompaniment was delicate while providing a solid foundation for the main theme.

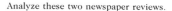

Analyze these two newspaper reviews.

Make a list of the aspects of the performance that the reviewer discusses.

Collect reviews of musical performances from a newspaper or magazine. Do your samples touch on the same topics as the reviews shown here?

Attend a local concert or performance of a musical, and write a review.

Oklahoma! by Rodgers and Hammerstein was produced with vitality and warmth by the Farnsworth State University Theater last weekend. The musical takes place in Oklahoma, shortly before it becomes a state of the Union, and deals with two sets of sweethearts, their families and friends. Pat Brooks, as Laurie, played her role with honesty and vigor. She gave her character personality, singing her love songs with the same good timing and high quality that she shows when she speaks. Barbara Mason, as the comic character Ado Annie, had tremendous energy, and Carol Shapiro, as the kind, no-nonsense Aunt Eller, gave strength to the musical. Also good were Brad Davis as Curly and Greg Murphy as Will. Tom Sonno, as the "heavy," Jud, succeeded in creating the moody character, and his "In My Room" was chilling and effective. The orchestra, directed by Elspeth Esterhazy, was professional and talented; the effective lighting was by Jo-Ann Corelli; the fine costumes by John Franklin; and the well-paced direction by Cindy Stewart.

48

The Lesson

1. Ask the students to open their books to page 48 and read the reviews prepared by a high school student. **What skills does a critic need?** (knowledge of the music being performed, an understanding of what constitutes a good performance, and an ability to express oneself clearly in writing)

2. Discuss aspects of a performance that could be critiqued:

   • overall quality
   • conductor's technique
   • performer's technique
   • expressiveness of the performance

3. **Do all critics agree?** (No, critics each have their own opinions and are responding to what they hear. Often two critics at the same concert will review it quite differently.) **Are the opinions of critics always correct?** (No. Some acknowledged masterpieces of great composers such as Beethoven, Wagner, Debussy, and Stravinsky were harshly criticized at premiere performances.)

4. Ask the students to bring concert and record reviews from newspapers and magazines. Post these on a bulletin board. Compare reviews of rock concerts and records with reviews of jazz and classical performances, and discuss similarities and differences among the reviews.

5. Plan to attend a concert as a class. Assign a critique as a homework assignment. *OPTIONAL*

The Record Collector

The big performance is over. The reviews have been written; the performers have continued their tour to another town. You can still remember the music . . . sort of. With a recording, you can have the performance, or one like it, at your fingertips.

The Record Collector

- sometimes goes shopping for a specific recording by a specific performer
- sometimes browses through the bins of the local record shop to discover recordings of all kinds of music
- sometimes goes to the public library to compare two performances of the same composition before purchasing a recording of one performance
- always takes good care of records (and tapes) to preserve their quality

Always pick up a record by the edges; never allowing your hands to touch it. Keep records free of lint. You may want to purchase a special cleaning cloth. Be sure that the record player needle is in good condition, or that the tape heads on the tape deck are clean. When placing the needle on a record, take care not to scrape it across the record; always put the needle down slowly and carefully.

LISTENING

The Great Gate of Kiev
by Modest Mussorgsky

Modest Mussorgsky (1839–1881) was a Russian composer of the romantic era. Among his best-known works are "A Night on Bald Mountain" and the opera *Boris Godunov*.

Listen to four different recordings of this music. How would you prepare information about each version for use by a record collector?

49

Lesson Focus
Expression: The expressiveness of music is affected by the way timbre, tempo, and texture contribute to the musical whole. *(D–S)*

Materials
○ **Record Information:**
- The Great Gate of Kiev, from *Pictures at an Exhibition* by Modest Mussorgsky (moo-**sorg**-skee), 1839–1881
  Record 2 Side A Bands a–d
  Band a: Paul Schenly, piano
  Band b: Kazuhito Yamashita, guitar
  Band c: New York Philharmonic Leonard Bernstein, conductor
  Band d: Tomita, synthesizer

○ **Other:** a pencil for each student
○ **Teacher's Resource Binder:**

Activity Sheets
- **Activity Sheet 10,** page A21
- Optional—
  Mainstreaming Suggestion 6, page M11

The Lesson

1. Write the following on the chalkboard: "The Record Collector: who, what, when, where, why." Ask the students to brainstorm regarding the recording artists involved, the musical selections, and so on; list their comments on the chalkboard. (Some students may be very sophisticated in their knowledge of recordings while others may be unaware of the variety, having limited their browsing and purchases to current popular recordings.)

2. Read and discuss the information on page 49. Set the following scenario. **Someone has asked you to pick up a recording of *Pictures at an Exhibition*. You stop at the record store and discover that there are four versions of the same piece. Will all the recordings be the same?** Play the opening section for each recorded version of "The Great Gate of Kiev." Modest Mussorgsky originally composed *Pictures at an Exhibition* for solo piano. The four recordings of the excerpt, "The Great Gate of Kiev," employ the original instrumentation (piano) and three variants; the orchestral transcription is traditional, and the guitar and synthesizer versions are contemporary arrangements.

3. Distribute Activity Sheet 10 (The Great Gate of Kiev). Ask the students to prepare information that would assist a record collector; they are to complete the activity sheet as they listen to the four versions of "The Great Gate of Kiev." Provide them with the title, composer, and performers. (See **Materials**. The other answers follow: Type of music—Classical; Instrumentation—1. piano, 2. guitar, 3. orchestra, 4. synthesizer; answers will vary for "Special features" and "Preference scale.")

Lesson Focus

Evaluation: Review concepts and skills studied in Unit 1. *(D–S)*

Materials

○ **Piano Accompaniment:** page 259

○ **Record Information:**
- When I'm on My Journey
  Record 2   Side A   Band 2
  Voices: treble voices
  Accompaniment: electric organ, electric guitar, piano, electric bass, percussion

○ **Teacher's Resource Binder:**

Evaluation
- **Review 1**, page Ev5
- **Musical Progress Report 1**, page Ev6

When I'm on My Journey

Afro-American Song

Verse

1. When I'm on my jour-ney, don't you weep af-ter me.
   When I'm on my jour-ney, don't you weep af-ter me.
   When I'm on my jour-ney, don't you weep af-ter me. I don't
   want you to weep af-ter me.

2. High upon the mountain, leave your troubles down below. (*3 times*)
   (*Refrain*)

3. When the stars are falling and the thunder starts to roll. (*3 times*)
   (*Refrain*)

4. Every lonely river must go home to the sea. (*3 times*)
   (*Refrain*)

50

The Lesson

1. Ask the students to begin by turning to page 50. Invite them to follow the notation for "When I'm on My Journey" while listening to the recording. **Is this a comfortable vocal range for all voices?** (probably not) Encourage everyone to attempt to sing this song. Ask the students to identify the *highest* and *lowest* pitches in the song. (G below middle C to the A above middle C) **What could be done to this song to make it easier for everyone to sing?** (Answers may vary. Guide the students to consider the following possibilities: transpose to another key; different vocal parts might sing only selected phrases; add harmony parts or entire chords to accompany the melody, as they learned to do in Musicianship 2 and 3. Encourage any of these suggestions by demonstrating each possible option.)

2. Challenge the students to create instrumental parts or improvise hand claps to enhance their performance of this song.

3. Arrange for the class to attend a band or choir rehearsal. If this is not possible, arrange to show a videotape of a rehearsal to the class. Ask the students to complete *Review 1;* they should record their observations of the rehearsal on the sheet, using the skills and knowledge learned in Unit 1.

4. Use the information gained from this evaluation and observations made throughout this unit to complete *Musical Progress Report 1.*

Unit 2

The Listening Experience

Unit Overview

In Unit 2, the students have opportunities to develop and refine their listening skills by studying music from the distant past to the present. Students will focus on the various aspects of music—instrumental and vocal timbre, rhythm, melody, and texture—and learn how these elements contribute to that special sound that distinguishes one era from another. The second part of this unit features three works from the world of musical theater—*The Play of Daniel, Madama Butterfly,* and *The Tender Land.* A discussion of audience etiquette and listening skills and how the students might apply these skills in an active social context completes the unit.

Lesson Focus

Time and Place: the way musical elements are combined into a whole reflects the origin of the music. *(D–I)*

Materials

○ **Record Information:**
  • Sound Prints
    Record 2 Side A Bands 0a–h
○ **Teacher's Resource Binder:**
  • Optional—
    Biographies 2–3, pages B3–B6

Listening to Music

We can listen to music
  • in the concert hall
  • on recordings
  • on the radio
  • on television
  • during a dance performance

Listening to music is like entering a time machine. We can be carried instantly out of our surroundings to any point in history.
We can

  • enter a medieval monastery at evensong
  • dance on the village green in merry old England
  • join the town choir as Bach prepares a new chorale
  • seat ourselves in a concert hall in Vienna, dressed in our gowns or tail coats and powdered wigs

Each generation has left behind a living music that says to us: This is how we thought . . . how we lived . . . who we were.
Listen carefully! Our music is part of you.
You will hear us in the sounds of your orchestras.
You will hear us in the melodies of your songs.
You will hear us, for we are still with you today.
Explore the music of past generations, for it is very much a part of today's music.
Listen to several musical examples from various periods of history. Can you guess when each selection was composed?

Look at the time line on the next few pages. Learn about people and events, and look at works of art from each era. Listen again to the musical compositions. Try to connect each musical example with the era in which it was written.

52

The Lesson

1. Begin the lesson by playing the recording of "Sound Prints." (See **For Your Information** for the sequence of the recorded excerpts.)

2. Invite the students to explore music of past generations. Read aloud the information on page 52. Ask the students to divide the top portion of a piece of paper by drawing three columns and labeling the columns *Long Ago, Past,* and *Recent.* Play the recording of "Sound Prints" again and ask the students to listen to each selection and place its number in the column that best describes the music. Play the recording as many times as needed. Assure the students that this is not a test; they may be surprised at how well they do! After the selections are labeled, compare notes. A correct grouping might be:

Long Ago	Past	Recent
1, 3, 5	2, 7	4, 6, 8

3. After discussing the broad categories used in Step 2, suggest that the students try to associate each composition with its specific time period. Invite students to explore each era. Ask them to examine the time line on pages 53–55 and learn about the people, the events, and a representative art piece from each time period shown.

4. After the students have examined the time line, ask them to copy the dates for each period in a row down the left margin of the lower part of their paper. Play "Sound Prints" again, and ask the students to place the number for each selection next to the time period they think most appropriate.

5. Invite the students to discuss their choices. Encourage them to develop appropriate vocabulary to describe what they hear. Suggest the terms *timbre, dynamics, instrumenta-*

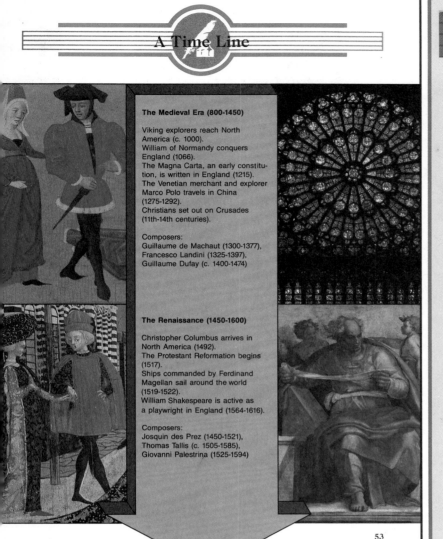

A Time Line

The Medieval Era (800-1450)

Viking explorers reach North America (c. 1000).
William of Normandy conquers England (1066).
The Magna Carta, an early constitution, is written in England (1215).
The Venetian merchant and explorer Marco Polo travels in China (1275-1292).
Christians set out on Crusades (11th-14th centuries).

Composers:
Guillaume de Machaut (1300-1377),
Francesco Landini (1325-1397),
Guillaume Dufay (c. 1400-1474)

The Renaissance (1450-1600)

Christopher Columbus arrives in North America (1492).
The Protestant Reformation begins (1517).
Ships commanded by Ferdinand Magellan sail around the world (1519-1522).
William Shakespeare is active as a playwright in England (1564-1616).

Composers:
Josquin des Prez (1450-1521),
Thomas Tallis (c. 1505-1585),
Giovanni Palestrina (1525-1594)

53

For Your Information

The excerpts on ''Sound Prints'' are heard in the following order:
1. *Hodie Christus Natus Est*— Medieval era (Gregorian chant)
2. ''Prelude to Act III'' from *Lohengrin*—Romantic era
3. *Canon in D*—Baroque era
4. ''*Canto Sotto*'' from *Stanzas, Book VII*—Twentieth century
5. *Fantasia in G*—Renaissance era
6. ''*Nacht*'' (Night) from *Pierrot Lunaire*—Twentieth century
7. First Movement from *String Quartet in B♭, K.458*—Classical era
8. *Reflections*—Twentieth century

tion, *harmony*, and *texture*, and define as needed. Comment on students' intuitive sense of historical style, if warranted. Explain that in this unit they will be exploring ways to place a piece of music in its historical context by listening for clues.

The Baroque Era (1600-1750)

The Pilgrims found Plymouth Colony (1620).
Robert de La Salle claims the Louisiana territory for France (1682).
Sir Isaac Newton discovers the law of gravity (1687).
The Industrial Revolution begins in England (1700's).

Composers:
Claudio Monteverdi (1567-1643),
Johann Sebastian Bach (1685-1750),
George Frederick Handel (1685-1759)

The Classical Era (1750-1800)

The French and Indian War is fought in North America (1754-1763).
The Declaration of Independence is written (1776).
The American colonies become an independent nation after winning the Revolutionary War (1775-1783).
The French Revolution begins (1789).

Composers:
Franz Joseph Haydn (1732-1809),
Wolfgang Amadeus Mozart (1756-1791),
Ludwig van Beethoven (1770-1827)

The Romantic Era (1825-1900)

Napoleon is crowned emperor (1804).
The United States and Britain fight the war of 1812 (1812-1815).
Mexican independence is declared (1821).
The California Gold Rush takes place (1848).
The Civil War is fought in the United States (1861-1865).
The telegraph, electric lightbulb, and telephone are invented.

Composers:
Hector Berlioz (1803-1869),
Robert Schumann (1810-1856),
Richard Wagner (1813-1883),
Johannes Brahms (1833-1897)

54

The Early Twentieth Century (1900-1950)

The Wright brothers fly the first airplane (1903).
Albert Einstein publishes his theory of relativity (1905).
The Bolshevik Revolution takes place in Russia (1917).
World Wars I and II are fought (1914-1918 and 1939-1945).
The United Nations is founded (1946).
Atomic power is developed.
The automobile, radio, sound movies, and television are invented.

Composers:
Claude Debussy (1862-1918),
Arnold Schoenberg (1874-1951),
Igor Stravinsky (1882-1971),
Aaron Copland (1900-   )

Later Twentieth Century (1950-present)

The age of the computer begins (1950).
The United States is involved in wars in Korea (1950-1953) and Vietnam (1964-1975).
The first earth satellite is launched by the Soviets (1957).
The United States lands astronauts on the moon (1969).

Composers:
Elliot Carter (1908-   ),
Luciano Berio (1925-   ),
Pauline Oliveros (1932-   ),
John Cage (1912-   ),
Ellen Zwilich (1939-   ),
Milton Babbitt (1916-   )

55

Lesson Focus

Timbre: The quality of a sound is affected by the material, shape, and size of the source.

Time and Place: A particular use of timbre reflects the origin of the musical whole. *(D–I)*

Materials

○ **Record Information:**
  • Instrumental Timbres
    Record 2   Side A   Band 4 a-g

○ **Teacher's Resource Binder:**

Activity Sheets
  • **Activity Sheet 11,** page A22
  • Optional—
    Biography 7, pages B13–14
    Enrichment Activity 5,
    page E15

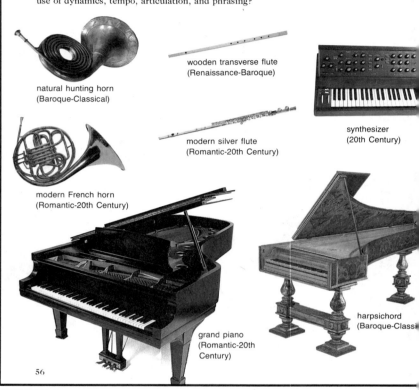

Clues to Musical Style: Instrumental Timbre

As you listen to music of different times, you may notice differences that are related to the sound of the instruments. Listen to the instruments pictured here. Compare the sounds of old and new. Describe the differences. Is the sound thin and straight or rich and full with little or much resonance?

Notice the expressiveness of the sound. Is there much contrast in the use of dynamics, tempo, articulation, and phrasing?

natural hunting horn
(Baroque-Classical)

wooden transverse flute
(Renaissance-Baroque)

synthesizer
(20th Century)

modern silver flute
(Romantic-20th Century)

modern French horn
(Romantic-20th Century)

grand piano
(Romantic-20th
Century)

harpsichord
(Baroque-Classi

56

The Lesson

1. Ask the students to open their books to page 56 and examine the pictures of the instruments. Many instruments will already be familiar to them; the shapes of others, however, may seem unusual. Discuss the fact that instruments, like many other things that we use today, have gradually changed over the years as people sought ways to alter them for different uses and expressive needs.

2. Ask the students to listen to bands 4a-b of "Instrumental Timbres" (the flute examples). Explain that the term "transverse" means that the flute is held crosswise rather than vertically, as with a recorder. Play the two examples and ask the students to offer observations as to differences they notice in the sound.

3. Play Band 4c and ask the students to compare the different horn timbres. The first version of the "Rondo" is played on a hunting or "natural" horn. The muted tones, resulting from using the hand or fist to alter the pitch, are distinguished from the open, natural tones. In the second version, played by a modern French horn, the timbre of the pitches remains consistent throughout the horn's register because many notes are performed by pressing down levers or valves.

4. Ask the students to identify the three keyboard instruments by listening to Band 4d (the examples for harpsichord, piano, and synthesizer). Discuss the differences in how the sound is produced by each keyboard. When the key is depressed on a harpsichord, the string is plucked by a *plectrum*. On the piano the strings are struck with a hammer.

The number and types of timbres that are combined influence the quality of sound and help us identify the period in which the music was composed.

Listen: can you identify which groups of instruments are playing and which period the music is from?

For Your Information

The excerpts for "Instrumental Timbres" are heard in the following order: **Band 4a:** *Owe Daz Nach Liebe Gat* by Master Alexander (late 13th century); Renaissance flute **Band 4b:** *Javanaise* by Claude Bolling (twentieth century); modern flute **Band 4c–d:** Rondo from *Concerto in E♭ No. 2* K. 417 by W.A. Mozart (Classical era); hunting horn and French horn **Band 4e–f–g:** *Two-part Invention in F* by J.S. Bach (Baroque era); harpsichord-piano-Moog synthesizer **Band 4h:** *Fantasia in G* by Alfonso Ferrabosco (Renaissance); consort of viols **Band 4i:** First Movement from *String Quartet in B♭,* K. 458 by W.A. Mozart (Classical era); **Band 4j:** *Javanaise* by Claude Bolling (twentieth century); flute-piano-double bass-percussion **Band 4k:** "*Canto Sotto*" from *Stanzas, Book* VII by Les Thimmig (twentieth century); flute-oboe-clarinet-French horn-bassoon-bass clarinet

57

On a synthesizer the sounds are produced electronically. Play the three examples; each instrument plays the same excerpt.

5. Ask the students to look at page 57 and listen to Bands 4e–h (examples of ensembles). Comment that musicians have always enjoyed playing together. Challenge students to identify the pictures for each recorded example.

6. Play Band 4e–f (the examples for the consort of viols and the string quartet) again. Ask the students to offer observations as to differences they notice in the sound. The *Fantasia in G* is played by six viols (two trebles, two tenors, two basses) commonly referred to as a "consort of viols."

7. Allow the students to enjoy the sound of the jazz quartet again (Band 4h). **This piece is an example of a jazz quartet. A common jazz quartet is made up of piano, percussion, double bass, and a solo instrument—usually a saxophone or trumpet.**

8. End the lesson by playing the woodwind sextet example again. Explain that this is a sextet because a bass clarinet has been added for this composition. It plays solo sections; the quintet (See **For Your Information**.) provides chordal responses.

LISTEN 3

Lesson Focus

Expression: Musical elements are combined into a whole to express a musical or extramusical idea. **(D–S)**

Materials

○ **Record Information:**
  • Prelude to Act III from *Lohengrin* by Richard Wagner (**vahg**-nuhr), 1813–1883
    Record 2   Side B   Band 1
  • First Movement from *Symphony No. 44* (excerpt)
    by Franz Joseph Haydn (**hide**-n), 1732–1809
    Record 2   Side B   Band 2
    Amsterdam Baroque Orchestra
    Ted Koopman, conductor

○ **Teacher's Resource Binder:**
  • Optional—
    Biography 2, page B3

LISTENING

Prelude to Act III from *Lohengrin*
by Richard Wagner

Richard Wagner (1813–1883) was one of the most important composers of the Romantic era. Wagner devoted most of his life to composing operas. He regarded opera as a total art work encompassing music, drama, and visual art. Wagner's opera *Lohengrin* is representative of certain aspects of music from the Romantic era. The large symphony orchestra featuring many contrasting timbres is the hallmark of the late nineteenth century. The prominent use of brass and percussion instruments, the chromatic melodic lines set in very high registers, and the dramatic climaxes add to the emotional quality of this truly romantic music.

1. The prelude opens with the vigorous "Festival Theme," played *fortissimo* by the entire orchestra and punctuated by crashes of cymbals. Notice the **chromatic** nature of the melody. The "Festival Theme" is stated twice.

2. The **tone color** of the French horns makes the introduction of the "March Theme" especially imposing.

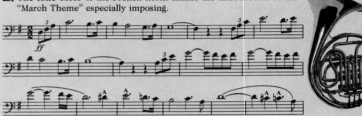

58

The Lesson

1. Invite the students to follow the call chart on pages 58–59 as they listen to the "Prelude to Act III" from *Lohengrin*. Discuss the characteristics of the Romantic style: the use of a large orchestra with many contrasting timbres; wide dynamic contrasts; many subtle changes of tempo; points of climax; frequency of chromaticism (the addition of pitches that do not normally belong to the major or minor scales used in a given composition) in melody and harmony.

2. To further illustrate the comparison between the Romantic and Classical styles, play the *Symphony No. 44* excerpt by Franz Joseph Haydn. Compare orchestration (reduced instrumentation), dynamics (fewer, less frequent changes), and harmony (less use of chromaticism).

58

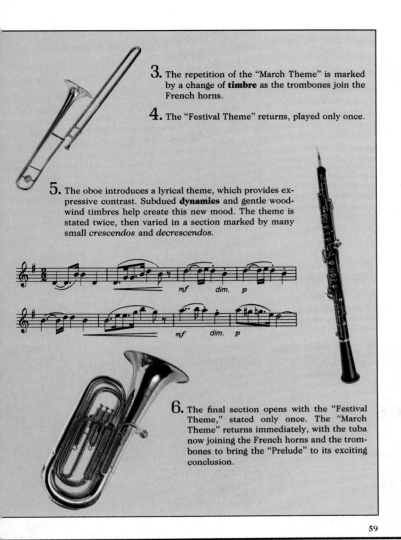

3. The repetition of the "March Theme" is marked by a change of **timbre** as the trombones join the French horns.

4. The "Festival Theme" returns, played only once.

5. The oboe introduces a lyrical theme, which provides expressive contrast. Subdued **dynamics** and gentle woodwind timbres help create this new mood. The theme is stated twice, then varied in a section marked by many small *crescendos* and *decrescendos*.

6. The final section opens with the "Festival Theme," stated only once. The "March Theme" returns immediately, with the tuba now joining the French horns and the trombones to bring the "Prelude" to its exciting conclusion.

59

For Your Information
If you wish to play another example of music from the Romantic era, refer ahead to the selections from *Madama Butterfly* (Record 4 Sides A, B Bands 1a–f, 1a-c).

Lesson Focus

Time and Place: The way musical elements are combined into a whole reflects the origin of the music. *(D–I)*

Materials

○ **Record Information:**
  • *The Play of Daniel*
    Record 3   Side B   Band 4b
    The Clerkes of Oxenford
    David Wulstan, director
  • *Madama Butterfly*
    by Giacomo Puccini (poo-**chee**-nee), 1858–1924
    Record 4   Side A   Band 1f
    Placido Domingo, tenor
    Philharmonic Orchestra
    Lorin Maazel, conductor

○ **Instruments:** piano

○ **Other:** pencil for each student

○ **Teacher's Resource Binder:**
  Activity Sheets • **Activity Sheet 12,** page A23
  • Optional—
    Biography 5, pages B9–10

Clues to Musical Style: Vocal Timbre

As you hear vocal music from various periods in history, you may find clues that are similar to the ones you noticed in instrumental music.

Listen to vocal music from the Medieval era and from the Twentieth century. As you listen carefully to each example, consider these characteristics:
The source of the sound

Soprano   Alto   Tenor   Baritone   Bass

The quality of the sound
    Is the sound rich and full? Does the singer use **vibrato?** Is the vibrato full or limited?
The expressiveness of the sound
    Is there much contrast in the use of dynamics, tempo, articulation, and phrasing?
The vocal style used by a singer is often influenced by the origin and style of the music. A sensitive performer may alter the vocal quality and the expressiveness of the sound to reflect the style of music being sung.

60

The Lesson

1. Ask the students to open their books to page 60 and read the discussion of clues to musical style. Examine the ranges of the voice parts. Play the lowest and highest pitch of each vocal range on the piano. The students may wish to categorize their own voices by comparing their ranges to the ranges shown on the pupil page. Be sure they understand the meaning of the word "vibrato"—the use of breath support to produce a controlled wavering of pitch. Invite students to demonstrate the difference between a limited vibrato sound and a full vibrato sound using the syllable "loo." Invite them to experiment with producing different kinds of vibrato.

2. Distribute two copies of Activity Sheet 12 (*Vocal Clues Chart*) and a pencil to each student. Play a short excerpt from *The Play of*

Daniel (Band a, first phrase sung by a tenor, remainder by a baritone). Follow this recording with an excerpt from *Madama Butterfly* (Band a, sung by a tenor). After students have marked their sheets, discuss the differences they have observed. Suggest that these differences in vocal performance style might have been dictated by the appropriate musical style for the historical period of each excerpt.

(The singers performing the Medieval excerpt use a limited vibrato sound and fewer dynamic contrasts. In comparison, the tenor performing the late Romantic opera excerpt sings with a full vibrato sound and uses a wide dynamic range.)

"Nacht" (Night) from *Pierrot Lunaire*, Opus 21

by Arnold Schoenberg

Arnold Schoenberg (1874–1951) was a major figure in Twentieth century music. He wrote for many kinds of instrumental and vocal ensembles and was an influential teacher, author, and painter, as well as a composer.

This composition for voice and chamber ensemble, first performed in 1912, introduced a new form of singing called *sprechgesang*. After you have listened, try to develop your own definition of this German word.

> Sinister giant black butterflies
> Shrouded the sun's bright rays.
> Like a sealed book of magic spells,
> The horizon rests . . . in silence.

Reverberation

Experiment with your own *sprechgesang*.
Use the ideas you gained while listening to "Night."
The following score may serve as a guide.

Solo Voice: Crossing it alone
In cold moonlight . . .
The brittle bridge
Echoes my footsteps.
Tagai

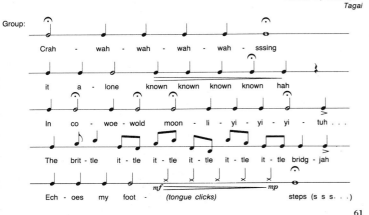

61

The Lesson

1. Play the recording of *"Nacht"* (Night) from Schoenberg's *Pierrot Lunaire* while the students follow the translation for the first verse in their books.

2. Discuss the meaning of the word *sprechgesang* ("spoken song" or "speech-song"). Ask the students whether they think this style is more or less effective than a traditional song style would be for this text. (Answers may vary.)

   Elements that help express the "night" mood include a free rhythmic flow, a wide range of dynamics, and melodic lines that are extremely chromatic and use wide skips. Vocal techniques used to express the text include "sliding" and "scooping" on certain words, changes in vocal sounds, elongating syllables, and the special use of diction.

3. Guide the students to develop their own accompaniment for "Reverberation." Distribute resonator bells to the students. Discuss whether the accompaniment should use sustained or short sounds, be rhythmically metered or free, or be *legato* or *staccato*. Experiment with a wide range of dynamics.

4. Choose a conductor and a soloist. The soloist reads the poem expressively; the group then performs the score following the conductor. The conductor is free to alter rhythms and may repeat words or syllables as desired. Encourage the soloists to experiment with the techniques used by the performer in *"Nacht."*

5. Listen to the recording of "Reverberation." Invite the students to explore different musical ideas to enhance their performance.

OPTIONAL

Lesson Focus

Expression: Musical elements are combined into a whole to express a musical or extra musical idea. *(C–E)*

Materials

○ **Record Information**
- *"Nacht"* (Night) from *Pierrot Lunaire*, Op. 21
  by Arnold Schoenberg
  (**shurn**-behrg), 1874–1951
  Record 2   Side B   Band 3
  Jan DeGaetani, voice
  Contemporary Ensemble
  Arthur Weissberg, conductor
- Reverberation
  Record 2   Side B   Band 4
  Voices: mixed voices
  Accompaniment: celesta, percussion

○ **Instruments:** resonator bells C, D, E, F♯, G♯, A♯, C′

○ **Teacher's Resource Binder:**
- Optional—
  Biography 3, page B5

Lesson Focus

Rhythm: A series of beats may be organized into regular or irregular groupings by stressing certain beats. *(D–I)*

Materials

○ **Record Information:**
- *Hodie Christus Natus Est*
  Record 3   Side A   Band 3
  Monks of the Benedictine Abbey
  En Calcat
- Reflections (excerpt) by Milton Babbitt, 1916–
  Record 2   Side B   Band 5
  Robert Taub, piano with synthesized tape
- First Movement from *String Quartet in Bb, K. 458* (excerpt) by Wolfgang Amadeus Mozart **(moet**-sahrt), 1756–1791
  Record 2   Side B   Band 6
  Juilliard String Quartet
- *Pavane "Belle qui tiens ma vie"* by Thoinot Arbeau (ahr-**boe**) 1519–1595
  Record 2   Side B   Band 7
  The Jaye Consort
- *"Nacht"* (Night) from *Pierrot Lunaire* **(Record 2   Side B   Band 3)**

○ **Teacher's Resource Binder:**

Activity Sheets • Activity Sheet 13, Page A24

(continued on next page)

The Lesson

1. Begin class by playing brief excerpts from *Hodie Christus Natus Est* and *Reflections.* Ask the students to identify the period of each (Medieval; Twentieth century) by listening to the quality of the sound. **Was there anything else in the music that might have helped you identify the period?** After the students have offered their suggestions, ask them to open their books to pages 62–63 and read the information on rhythm.

2. Before playing the four selections cited in **Materials,** be sure students understand the terms and their illustrations by challenging them to try performing each rhythm example.

3. Distribute two copies of **Activity Sheet 13** (*Rhythm Clues*) to each student. Play each of the following recorded selections, allowing

---

Clues to Musical Style: Rhythm

When we listen to music of different periods, we may first notice the different sounds of instruments and voices. Next we may notice differences in the way rhythm is organized. Listen to a

- religious chant from the Medieval era
- pavane from the Renaissance
- minuet from the Classical period
- twentieth-century vocal work with instruments

As you listen to each piece, notice how rhythmic characteristics are used:

Does the underlying beat occur at

- regular intervals?

- irregular intervals?

Do accents occur

- regularly?

- irregularly?

62

---

time for students to mark their charts before proceeding to the next selection.

Hodie Christus Natus Est (Medieval)
  Beat: irregular; not strongly felt
  Accents: occur according to word stress
  Flow: also according to word stress
  Interweaving of lines: none
Pavane (Renaissance)
  Beat: regular, strongly felt
  Accents: occur regularly
  Flow: moves regularly in relation to the underlying pulse
  Interweaving of lines: closely related
First Movement from *String Quartet in Bb, K. 458* (Classical)

The students will probably describe rhythmic characteristics for this selection in the same way as for the *Pavane.* Discuss the fact that although the First movement from

Is the beat strongly heard or almost absent?

Does the flow of the rhythmic line move

- in even, regular patterns in relation to the underlying beat?

- freely, with no recurring beats?

Do the rhythmic lines interweave by moving

- in even relationships to each other and to the beat?

- unevenly, as though unrelated to each other?

- in mixed fashion, with some even and some uneven rhythmic lines?

Materials *(continued)*
- Optional—
Biography 3, page B5
Mainstreaming Suggestion 7, page M14

String Quartet in B♭ is not actually a dance, it is very dancelike and, therefore, has strong, regular rhythms.

Reflections
Beat: irregular, if not completely absent
Accent: irregular
Flow: free
Interweaving of lines: seemingly unrelated

4. Discuss students' answers. As the characteristics of each selection are mentioned, emphasize that it is possible for the rhythm of music from the same period to be organized quite differently.

Lesson Focus

Time and Place: A particular use of rhythm reflects the origin of the musical whole. *(P–E)*

Materials

○ **Record Information:**
- *Pavane*
  (Record 2   Side B   Band 7)
- *Menuetto* from *Don Giovanni* by Wolfgang Amadeus Mozart (**moet-sahrt**), 1756–1791
  Record 2   Side B   Band 8
  Ensemble conducted by Buryl Red
- *The Emperor Waltz*
  by Johann Strauss (the younger) (**shtrouss**), 1825–1899
  Record 3   Side A   Band 1
  Eduard Strauss and his orchestra
- *Twelfth-Street Rag*
  by Euclay L. Bowman, 1887–1949
  Record 3   Side A   Band 2
  Elmer Snowden, banjo, and ensemble

○ **Instruments:** drum and mallet

○ **Teacher's Resource Binder:**
- **Activity Sheets 14a-c,** pages A25-A27
- Optional—
  Biography 4, page B7

Rhythm and Dance

One of the important influences on the musical style of a society is its dance forms. As nearly as we can tell, the earliest instrumental music was developed as an accompaniment to the dance. Dance accompaniment continues to be an important function of social music.

Listen to dance music of four different eras. Learn each dance. Discuss ways in which

- the dance steps reflect the rhythms in the music
- the form of the dance reflects the musical form

In the Renaissance Era:
The Pavane
Belle qui tiens ma vie
by Thoinot Arbeau
Thoinot Arbeau (1519–1595) was a French composer of dance music. Arbeau was also an author and wrote instructions for the dances of his time.

In the Classical Era:
The Minuet
"Menuetto" from *Don Giovanni* by Wolfgang Amadeus Mozart
Wolfgang Amadeus Mozart (1756–1791) is considered by many to be one of the greatest composers that ever lived. This minuet is from one of his many operas. Mozart also composed a large body of solo keyboard pieces, instrumental sonatas, music for various chamber ensembles, and sacred music for chorus and orchestra.

64

The Lesson

1. Review the discoveries made in the previous lesson about musical clues. (Dances have regular, strongly felt beats; accents occur regularly; rhythms flow regularly in relation to the underlying pulse; interweaving of lines is closely related.) Focus attention especially on *Pavane* and "*Menuetto*" from *Don Giovanni*.

2. Call attention to the first two paragraphs on page 64. Then ask the students to examine the illustrations on pages 64–65. **How would you expect the music for each of the dances to differ, based on what you see in each of the pictures?** (The pavane and the minuet look more courtly and regal. The waltz appears to be somewhat subdued, while the Charleston appears to be very animated.)

3. Have the students learn to dance the pavane. Guide them by playing this pattern on a drum.

$$\frac{2}{4} \quad \text{♩} \quad \text{♫} \quad :\|$$

Display the transparency prepared from Activity Sheet 14a (*Period Dances*). While playing the drum pattern, walk the students through the dance steps as described on the activity sheet; then have them perform the pavane with the recording.

4. Display the transparencies prepared from Activity Sheets 14a–c (*Period Dances*) and help the students learn the other dances. After having the students practice all the steps and walk through each of the dances, have them perform each dance with the recording. Discuss the differences observed among these four

**In the Romantic Era:
The Waltz**
The Emperor Waltz
by Johann Strauss, Jr.
Johann Strauss, Jr. (1825–1899) was a Viennese composer known for his waltzes and operettas. Strauss was very popular in his lifetime and was referred to as "the king of the waltz."

**In the Twentieth Century:
The Charleston**
Twelfth-Street Rag
by Euclay L. Bowman
The Charleston was a dance of the 1920s, probably named after the city in South Carolina. Bowman (1887–1949) was one of many composers at this time who wrote popular music for dance.

65

dances. **Were the differences what you expected from seeing the pictures on pages 64 and 65?** (Answers may vary.)

Lesson Focus

Time and Place: A particular use of melody reflects the origin of the musical whole. *(P–E)*

Materials

○ **Record Information:**
  • *The Emperor Waltz*
    (Record 3   Side A   Band 1)
  • *Pavane*
    (Record 2   Side B   Band 7)
  • *Nacht* from *Pierrot Lunaire*
    (Record 2   Side B   Band 3)
  • First Movement from *String Quartet in B♭, K. 458* (excerpt)
    (Record 2   Side B   Band 6)
  • *Reflections* (excerpt)
    (Record 2   Side B   Band 5)

○ **Other:** a pencil for each student

○ **Teacher's Resource Binder:**
  | Activity Sheets | • **Activity Sheet 15**, page A28 (Prepare four copies for each student.)
  • Optional—
    Biographies 3, 4, pages B5, B8
    Mainstreaming Suggestion 8 page M14

Clues to Musical Style: Melody

Next to rhythm, the most important and interesting musical element is probably **melody**. You discovered that rhythmic organization may sometimes be a clue to the musical style. The way a melody is organized may also help you identify its historical period. Listen to a melody. As you listen, try drawing its **shape**. Could the contour you drew be described as

undulating?   arched?   terraced?   irregular or   ?

Another characteristic of melody is **range**.

Listen again. Does the distance between the highest and lowest pitches seem to be

very wide?   moderate?   very narrow?

A melody may also be described as having **motion**.

As you listen a third time, think about the distance between the individual pitches. Did the melody usually move by

skips?   steps?   a combination of both?

66

The Lesson

1. Play the opening of *The Emperor Waltz* by Johann Strauss. Ask the students to offer clues they might use toward determining the historical period of this composition. **Can you decide by listening to the sound of the instruments? by noticing the way the rhythm is organized? What else draws your attention to this music?** (Answers may vary. Students may comment on the melody as being particularly distinctive.)

2. Ask the students to open their books and read the discussion of melody at the top of page 66. Distribute four copies of **Activity Sheet 15** and ask the students to listen to *The Emperor Waltz* again and try to draw its contour.

3. Ask the students to compare the shape of this melody with the shapes shown in the book. Conclude that this melody could probably be described as "undulating." Read about the next characteristic: range. Play the Strauss excerpt again, and ask the students to decide whether they think the melody is very wide or very narrow (probably "moderate"). After reading the discussion about motion, listen again and conclude that the motion is a combination of steps and small skips.

4. Follow the next suggestion for "central pitch" on page 67. Ask the students to turn the activity sheet over and draw a "central pitch" line across the sheet. **Draw the melodic contour again, this time in relation to the central pitch.** (The melody returns to the central pitch infrequently.)

5. Follow a similar procedure with each of the following recorded examples. Play each exam-

In many melodies, the pitches will often move in relation to a **central pitch.** Draw a line across your sheet of paper to represent the central pitch (the pitch to which all other pitches seem to return in a given key). Then draw the contour of the melody as you listen again. Show the melody as it moves above, moves below, and returns to that central pitch.

Does it seem to return frequently to the central pitch?

central pitch

Or does no one pitch seem to be more important than another?

central pitch

By listening carefully to music of various periods, you may be able to describe some differences in the way melodies are organized.

Listen to and compare the melodies of

- The Renaissance
- The Romantic era
- The Classical period
- The Twentieth century

67

ple several times so that the students have time to draw the shape, listen for the range and motion, and then draw the shape again in relation to the central pitch. After each example is heard, discuss the students' conclusions. As with rhythm, be sure that the students understand that other examples from the same historical period might reveal different ways of organizing melodies. (*Pavane:* shape—arched or undulating; range—narrow; motion—mostly steps; central pitch—at ends of phrases. *"Nacht"* (Night) from *Pierrot Lunaire*: shape—irregular; range—wide; motion—many large skips; central pitch—not apparent. First Movement from *String Quartet in D, K.155:* shape—undulating; range—moderate; motion—steps and small skips; central pitch—beginnings and ends of phrases. *Reflections:* shape—irregular; range—very wide; motion—constantly changing; central pitch: not apparent)

Lesson Focus

Texture: Musical quality is affected by the number of and the degree of contrast between musical lines occurring simultaneously. *(D–S)*

Materials

○ **Piano Accompaniment:** page 260
○ **Record Information:**
   • *Hodie Christus Natus Est*
   Record 3   Side A   Band 3
   Monks of the Benedictine Abbey En Calcat
   • Procession from *A Ceremony of Carols*
   Record 3   Side A   Band 4
   Voices: boys's choir
   Accompaniment: harp

Clues to Musical Style: Texture

For nearly a thousand years, music of the Western tradition has been composed of several lines moving in relation to each other, not of just a single melodic line.

The relationship of these lines can be a clue to the historical period of the music.

Can you define these three different types of **texture** just by looking at musical examples?

Monophony

Homophony

Polyphony

68

The Lesson

1. As the students examine the examples shown on page 68, help them define these terms:
   monophony—"one line, no accompaniment" (*mono* means "one")
   homophony—"a main melody (or melodies) with supporting accompaniment" (*homo* means "the same")
   polyphony—"two or more independent melodic lines occuring simultaneously" (*poly* means "many")

2. Listen to the recording of *Hodie Christus Natus Est* as the students follow the notation on the upper half of page 69. **What do you notice about the music?** (It is sung in a very *legato*, unmetered manner by unison male voices.) Adjust the balance of the record player so that the students can hear only the vocal channel of Britten's "Procession" from

A Ceremony of Carols. **How is this version different?** (The boy's voices are an octave higher than the men's voices; the music is still *legato* but seems to be somewhat metered.) Explain to the students that both recorded versions are monophonic because they are unaccompanied. Readjust the balance of the stereo so that the students may hear the accompaniment for the "Procession." **Benjamin Britten used this Gregorian chant to both open and close his choral work, *A Ceremony of Carols*. Can you decide in what style the accompaniment is played?** (Homophonic: although it does not always follow the rhythm of the melody exactly, the harp part moves in chordal style rather than as an independent melodic line.)

3. Learn to sing the melody of the "Procession" with the recording. The students should sing

Procession (Hodie Christus Natus Est) from A Ceremony of Carols

Music by Benjamin Britten

Benjamin Britten (1913–1976) was a prominent English composer of this century. The Gregorian chant, *Hodie Christus Natus Est* was used by Britten in his composition, *A Ceremony of Carols.* The "Procession" is based on church music from the Medieval era.

69

For Your Information

The four-line stave shown at the top of page 69 was a predecessor of today's five-line musical staff. It is frequently used today for reading plainsong or Gregorian chant. Each group of notes is read from the bottom up. When the note heads are attached to each other, this usually indicates a *melisma* (two or more notes to be sung on one syllable). The students will be able to compare the plainsong notation with the standard notation on the lower half of the page. This is the composer Benjamin Britten's transcription of the original chant. The concluding "Alleluia!" was added by the composer.

only the lines of the melody that lie within their vocal range. Notice that the fourth line of the melody shows optional notes an octave lower. These lower notes were indicted by the composer, Benjamin Britten. The last line of the melody is an additional "Alleluia" composed by Britten. The performance style of the melody should always be as *legato* as possible with phrases occurring where each new breath is indicated.

Lesson Focus

Texture: Musical quality is affected by the number of and the degree of contrast between musical lines occurring simultaneously. *(D–S)*

Materials

○ **Piano Accompaniment:** page 262
○ **Record Information:**
  • Morning Has Broken
    Record 3 Side A Band 5
    Voices: mixed choir
    Accompaniment: organ
  • First Movement from *String Quartet in B♭, K. 458* (excerpt)
    (Record 2 Side B Band 6)
  • ''Prelude to Act III'' from *Lohengrin*
    (Record 2 Side B Band 1)
  • *Reflections* (excerpt)
    (Record 2 Side B Band 5)
○ **Teacher's Resource Binder:**
  Activity Sheets
  • **Activity Sheet 16,** page A29
  • Optional—
    Biography 2, page B3

Morning Has Broken

Words by Eleanor Farjean

Gaelic Melody
Arranged by Buryl Red

Perform this composition in a homophonic style by

• singing the melody in unison with piano accompaniment
• performing it as a four-part hymn

Listen to a contemporary performance of this melody. Is it still in a homophonic style?

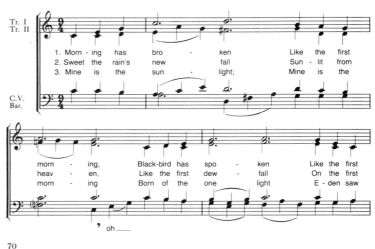

Tr. I
Tr. II

1. Morn - ing has bro - ken   Like the first
2. Sweet the rain's new fall   Sun - lit from
3. Mine is the sun - light;   Mine is the

C.V.
Bar.

morn - ing,   Black-bird has spo - ken   Like the first
heav - en,   Like the first dew - fall   On the first
morn - ing   Born of the one light   E - den saw

' oh ——

70

The Lesson

1. The arrangement of "Morning Has Broken" on pages 70–71 is designed so that any combination of voice parts will yield musical results. The students may learn to sing the top line in unison, and then add any or all of the harmony parts.

2. **OPTIONAL** A contemporary version of this traditional hymn was made popular by Cat Stevens during the late 1970s. If possible, bring a recording of this version into class and ask the students to determine whether it is in a homophonic style. (yes)

3. Examine the designs shown at the bottom of page 68. Discuss other characteristics of the texture, such as the presence of parallel or contrary motion and the number of musical lines occurring simultaneously. These relation-ships constitute the difference between a thick or thin texture.

4. Distribute four copies of Activity Sheet 16 *(Clues to Texture)* and a pencil to each student. Listen to the recording of "Morning Has Broken." Help the students fill out the activity sheet. If necessary, they may refer to the music on pages 70–71. Discuss their findings and verify the answers by listening again. (See **For Your Information.**)

5. Following the procedure in Step 4, ask the students to complete additional copies of the activity sheet as they listen and record information about each of the following selections:
First Movement from *String Quartet in B♭, K.458*
"Prelude to Act III," from *Lohengrin*
Reflections

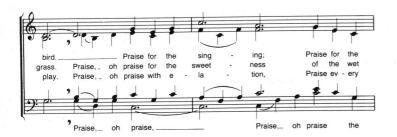

bird. _____ Praise for the sing - ing; Praise for the
grass. Praise, _ oh praise for the sweet - ness _____ of the wet
play. Praise, _ oh praise with e - la - tion, Praise ev - ery

Praise, _ oh praise, _____ Praise, _ oh praise the

morn - ing; Praise for them spring - ing Fresh from the Word. _
gar - den, Sprung in com - plete - ness Where his feet pass. _
morn - ing, God's re-cre - a - tion Of the new day. _

'oh _

Can you identify homophonic, monophonic, and polyphonic textures just by listening? Notice other characteristics of texture:

- **the number of lines**

motion

- parallel

- contrary

texture

- thick

- thin

71

For Your Information

The correct answers for the activity sheet follow:

"Morning Has Broken"
Number of lines: many
Motion: parallel and contrary
Texture: moderately thick, basically homophonic

First Movement from *String Quartet in Bb, K. 458*
Number of lines: few
Motion: parallel and contrary
Texture: moderately thick, homo-phonic and polyphonic

"Prelude to Act III" from *Lohengrin*
Number of lines: many
Motion: parallel and contrary
Texture: thick, mostly homophonic

Reflections
Number of Lines: varies
Motion: varies
Texture: varies, alternately mono-phonic and polyphonic

Lesson Focus

Texture: Musical quality is affected by the number of and degree of contrast between musical lines occurring simultaneously. *(P–S)*

Materials

○ **Piano Accompaniment:** page 264
○ **Record Information:**
   • *So Ben Mi Ch'à Bon Tempo* by Orazio Vecchi (**veck**-ee), 1550–1605
     Record 3   Side A   Band 6
     Rome Polyphonic Choir
○ **Instruments:** soprano, alto, and tenor recorders; violin; viola; cello or guitar
○ **Teacher's Resource Binder:**
   | Evaluation | **Checkpoint 2,** page Ev7

The Lesson

1. Review Step 1 of Listen 9. Help the students discover that the excerpt found at the bottom of page 68 is from the madrigal on pages 72–73. Listen to the recording of "*So Ben Mi Ch'à Bon Tempo,*" then play or sing each part. (See **For Your Information**.) Discuss whether each of the parts seems to have a life of its own as an independent melody. Point out the change in texture from a basically homophonic to polyphonic style in the last phrase (last four measures) of the madrigal. Compare the independent nature of the vocal lines in this phrase with the more chordal motion in the first three phrases.

2. Discuss with the students the fact that this Italian madrigal includes an example of the typical "fa-la-la" refrain. This type of refrain is characterized by repetitions—polyphonic vocal parts that contrast with the homophonic verse—where the lower parts support the main melody (as sung by the Treble I voices).

Guide the students to note that this piece is in E minor, but that various pitches are raised a half-step throughout the madrigal. This type of chromatic alteration is typical of Renaissance music. The major and minor keys as we know them did not come into general use until the Baroque period.

3. Assign vocal parts (see **For Your Information**) and learn to sing the madrigal. Point out to the students that there are no markings for dynamics or articulations. Explain that often composers of the Medieval and Renaissance periods normally left all decisions about expression to the performer. Guide the students

2. So ben ch'è favorito, so ben ch'è favorito,
   Fa la la la . . .
   Ahimè no'l posso dir, ahimè no'l posso dir,
   Fa la la la . . .

3. O s'io potessi dire, o s'io potessi dire,
   Fa la la la . . .
   Chi va, chi sta, chi vien, chi va, chi sta, chi vien,
   Fa la la la . . .

73

For Your Information

Madrigals are vocal settings of poems on a variety of topics, from love and sorrow to nature; some are humorous or political. Madrigals were popular in Europe from the end of the 13th to the beginning of the 17th centuries. People gathered to enjoy the latest madrigals much as people today might enjoy the newest recordings of popular tunes.

Part assignments for ''*So Ben Mi Ch'à Bon Tempo*'' follow:

Tr. I —soprano (first line)
Tr. II—alto (second line)
C.V.—tenor (third line)
Bar.—bass (fourth line, bass clef)

Phonetics for ''*So Ben Mi Ch'à Bon Tempo*'' follow:

1. soe ben mee kah bawn **tem**-poe, fah lah . . . ahl soe mah **bah**-stah moe, fah lah . . .
2. soe ben keh fah-vaw-**rree**-toe, fah lah . . . ah-ee **may** nohl poh-ssoe deer, fah lah . . .
3. oh see-oe poh-**teh**-ssee **dee**-ray kee vah kee stah kee vee-ehn

to consider appropriate dynamics, articulations, and tempo in their performance of this madrigal.

4. Although madrigals are most often performed *a capella* (unaccompanied), they can be performed by any combination of voices and instruments. Student instrumentalists may enjoy playing an arrangement of this madrigal; any voice part may be doubled. One appropriate combination would be:

Soprano part: voices and soprano recorder
Alto part: alto recorder, violin or viola
Tenor part: tenor recorder or viola
Bass part: cello or guitar

OPTIONAL

Lesson Focus

Expression: Musical elements are combined into a whole to express a musical or extramusical idea. *(D–E)*

Materials

○ **Record Information:**
• Overture from *Man of La Mancha*
Record 3 Side A Band 7
Original Broadway Cast Recording

For Your Information

In the musical, *Man of La Mancha,* Cervantes, imprisoned, invents a drama for his fellow prisoners in which he becomes Don Quixote, a dauntless knight complete with a squire, Sancho, and the "lady of his dreams," Aldonza. The drama ends when Don Quixote lies dying. He has won over his fellow prisoners with his vision of goodness, justice, and hope. The musical ends when Cervantes is led off to his trial by the Inquisition.

Music and Drama

Music has been an important part of the theater for hundreds of years. From **miracle plays** to **opera** to **Broadway musicals**, creators of drama have turned to music to help tell story, create a mood, and convey the feelings of characters in their stories.

Whether the composer was a medieval monk in a monastery or is a contemporary artist writing for television, some musical devices used to express dramatic ideas have remained the same.

In this chapter you will

- describe the differences in musical theater of various times and places
- identify characteristics of musical theater
- participate in informal dramatizations of musical theater

Review . . .   *Big River*—a Broadway musical of the eighties
Listen to . . .   *The Play of Daniel*—a miracle play of the 12th century
    Madama Butterfly—an opera composed at the turn of this century
    The Tender Land—an American folk opera of the 1950s
Compare . . .   the ways music helps to tell the story, create a mood, convey feelings
Begin . . .   by listening to an overture from a Broadway musical. How does this overture help set the scene? create mood? identify characters? predict plot?

74

The Lesson

1. Using the information found at the top of page 74 as a guide, identify the different types of musical drama with which the students may be familiar (musicals, operettas, operas, rock operas, and so on).

2. Begin by introducing students to the overture. Explain that often the purpose of the overture is to help set the scene and the mood and to introduce the drama by presenting a sampling of melodies from the music to follow. Invite students to listen to the overture from the musical *Man of La Mancha* without identifying the selections. **In what country would you expect this drama to take place?** (Syncopated rhythms and castanets might suggest a Latin country such as Spain.)

3. Briefly tell the story. (See **For Your Information**.) Explain to the students that four of the

melodies from the drama to follow are heard in the overture. The melodies represent: 1) the hero loudly proclaiming who he is; 2) a love song; 3) a song in which the heroine, Aldonza, protests, "I'm no lady"; 4) the noble dream. Change the sequence of these ideas and write them on the chalkboard. Then challenge the students to determine which melody might be used for each of these ideas. They should listen and be prepared to justify their decisions based on the way the musical ideas were used. (strong, majestic sounds for melody 1, and so on) After a discussion of their decisions, identify each of the melodies in sequence as presented in the overture:
1) "I, Don Quixote;" 2) "Dulcinea;" 3) "Aldonza;" 4) "To Dream the Impossible Dream."

The Play of Daniel

Musical drama has been popular for centuries. This play is nearly eight hundred years old. It was probably first performed in one of the medieval cathedrals of France. The music combines characteristics of religious and secular music of the time.

Ductia

Although the music heard on the recording was not part of the original play, music of this type probably accompanied sections of the drama. Listen for each of these medieval instruments.

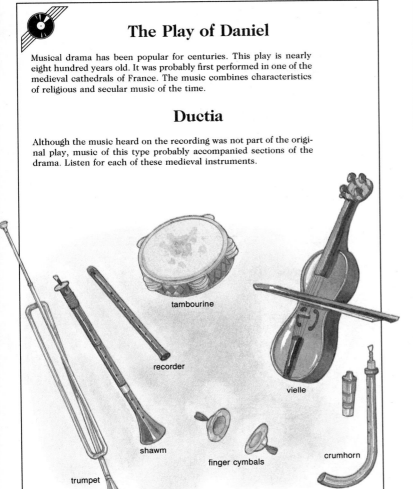

tambourine

recorder

vielle

shawm

finger cymbals

crumhorn

trumpet

75

Lesson Focus

Expression: Musical elements are combined into a whole to express a musical or extramusical idea. *(P–S)*

Materials

○ **Record Information:**
- *Ductia*
  Record 3   Side B   Band 1a
  N.Y. Pro Musica
  Noah Greenberg, director
- *The Play of Daniel*
  Record 3   Side B   Bands 1b-4d
  The Clerkes of Oxenford
  David Wulstan, director

○ **Instruments:** soprano recorders; triangle and striker; small hand drum (or bongos); finger cymbals; sleigh bells; large hand drum (or bass drum); tambourine; metallophones (soprano, alto, or bass) and mallets; autoharp or guitar

○ **Teacher's Resource Binder:**
- Optional—
  Enrichment Activity 6, page E15

The Lesson

1. Introduce the students to the style of the music found in *The Play of Daniel* by listening to the *Ductia*. The students should focus their attention on page 75 as they listen. **Which of the instruments shown do you hear?** (The piece begins with a trumpet introduction punctuated by finger cymbals. The following sequence of instruments then play the same melody or a variation of it: shawm, soprano recorder, shawm and recorder, tenor vielle, recorder and vielle, shawm, recorder, vielle, and crumhorn. Small percussion instruments accompany the wind instruments throughout.)

2. Continue to explore the style of the music by singing "Long live the King!" (*"Rex, in eternum vive!"*) If a trumpet player is available, the trumpet part may be used as an introduction to the sung fanfare. (If a B♭ trumpet

is used, the trumpet player will need to play each of the notes one whole step higher: E—E—B—E—B—E'.) This fanfare is used throughout the drama to announce the King. Ask the students to scan the text on pages 77–81 to find each place where the fanfare would be performed. (bottom of page 78, top of page 81) Although the fanfare occurs only twice in the excerpted version in this lesson, it is heard a total of eight times in the full version. Play the recording of the fanfare (Band 2). The students should compare their performance of the opening fanfare to the recording.

3. Listen to Band 3 of the recording "*Ecce Rex Darius*." Near the end of this band, the students will hear the chorus at the bottom of page 76 ("Let Us All Give Thanks Together"). Teach them to sing this song (in Latin) in four parts. When the students feel secure performing the song, add the accompaniment shown

For Your Information

Miracle plays such as *The Play of Daniel* originate in the liturgy of the medieval Christian church. Beginning in the 10th century, monks composed textual additions in Latin to comment or expound on the ideas presented in the liturgy. Music was composed for these textual additions.

These additions of textual commentary into the liturgy were usually called *tropes*. Tropes for the Christmas and Easter *Introits* (the introductory text and music in the Mass) were very important in the evolution of the miracle play. *Introit tropes* were written as dialogues based on Biblical events or stories.

Drama, as inherited from the Greeks and Romans, had been considered pagan by the early Church; these small Introit insertions, therefore, constituted a radical change in the medieval Mass. A substantial drama inserted into the Mass would make the service too long, and the monks turned instead to the Offices, another type of church service.

By the 12th century liturgical dramas had attained the grandeur that can be observed in *The Play of Daniel*. *The Play of Daniel* was performed during the Christmas season at the end of *Matins*, an early morning Office. An extensive drama, such as *The Play of Daniel*, eventually provided the basis for the development of drama as a secular creative endeavor, beyond the confines of the Church.

Long Live the King (Fanfare)

Let Us All Give Thanks Together

76

at the top of page 77. Use many players for each part, if feasible.

4. Assign students to read the narration that precedes each of the recorded excerpts. Suggest that the students also read the English translation as they listen to and follow the Latin text. Play the recording with the narration read by assigned students between each band.

5. After the students have listened to the complete recording, identify the different types of music heard: processionals, chants, and dances. Explain to the students that, here, as in opera, certain types of music are used for different aspects of the play. (processionals for entrances and exits; freely flowing chantlike melodies for dialogue; songs with a clearly defined rhythmic structure to express the feelings of the characters)

Discuss the general characteristics of this music:

- Melodies usually move stepwise or in small skips (thirds) and usually return to a central pitch at the end of each phrase.
- The rhythm of the words usually dictates the rhythm of the melody.
- All roles are performed by men and boys in musical theater of this period.
- In processionals, the rhythm patterns are often uneven.

"Jubilemus . . . " (pages 77–78) This dance-like processional (or *conductus*) is a typical form in medieval music. It provides the opportunity for colorful processionals.

The music is mostly accompanied by percussion. The recorder, vielle, bells, and percussion were traditionally associated with the pagan groups in medieval plays.

Recorder (soprano or alto): Play Treble I part.
Triangle, small and large drums, and finger cymbals: Play stems up on the percussion part below.

Tambourine: Play stems down.

Metallophone:

Cast

King Belshazzar, *king of Babylon*	**Counselors**
Satraps, *noble lords*	**Soldiers**
Queen	**Princes**
Daniel, *a Jewish prophet*	**Musicians**
King Darius, *the new king*	**Angels**
Habakkuk, *a Jewish prophet*	

The play opens as the king, Belshazzar, ascends his throne while the Satraps sing and bring forth vessels stolen from the Temple of the Jews.

Satraps: Jubilemus Regi nostro
magno ac potenti!
Resonemus laude digna
voce competenti!

Let us praise our King,
great and powerful!
Let us resound with worthy praise
and fitting song!

Resonet jocunda turba
solemnibus odis!
Cytharizent, plaudant manus,
mille sonent modis!

Let the merry throng break forth
in solemn chants;
Let them play their harps, clap their hands,
sing a thousand tunes.

Pater ejus destruens
Judaeorum templa,
Magna fecit, et hic regnat
ejus per exempla.

His father destroyed
the Temple of the Jews,
And now this one reigns
by his father's example.

Pater ejus spoliavit
regnum Judaeorum;
Hic exaltat sua festa
decore vasorum.

His father took great booty
from the kingdom of the Jews;
Now he can make his feasts more splendid
with such handsome vessels.

77

"Rex, in eternum . . ." (page 78) The trumpet is always associated with royalty, whether the royal person is speaking or being spoken to.

"Tune Daniel" (page 78) This is an example of the close relationship between text and melody. Notice that each syllable of the words has been set to one pitch of the music.

"Rex, tua nolo . . ." (page 79) Daniel's singing is accompanied by stringed instruments, such as the psaltery and harp, and also by the portative (chamber) organ. These instruments are usually used to accompany the characters that are considered holy. The freely-flowing rhythm, dictated by the rhythm of the words, is unmetered.

"Ecce Rex Darius . . ." (page 79) As Darius and his court approach the court of Belshazzar, each strophe (verse) of this processional is more powerful than the preceding strophe, building to a strong climax. Suggest to the students that they visualize a colorful procession with elegant clothing, flashing jewelry, and brilliant banners.

"Nunquam vobis . . ." (page 80) Focus the students' attention on the way the music conveys the contrasting moods of the saddened king and the envious counselors.

"Hujus Rei . . ." (page 80) This metered lament suggests Daniel's mood and feelings as he faces the lions.

"Surge, Frater . . ." (page 80) This melody is sung by Habakkuk, a holy man, and is accompanied by stringed instruments.

"Rex, in aeternum . . ." (page 81) Note the use of the trumpet in Daniel's conversation with King Darius.

Haec sunt vasa regia
    quibus spoliatur
Jerusalem, et regalis
    Babylon ditatur.
	These are the royal vessels
	    which were taken
	From Jerusalem, and now adorn
	    regal Babylon.

Ridens plaudit Babylon,
    Jerusalem plorat;
Haec orbatur, haec triumphans
    Belshazzar adorat.
	With laughter, Babylon rejoices;
	    Jerusalem weeps.
	She has been deprived of her children,
	    while Babylon in triumph venerates
	    King Belshazzar.

Omnes ergo exultemus
    tantae potestati
Offerentes Regis vasa
    suae majestati.
	Therefore, let everyone rejoice
	    at such great power,
	Offering these royal vessels
	    to his majesty.

Suddenly, a hand appears and writes on the wall:
    Mane, Thechel, Phares.
The king is in terror and assures the court that anyone knowing the meaning of these words will be given power over Babylon, but his wise men are of no help.

The queen enters and suggests that Daniel, a captured prophet of the Jews, might be able to interpret the words. The soldiers bring Daniel before Belshazzar.

| **Daniel:** | Rex, in eternum vive! | Long live the King! |
| **Belshazzar:** | Tune Daniel nomine diceris,
Huc adductus cum Judaeae
    miseris?
Dicunt te habere Dei spiritum
Et praescire quodlibet
    absconditum.
Si ergo potes scripturam
    solvere,
Immensis muneribus ditabere. | Are you not called Daniel,
Brought here with the wretches of Judea?
They say you have the spirit of God
And foresee whatever is hidden.
If then you can solve this writing,
You will be enriched with countless gifts. |

78

"Merito haec patimur . . . " (page 81) The style of this music is derived from the ancient liturgy, and the melody is in a rhythm typically associated with chants.

"Deum Danielis . . . " (page 81) The short melodies used for this conclusion proceed with a strong rhythmic flow that follows the natural accents and cadence of the text.

6. Invite the students to follow the script and improvise their own performance, using small percussion and dronelike instruments as accompaniment. (For a drone, play the G minor and G major chords at the same time on the autoharp, or play fifths on a guitar or metallophone.) The students might choose to select a myth or familiar tale and develop their own medieval drama. Suggest that they in-

OPTIONAL

clude processionals, chantlike melodies, and rhythmic songs. Use classroom instruments as suggested above for accompaniment.

Daniel:

Rex, tua nolo munera;
Gratis solvetur litera.
Est autem haec solutio:
Instat tibi confusio.
Pater tuus prae omnibus
Potens olim potentibus,
Turgens nimis superbia
Dejectus est a gloria
Et Mane, dicit Dominus,
Est tui regni terminus.
Thechel libram significat
Quae te minorem indicat.
Phares, hoc est divisio,
Regnum transportat alio.

O King, I wish not your gifts;
Unrewarded I will solve the letters.
This is the solution:
Affliction awaits you.
Your father above all others
Once was powerful.
Swollen with excessive pride
He was cast down from glory.
For *Mane,* says the Lord,
Is the end of your kingdom;
Thechel means a measuring weight,
Which means you are weaker;
Phares, that is division,
Your kingdom will be given to another.

Belshazzar:

Qui sic solvit latentia
Ornetur veste regia.

Let him who has solved the secret
Be adorned with regal robes.

Daniel returns to his quarters. The king orders the stolen Jewish vessels removed from his court and brought to Daniel.

Suddenly, King Darius appears in Belshazzar's court. Before Darius enters, his princes and musicians march in, singing Darius' praises.

Ecce Rex Darius
Venit cum principibus,
Nobilis nobilibus.

Behold King Darius
Approaching with his princes,
The noble with his nobles.

Ejus et curia
Resonat laetitia,
Adsunt et tripudia.

And his entire court
Resounds with joyousness,
And dances are there too.

Hic est mirandus,
Cunctis venerandus.
Illi imperia
Sunt tributaria.

He is admired,
Venerated by all.
There are many kingdoms
Subject to him.

Regem honorant
Omnes et adorant.
Illum Babylonia
Metuit et patria.

All honor the King
And adore him.
Him Babylon fears
And his fatherland.

Simul omnes gratulemur;
Resonent et tympana;
Citharistae tangant cordas;
Musicorum organa
Resonent ad ejus praeconia.

Let us all give thanks together;
Let the drums sound forth;
Let the harp players pluck their strings;
Let the instruments of the musicians
Resound in his praise.

79

Daniel's prophecy is fulfilled with the capture of Belshazzar by King Darius. The court informs the new king of Daniel's powers. The king calls for Daniel and appoints him as his counselor.

Daniel's good fortune has aroused the jealousy of others in the court. They claim that Daniel has defied the king's decree that no other gods should be worshipped save the king himself. Darius attempts to defend Daniel, but the envious counselors prevail.

Darius: Nunquam vobis concedatur
Quod vir sanctus sic perdatur.

It will never be granted to you
That this holy man should perish so.

Counselors: Lex Parthorum et Medorum
jubet in annalibus
Ut qui sprevit quae decrevit
Rex, detur leonibus.

The law of the Parths and the Medes
in the annals does command
He who heeds not the King's decree
to the lions should be thrown.

Darius: Si sprevit legem quam
statueram
Det poenas ipse quas decreveram.

If he disdained the law proclaimed
Let him be punished as ordained.

As Daniel is thrown in the lion's den, he calls out:

Daniel: Hujus rei non sum reus;
Miserere mei Deus;
eleyson.
Mitte, Deus, huc patronum
Qui refrenet vim leonum;
eleyson.

For this charge I am not guilty;
Have mercy on me, O God;
eleison.
Send, O God, a protector here
To restrain the lions' power;
eleison.

An angel appears and shields Daniel from the lions.

Another angel brings Habakkuk the prophet to Daniel, bearing food.

Habakkuk: Surge, frater, ut cibum capias;
Tuas Deus vidit angustias;
Deus misit, da Deo gratias,
Qui te fecit.

Rise up, brother, and take the food;
God has seen your afflictions;
God has sent it, give thanks to God,
The God who made you.

80

In sadness, the king comes to the lion's den to ask Daniel if he thinks his God will save him. Daniel replies:

Daniel: Rex, in eternum vive!

Long live the King!

Angelicum solita misit
  pietate patronum,
Quo Deus ad tempus conpescuit
  ora leonum.

An angelic protector He has sent
  in His customary mercy
By whom God constrained in time
  the mouths of the lions.

Darius: Danielem educite,
Et emulos immittite.

Bring Daniel out,
Throw the envious in.

Counselors: Merito haec patimur, quia
  peccavimus in sanctum Dei,
Injuste egimus,
  iniquitatem fecimus.

We suffer justly for we have sinned
  against this holy man of God,
We have acted wickedly,
  we have done iniquity.

Darius: Deum Danielis qui regnat in
  saeculis
Adorari jubeo a cunctis populis.

I command that the God of Daniel
Who reigns forever be adored by all.

Prepare your own performance of *The Play of Daniel,* or choose another ancient story and compose a play in a similar style.

Use medieval modes as the basis for your melodies.

Dorian

Mixolydian

Discuss the characteristics of the music from *The Play of Daniel* and try to incorporate these ideas into your own composition.

81

Lesson Focus

Expression: Musical elements are combined into a whole to express a musical or extramusical idea. **(D–S)**

Materials

○ **Record Information:**
- *Madama Butterfly*
  by Giacomo Puccini (poo-**chee**-nee), 1858–1924
  Record 4   Sides A, B   Bands 1f, 1c
  Renata Scotto, Placido Domingo, Ambrosian Opera Chorus, Philharmonic Orchestra, Lorin Maazel, conductor

○ **Teacher's Resource Binder:**
- Optional—
  Biography 5, page B9
  Kodaly Activity 12, page K17

LISTENING

Madama Butterfly

Libretto by L. Illica and G. Giacoso
Music by Giacomo Puccini

Giacomo Puccini (1858–1914) was the last major Italian operatic composer in the Romantic tradition. Puccini's best-known operas include *La Boheme, Tosca, Manon Lescaut,* and *Turandot.*

Cast of Characters

Madama Butterfly (Cio-Cio-San), *a young Japanese bride*
Lieutenant F.B. Pinkerton, *an American Naval Officer*
Sharpless, *U.S. Consul at Nagasaki*
Goro, *a marriage broker*
Suzuki, *Butterfly's servant*
Price Yamadori, *a suitor*
Bonzo, *Butterfly's uncle, a priest*
Butterfly's child
Friends and relatives
Kate Pinkerton

This opera takes place in Japan in the late 1800s, when Japan had begun to allow foreign ships to enter Japanese ports and engage in trade. American sailors found Japan to be an exotic country, with traditions and customs very different from the ways at home.

This story concerns an American naval officer and his marriage to a young Japanese woman. As you read the drama and listen to excerpts from the opera, think about whether this story could have been set in another country at another time.

Act I

The setting is a house with a terrace and garden on a hill near Nagasaki. The harbor and the city can be seen at the rear of the set. Goro, a marriage broker, is showing the house to U.S. Navy Lieutenant Pinkerton. Goro has arranged a marriage between Pinkerton and a geisha girl, Cio-Cio-San.

82

The Lesson

1. Prepare the students for the study of *Madama Butterfly* by discussing the historical and cultural context of the opera. (See **For Your Information.**) You may wish to assign your students to research the history of Japan, the customs of the period (both American and Japanese), and the effect of the arrival of the Americans, as well as other foreigners, on Japanese society.

2. There are many ways of introducing the opera to students: one would be to listen without interruption to the opera as excerpted here, so that the students get the impact of the story in its entirety. Assign a narrator in advance to read the synopses when they appear in the pupil book. Be certain that the students understand that in an actual performance of the opera all parts would be sung.

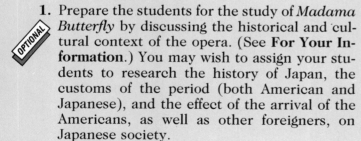

3. Suggest to students that they follow the Italian the first time they listen before looking at the English translation. **Can you grasp any of the story line or the emotions of the singers by listening to the Italian words?**

4. After the opera has been heard once, engage the students in a discussion, replaying sections as needed. Some possible lines of discussion might include the following:

   - **Describe the personality and character of each individual. What provided you with clues—the music? —the dialogue?**
   - **At what point did you realize that Pinkerton was not going to be faithful to his Japanese wife?**
   - **Give examples of places where the vocal line itself (not the words) helped the listener grasp the story or the mood.**
   - **How did the orchestral accompaniment**

Pinkerton:	Is everything ready?	
Goro:	Everything. The registrar and consul are coming, along with your bride-to-be and her relatives. All you have to do is sign the contract and your wedding is over.	
Sharpless:	*(enters, breathing heavily)* I'm getting too old to climb these rocky hills.	
Pinkerton:	How do you like my house? I bought it for 999 years, with the option of breaking the contract every month. Then, with Goro's help, I'm to be married in the Japanese manner—also for 999 years; and also, with the option to annul this contract in any month I choose.	

Pinkerton:	Dovunque al mondo lo Yankee vagabondo si gode e traffica sprezzando rischi. Affonda l'áncora alla ventura . . . Milk-punch, o Whiskey? Affonda l'áncora alla ventura finché una raffica scompigli nave e ormeggi, alberatura. . . . La vita ei non appaga se non fa suo tesor i fiori d'ogni plaga . . .	We Yankees roam the world, enjoying ourselves, laughing at risks, taking the profits. We drop anchor wherever we please . . . *(pausing to offer a drink)* . . . Milk-punch or whisky? . . . until it's time to move on. All the treasures and flowers of every shore are ours . . .
Sharpless:	È un facile vangelo . . .	That's an easy creed . . .
Pinkerton:	. . . d'ogni bella gli amor.	. . . girls wherever we go . . .
Sharpless:	È un facile evangelo che fa la vita vaga ma che intristisce il cor . . .	an easy creed for a pleasant life, but it saddens the heart . . .
Pinkerton:	Vinto si tuffa, la sorte racciuffa. Il suo talento fa in ogni dove. Così mi sposo all'uso giapponese per novecentonovantanove anni. Salvo a prosciogliermi ogni mese.	If unsuccessful, we're up and away, looking for whatever might come along. So, I'm marrying Japanese style, with the right to leave every month.
Sharpless:	È un facile vangelo.	An easy creed.
Pinkerton:	America for ever!	*(toasts with his glass)* America forever!
Sharpless:	America for ever!	America forever!

83

For Your Information

The English translation printed opposite the Italian text in the pupil book is not an exact translation, but simply a restatement of the ideas in the English language.

During the 19th century, life in Japan was still structured by ancient customs and religious rituals. Important to the study of this opera is some understanding of the woman's place in Japanese society of the period. A woman was considered the property of her parents or husband. Parents, in consultation with a marriage broker, would arrange for a husband for their daughter. Often they were paid a sum of money for her. Divorce laws allowed the husband to dispose of her for any reason, or for no reason, simply by declaring that he was no longer responsible for her.

At the same time, America was at the height of its imperialism. American ships sailed over the world, establishing colonies and spheres of influence. It was a time of optimism, prosperity, and expansion. Small wonder, then, that America's representatives on the seas saw themselves, as Pinkerton does, as superior, free to do as they wished, claim their bounties, and sail away again.

provide clues to the story? To the mood?
• Could this same story have been placed in another setting? Might it take place today? What elements might have been changed?

Encourage students to exchange opinions.

5. While students may resist listening to opera initially, some aspects may interest students and increase their enjoyment of this genre now or in later life. Some students may enjoy

OPTIONAL

• learning portions of the text and the music
• producing a filmstrip to illustrate the story
• rewriting the script to provide for a different ending
• researching how Puccini became familiar with the original story (Puccini went to a performance of a play by an American playwright when he was in London preparing for another of his operas. Just as most students in the class will not understand the Italian language used in the opera, neither did Puccini understand the English language used in the play, but he was so moved by the play itself that he secured the rights to compose an opera from the play.)

• researching Japanese opera and comparing it to Italian opera
• listening to other operas by Puccini
• listening to different soloists perform the same arias from *Madama Butterfly* and comparing the performances (It may interest students to know that on the opening night, *Madama Butterfly* was booed, and Puccini hid backstage in a dressing room to shut out the noise! Three months later, after reworking the opera, changing 30 or so pages, streamlining some parts, changing melodies, and dividing the second act into two scenes, Puccini again presented *Madama Butterfly*. This time it was a very great success!)

Sharpless is concerned about Pinkerton's bride. He doesn't want Pinkerton to take advantage of her. Sharpless toasts Pinkerton's happiness, but Pinkerton adds a toast to the day when he will marry a real American wife. Butterfly appears with her friends and kneels at his feet. She sings of being the happiest maiden in Japan.

Butterfly:	Siam giunte. F. B. Pinkerton, Giù.	*(to her friends)* Down.
Friends:	Giù.	*(kneeling)* Down!
Butterfly:	Gran ventura.	*(to Pinkerton)* Good fortune to you.
Friends:	Riverenza.	At your service.
Pinkerton:	È un po' dura la scalata?	Was the climb hard?
Butterfly:	A una sposa costumata più penosa è l'impazienza.	Nothing is too hard to do for my husband.
Pinkerton:	Molto raro complimento.	A nice compliment.
Butterfly:	Dei più belli ancor ne so.	I know better ones!
Pinkerton:	Dei gioielli!	What a jewel!

84

| **Butterfly:** | Se vi è caro sul momento . . . | Shall I say another? |
| **Pinkerton:** | Grazie, no. | Thank you, no. |

Questioned about her family, Butterfly explains that her family used to be rich, but that bad times came upon them. She has worked as a geisha girl to support herself. She tells him that she is fifteen years old. Her mother is living, but her father is dead. While she takes some items she has brought (including a sword) into the house, Goro explains that the sword is the one that was given to her father by the Mikado. As Butterfly returns she sings:

Butterfly:	Ieri son salita tutta sola, in secreto, alla Missione. Colla nuova mia vita posso adottare nuova religione. Lo zio Bonzo nol sa, nè i miei lo sanno. Io seguo il mio destino, e piena d'umiltà, al Dio del signor Pinkerton m'inchino. È mio destino. Nella stessa chiesetta in ginocchio con voi pregherò lo stesso Dio. E per farvi contento potrò forse obliar la gente mia. Amore mio!	Yesterday, I climbed to the Mission. No one knew I went, not even my uncle, the priest. To make you happy, I am giving up my religion and kneeling before your God.
Goro:	Tutti zitti!	Quiet everyone! *(The ceremony begins.)*
Commissioner:	È concesso al nominato Benjamin Franklin Pinkerton, Luogotenente nella cannoniera "Lincoln", marina degli Stati Uniti America del Nord; ed alla damigella Butterfly del quartiere d'Omara, Nagasaki, d'unirsi in matrimonio, per dritto il primo, della propria volontà, ed ella per consenso dei parenti qui testimoni all'atto.	It is granted to Benjamin Franklin Pinkerton, Lieutenant of the gunboat "Lincoln," United States of America, and to Butterfly, living in Omara, Nagasaki, to be joined in marriage. Lieutenant Pinkerton, by his own free will, and Butterfly, with the consent of her relatives, who witness the contract.
Goro:	Lo sposo. Poi la sposa. E tutto è fatto.	*(indicating where to sign)* The husband. Now the wife. And it's all settled.
Friends:	Madama Butterfly!	Madame Butterfly!
Butterfly:	Madama F. B. Pinkerton.	Madame F. B. Pinkerton!

Pinkerton proposes a toast to the marriage, to which all respond.

| **Mother:** | O Kami! O Kami! | O Kami! O Kami! |
| **Cousin:** | Beviamo ai novissimi legami. | Let us drink to the new union. |

85

The wedding has taken place and the celebration has begun. It is interrupted by the arrival of Butterfly's enraged uncle, Bonzo, a Shinto priest. He curses Butterfly for having left her religion to marry a foreigner.

Priest:	Ciociosan! Ciociosan! Abbominazione!	Cio-Cio-San! You are cursed!
Friends:	Lo zio Bonzo!	It's her uncle, Bonzo!
Goro:	Un corno al guastafeste!	He'll spoil everything!
Priest:	Ciociosan!	Cio-Cio-San!
Goro:	Chi ci leva d'intorno le persone moleste?	How can we get rid of him?
Priest:	Ciociosan! Ciociosan! Che hai tu fatto alla Missione?	Cio-Cio-San! What did you do at the mission?
Cousin:	Rispondi, Ciociosan!	Answer, Cio-Cio-San!
Friends: **Pinkerton:**	Che mi strilla quel matto?	What is that maniac yelling about?
Priest:	Rispondi, che hai tu fatto?	Answer, what have you done?
Friends: **Relatives:**	Rispondi, Ciociosan!	Answer, Cio-Cio-San!
Priest:	Come, hai tu gli occhi asciutti? Son dunque questi i frutti? Ci ha rinnegato tutti!	Why aren't you crying? Aren't you ashamed? You have given up everything!
Friends: **Relatives:**	Hou! Ciociosan!	*Oh! Cio-Cio San!*
Priest:	Rinegato vi dico, il culto antico.	You have given up your religion!
Friends: **Relatives:**	Hou! Ciociosan!	*Oh! Cio-Cio San!*
Priest:	Kami sarundasico!	You are cursed!

Seeing that Butterfly has become very upset, Pinkerton orders everyone to leave the house. As they leave, the guests repeat angry cries, and Butterfly bursts into tears.

Pinkerton:	Bimba, bimba, non piangere per gracchiar di ranocchi.	Sweetheart, don't cry about the croaking of a few frogs.
Butterfly:	Urlano ancor!	I can still hear them.
Pinkerton:	Tutta la tua tribù e i Bonzi tutti del Giappon non valgono il pianto di quegli occhi cari e belli.	All your family and all the Bonzos in Japan aren't worth a single tear from your dear and beautiful eyes.

86

Butterfly is consoled by Pinkerton's words, and as night falls the pair take comfort in being together.

Pinkerton: Dammi ch'io baci le tue mani care Mia Butterfly! Come t'han ben nomata Tenue farfalla.

Give me your hands and let me kiss them. My Butterfly, how like a slender butterfly you are!

Butterfly: Dicon ch'oltre mare Se cade in man dell'uom, Ogni farfalla da uno Spillo è trafitta Ed in tavola infitta!

They say that in your country, people catch butterflies and fasten them with pins and set them in display cases.

87

Pinkerton:	Un po' di vero c'è. E tu lo sai perchè? Perchè non fugga più. Io t'ho ghermita. Ti serro palpitante. Sei mia.	Only to keep them from flying away. I have caught you . . . *(He clasps Butterfly in his arms.)* and you are mine.
Butterfly:	Sì, per la vita.	Yes, for my whole life.
Pinkerton:	Vieni, vieni. Via dall'anima in pena L'angoscia paurosa È notte serena! Guarda: dorme ogni cosa!	Come to me and forget all your fears. The night is clear and everything is sleeping.
Butterfly:	Ah! Dolce notte!	Ah, what a lovely night!
Pinkerton:	Vieni, vieni.	Come to me.
Butterfly:	Quante stelle! Non le vidi Mai sì belle! Trema, brilla Ogni favilla Col baglior D'una pupilla. Oh!	What stars! I have never seen so many stars shining so beautifully.
Pinkerton:	Via l'angoscia dal tuo cor!	Forget all your fears.
Butterfly:	Quanti occhi Fisi attenti, . . .	The stars are like eyes, looking at us . . .
Pinkerton:	Ti serro palpitante. Sei mia. Ah!	You are mine.
Butterfly:	D'ogni parte A riguardar!	The stars gaze from all sides . . .
Pinkerton:	Vien, vien, sei mia, ah!	Come, you are mine.
Butterfly:	Pei firmamenti, Via pei lidi, Via pel mare.	From heaven, on land, on sea . . .
Pinkerton:	Vieni, guarda: Dorme ogni cosa! etc.	See how everything is sleeping. (etc.)
Butterfly:	Ah! Quanti occhi Fisi, attenti! etc. Ride il ciel! Ah! Dolce notte! Tutto estatico d'amor.	So many stars, gazing like eyes. (etc.) The sweetest, most beautiful night!
Pinkerton:	Ah! Vien! Sei mia!	Come to me! Be mine!

As the newlyweds walk slowly from the garden toward the house, the curtain falls on Act I.

Act II

Three years have passed. Pinkerton has gone to America, but has promised to come back someday. Inside Butterfly's house, Suzuki is praying for Pinkerton's return. Butterfly, on the other hand, is very trusting and sings of the day when she will see her husband again.

Butterfly:

Un bel dì, vedremo
Levarsi un fil di fumo
Sull'estremo confin del mare.
E poi la nave apparè.
Poi la nave bianca
Entra nel porto,
Romba il suo saluto.
Vedi? È venuto!

One lovely day, we'll see smoke rising over the horizon. A white ship will appear and enter the harbor. The guns will thunder a salute: "You see? He has come!"

Io non gli scendo incontro. Io no. Mi metto là sul ciglio del colle e aspetto, e aspetto gran tempo e non mi pesa la lunga attesa.

I won't go down to meet him. I'll stand at the top of the hill and wait a long time.

È uscito dalla folla cittadina un uomo, un picciol punto s'avvia per la collina.

At last, a tiny figure will appear making his way up the hill.

Chi sarà? Chi sarà? E come sarà giunto che dirà? Che dirà? Chiamerà Butterfly dalla lontana. Io, senza dar risposta me ne starò nascosta un po' per celia, e un po' per non morire al primo incontro, ed egli alquanto in pena chiamerà, chiamerà: "Piccina mogliettina olezzo di verbena" i nomi che mi dava al suo venire.

Who is it? And what will he say? He will call "Butterfly" from the distance. I will stay hidden, to tease him, but also so that I don't die of joy. And he will call me again: "My little wife, my little sweet flower"—all the names he used to call me.

Tutto questo avverrà, te lo prometto.

All this will happen; I promise you.

Tienti la tua paura, io con sicura fede l'aspetto.

Keep your fears to yourself. I wait for him with complete faith.

89

Goro, the marriage broker, brings Yamadori, a wealthy Japanese man who hopes to marry Butterfly. She rejects the idea, saying that she is married to Pinkerton and is bound by the laws of America, not Japan. Sharpless also comes to Butterfly's house with a letter from Pinkerton. Butterfly becomes so excited, that she does not realize that Sharpless is trying to prepare her for bad news. Sharpless angers Butterfly when he suggests that Pinkerton has forgotten her. He urges her to marry Yamadori. Butterfly rushes out and returns with a blond-haired, blue-eyed child. She explains that Pinkerton is unaware of his son because the baby was born after Pinkerton was reassigned to America. She asks Sharpless to write and tell Pinkerton of his son. She is certain that he will return to the two of them.

A cannon shot is heard from the harbor announcing the arrival of a ship. Butterfly and Suzuki rush to decorate the house with flowers in Pinkerton's honor. Butterfly dresses in her wedding gown, puts a scarlet poppy in her hair, and has Suzuki dress the little boy. As the curtain falls, Suzuki and the child have fallen asleep, leaving Butterfly awake, motionless and watching.

Act III

As the curtain rises, the child and Suzuki are still asleep, and Butterfly silently waits for Pinkerton. It is dawn, and the room gradually fills with light.

Suzuki:	Già il sole, Ciociosan!	It is morning, Cio-cio-san!
Butterfly:	Verrà, verrà, vedrai.	He's coming! *(She picks up the child and carries him from the room.)*
Suzuki:	Salite a riposare, affranta siete . . . al suo venire vi chiamerò.	You're so tired; you must rest . . . I'll wake you when he comes.
Butterfly:	Dormi amor mio, dormi sul mio cor. Tu sei con Dio Ed io col mio dolor. A te i rai degli astri d'or, Bimbo mio dormi!	Sleep, little one, sleep. You are with God, while I am with my grief. But on you shine the star's bright rays. Sleep, my darling, sleep.
Suzuki:	Provera Butterfly. Chi sia? Oh!	Poor Butterfly. *(There is a knock at the door and Suzuki slides the panel back.)* Who is it? Oh!

90

Sharpless:	Stz!	Hush!
Pinkerton:	Zitta! Non la destar.	Quiet! Don't disturb her.
Suzuki:	Era stanca si tanto! Vi stette ad aspettare tutta la notte col bimbo.	She stood watching for you all night with the child.
Pinkerton:	Come sapea?	How did she know?
Suzuki:	Non giunge da tre anni una nave nel porto che da lunge Butterfly non ne scruti il color, la bandiera.	Not a ship has entered the harbor for three years without her knowing.
Sharpless:	Ve lo dissi?	Didn't I tell you?
Suzuki:	La chiamo.	I'll call her.
Pinkerton:	No, non ancor.	No, not yet.
Suzuki:	Lo vedete, ier sera, la stanza volle sparger di fiori.	Last night, she scattered flowers all over for your arrival.
Sharpless:	Ve lo dissi?	Didn't I tell you?
Pinkerton:	Che pena!	This is terrible!
Suzuki:	Chi c'è là fuori nel giardino? Una donna!	Who's in the garden? A woman!
Pinkerton:	Zitta!	Hush!
Suzuki:	Chi è? Chi è?	Who is she? Who is she?

As Pinkerton leaves, his wife Kate and Butterfly enter. After a few moments, Butterfly realizes who Kate is. Kate explains that Pinkerton wants to take the child back to America with them. Butterfly is heartbroken but agrees on the condition that Pinkerton meet her alone in half an hour. Sharpless and Kate exit; Butterfly tells the weeping Suzuki to go and keep the child company. Butterfly kneels before the statue of Buddha. She then goes and takes down her father's sword, kisses the blade ceremoniously, and reads the inscription on the sword:

Butterfly:	"Con onor muore chi non puo serbar vita con onore."	"To die with honor when one can no longer live with honor."

She raises the sword to her throat. The door opens, and Suzuki pushes the child inside. He runs toward his mother. Butterfly throws down the sword and flings her arms around him.

91

Butterfly: Tu? Tu?

Piccolo Iddio! Amore mio, fior di giglio e di rosa.

Non saperlo mai per te, pei tuoi puri occhi, muor Butterfly, perchè tu possa andar di là dal mare senza che ti rimorda ai di maturi, il materno abbandono. O a me, sceso dal trono dell'alto Paradiso, guarda ben fiso, fiso di tua madre la faccia! Che te'n resti una traccia, guarda ben! Amore, addio! Addio, piccolo amor! Va. Gioca, gioca.

You? You?

My little idol! I love you, my beloved flower.

This terrible scene is not for your innocent eyes. You must go far away across the sea without a mother's death to haunt you as you grow.

But look carefully at your mother's face now, so that you will have a faint memory of it. I love you. Farewell, my little love. Farewell.

She sets the child on a rug, gives him an American flag to play with, and blindfolds him. Taking her father's sword, she goes behind the screen. The sound of the sword is heard falling and Butterfly staggers out from behind the screen toward her son. She kisses him before she collapses by his side. Pinkerton's voice is heard from outside: Butterfly! Butterfly! Butterfly! The door flies open and Pinkerton and Sharpless burst in. They run towards Butterfly who points weakly to the child and dies. Pinkerton drops to his knees, in despair. Sharpless takes the child into his arms and kisses him as the curtain falls.

92

The Tender Land

Libretto by Horace Everett
Music by Aaron Copland

Aaron Copland (1900–) was born in Brooklyn, New York. He studied in Paris with Nadia Boulanger, who taught some of the most famous composers of the twentieth century. His best-known works include the ballets *Appalachian Spring* and *Rodeo* and the film score for *The Red Pony*.

The action takes place on a farm in the Midwest. The time is the early 1930s; the month is June, the time of Laurie's graduation and the spring harvest.

Cast of Characters

Laurie Moss, *a high school senior*
Ma Moss, *Laurie's mother*
Beth Moss, *Laurie's little sister*
Grandpa Moss, *Laurie's grandfather*
Martin and Top, *two drifters looking for work*
Mr. and Mrs. Jenks, *the Moss's neighbors*

93

Lesson Focus

Expression: Musical elements are combined into a whole to express a musical or extramusical idea. *(D–S)*

Materials

○ **Record Information:**
  • The Tender Land (excerpts)
    Record 5 Sides A, B Bands 1–5, 1a–b
    Choral Art Society
    New York Philharmonic
    Aaron Copland, conductor
○ **Teacher's Resource Binder:**
  [Activity Sheets]
  • **Activity Sheet 17,** page A30

The Lesson

1. This lesson engages students in four types of activities: reading the plot summaries, following the notated score, performing the musical examples, and listening to the musical excerpts. As each notated song appears, help students learn to sing these excerpts by following the suggestions provided for each song, or prepare them to read the score while listening to the recording. You may wish to learn and discuss all the songs first and then return to follow the plot.

2. *OPTIONAL* The students may take turns reading the plot summaries, or you may wish to give the class time to read them silently before proceeding to the next musical selection.

3. All the action takes place in the house and yard of a farm in the Midwest. As the opening instrumental section of the opera is heard, set the scene for students by reading the following comments:

The curtain rises on a farmhouse and yard in the Midwest. The child, Beth, is dancing by herself, acknowledging a doll as a partner. Ma Moss is seated in the porch rocker, and is sewing. Laurie comes in with her books in a strap. She lays them on the steps and walks around the yard eyeing all the familiar things in a new way.

• "Once I thought I'd never grow . . . " (Laurie's song, page 94) The students may follow the text on the pupil page 98. Distribute Activity Sheet 17 (*Laurie's Song*). Listen to the song. Guide the students to discover that this song flows with much "up and down" motion. There are many notes of the same duration with the rhythmic interest

For Your Information

Aaron Copland (1900–) was raised in Brooklyn, New York. When he was fifteen, Aaron Copland decided to become a composer. As the first step toward this goal, he tried to learn harmony through a correspondence course. After a few lessons he realized he needed more substantial instruction and sought a qualified tutor. In his early twenties, Copland studied in Paris and came to be recognized as a talented composer who followed experimental paths. Early in his career, Copland was concerned about writing music that would be, above all, American. He began by using a jazz idiom in his symphonic works. Later he felt that this was too limiting and began to compose works that were influenced by Igor Stravinsky. He then felt that he was turning out pieces that were not reaching the average listener. He became dissatisfied with the relationship between the music-loving public and the living composer. Composers were ''in danger of working in a vacuum.'' Meanwhile, a new public for music had grown up around the radio and phonograph, and Copland said, ''It made no sense to ignore them and to continue working as if they did not exist. I felt that it was worth the effort to see if I couldn't say what I had to say in the simplest possible terms.'' During this time Copland wrote many of the works that are *(continued on next page)*

Act 1

The isolated world of this rural family revolves around the graduation of Laurie, but she is unsure of her place in the world. It is late afternoon of the day before her high school graduation. *(Laurie strolls home from school. Ma Moss and Beth are on the porch.)*

Laurie: Once I thought I'd never grow tall as this fence. Time dragged heavy and slow. But April came, and August went before I knew just what they meant, and little by little I grew. And as I grew, I came to know how fast the time could go.

Now the time has grown so short; the world has grown so wide. I'll be graduated soon. Why am I strange inside? What makes me think I'd like to try to go down all those roads beyond that line above the earth and 'neath the sky? Tomorrow when I sit upon the graduation platform stand, I know my hand will shake when I reach out to take that paper with the ribboned band.

Now that all the learning's done, oh, who knows what will now begin? It's so strange, I'm strange inside. The time has grown so short, the world so wide.

created by occasional sustained pitches (*fermatas*) held at the end of phrases. Ask the students to follow the first part of Laurie's song by sliding a finger along the lines on the contour score. Suggest to them that the wandering nature of the pitches (few with no repeated patterns, no sense of a return to a central pitch) might musically express the unsettled emotions referred to in the lyrics.

• "A stranger may seem strange . . . " (Trio for Martin, Top, and Grandpa, pages 95–96.) **Look at the notation. Predict what you might hear just by looking at the music.** Ask questions such as the following:

Will this be sung as smoothly and freely as Laurie's song? (no) **How can you tell from the music?** (no ties or slurs indicated, rhythm very straight, accented beats, volume markings suggesting robust singing) **Where has imitation been used in the vocal**

parts? (much use of imitation, both melodic and rhythmic, beginning measures 10, 20, 24) **How does this use of imitation help express the text?** (suggests the urgency of getting the harvesting job and the gradual realization by Grandpa that these men are suited to the work)

• "Stomp your foot . . . " (full ensemble, page 97) **Follow the notation. Listen as the first section is introduced. And sing along when the section is repeated.** Draw students' attention to the melody line of this section. Measures 1, 3, and 5 begin with a dramatic octave leap. Ask all students to sing the song, using the octave skip as written. Then have them sing the song again without the octave skip, remaining on the same note. **Why do you suppose Copland used this octave skip when the melody could have begun on the same pitch?** (The octave skip conveys a feel-

(Ma Moss and Beth go into the house. Laurie starts to follow, but hides when she hears two strangers approaching.)

Top and Martin are two hungry drifters who have come to the farm looking for work in the harvest. They see Laurie behind the porch and humorously tease her, trying to wrangle an introduction. Not many strangers come to the farm, so Laurie is timid and skeptical. She asks where they are from.

Top: We've been north, we've been south. We're goin' east,
Martin: we're goin' west. We've been here, we're goin' there.
            That's where we've been and that's where we're goin'.

Martin and Top are explaining to Laurie that they are looking for work when Grandpa returns. The young men ask for a job in the spring harvest. Grandpa is a bit suspicious about hiring strangers and says, "They bring no good, somehow."

95

For Your Information *(continued)*
best known today—the film score for *The Red Pony* and the ballets *Rodeo* and *Appalachian Spring.* The opera *The Tender Land* is another example of Copland's efforts to express musically the drama in the daily lives of ordinary people in America.

ing of excitement, suggesting the leaping and jumping of dancers. The song seems to lose excitement when sung on the same pitches.)

• "The plains so green . . . " (Duet—Martin and Laurie, pages 99–100) Ask the students to look at the rhythmic relationship between the two parts of the duet in the score. Ask them to ignore the final eight measures for the moment.

After the class silently studies the notation, divide the students into two groups. Group 1 is to rhythmically read Laurie's part; Group 2, Martin's part. Both groups are to tap short sounds on their legs as they chant the words to each part. (The short sound will be the quarter note.) The students will discover that the following rhythmic pattern is repeated and imitated until the meter change.

If the students wish to rhythmically read the remaining eight measures of the song, they should change the shortest sound to an eighth note. To perform this duet, the students will need at times to select pitches that are within their range.

4. Read the information on Aaron Copland (pupil page 93) and provide the students with additional information on the composers' life as needed. (See **For Your Information**.)

95

Grandpa: When you put it like that I'll have to admit. You're right for the work and besides bein' fit you're not such a stranger, not such a stranger, not such a stranger anymore . . .

Act II

Family and guests are seated around a large table loaded with food. Ma Moss tries to encourage everyone to have a second helping.

Top: Not for me, Missus Moss, I've already had three helpin's.

Mrs. Jenks: Did you see him put that food away? He must have hid it somewhere.

Top: Where I hid it . . . you'll never find it.

Mrs. Jenks: How many boardin' houses have gone bankrupt 'cause of you two?

Top: Let's see: one, two, three, four . . .

Martin: Five boardin' houses and two jails!

All: Tall tales, tall tales, five boardin' houses and two jails!

Grandpa: Try makin' peace with some of my wine—finest wine anywhere, berry wine.

Mr. Jenks: Let's drink to a good spring harvest!

Grandpa: The first of our family that's ever graduated, and *that's* what I'm drinkin' to tonight, Mr. Jenks!

Mr. Jenks: To Laurie then!

All: Laurie, Laurie . . . Laurie Moss!

Laurie: (*seated quietly behind the table, now steps forward, revealing her new dress*) Thank you, thank you all.

(The group prepares for a dance. Top pulls Martin aside.)

Top: Remember what I told you. You have a dance while I start with the old man, then you take him over. (*looking at Laurie*) Gee, she's a pretty thing.

Martin: Take it easy, Top, don't lose us our jobs. (*to himself*) She *is* a pretty thing.

The festive atmosphere continues with a square dance.

Stomp your foot up - on the floor. Throw the win - dows o - pen.

Take a breath of fresh June air, and dance a - round the room,

and dance a - round the room. _____

97

After the dance, all gather around Top, who seems to be telling another story. Martin and Laurie walk away from the group.

Martin: The world seems still tonight. (*He takes Laurie's hand and they go to the porch. At the bottom of the steps he kisses her tenderly.*)

Laurie: Oh, Martin. I should say something.

Martin: Quiet, quiet . . . tomorrow you'll be graduated and like you ma says, "you won't be nervous anymore."

98

Martin begins to dream wistfully and tells Laurie that someday he would like to have a wife who would walk out on the land with him at the end of each day.

Martin: Oh, Laurie, are you ready for settlin' in with me? Do you feel in love that way I do?

Laurie: In love? In love? Yes, yes, I do love you. You came and made me feel in love. I feel so many, many, things, Martin. Tomorrow after graduation . . . perhaps I'll know.

Martin: Laurie, Laurie! I'll be goin' soon.

Laurie: Don't talk of that, Martin. Oh please, I don't want you to go. Harvest is through so quickly.

Martin: I'll stop here 'till harvest's done. If you love me, then this is where I'll stay.

Laurie: Martin, yes, I want you . . . I need you.

Martin: I love you . . . I'll stay.

Laurie: I love you . . .

99

Grandpa discovers that Laurie and Martin are not with the group. He jumps to false conclusions and calls the two drifters "dirty strangers" and "bums." Laurie tries to defend Martin. The party ends abruptly because of the argument. Grandpa orders Martin and Top to leave at daybreak. Laurie turns and runs into the house. Later, Martin and Laurie meet. Laurie convinces Martin to take her with him in the morning. Laurie goes into the house, and Martin is left alone.

100

Martin: Daybreak will come in such short time. Why do I hope the hours pass slow? Oh, will I find that when I stayed, I meant to go? (*Top enters, having overheard Martin.*) Laurie, I love you, I love you.

Top: What you doin' sittin' here? Don't you want to get some sleep before we hit the road?

Martin: (*dazed, not looking at Top*) Laurie . . . Laurie . . .

Top: What's the matter with you? What's this about Laurie?

Martin: (*still not looking at Top*) She's comin' with us, Top.

Top: Are you crazy? She can't come with us! That Grandpa of hers would have us in jail 'fore we was a mile off! Think, Martin, think . . . our kind's no good for a girl like her. She don't fit with guys like us. She belongs in a soft, white dress up on that graduation stand, with a mother and a grandpa to make a fuss, when she gets that roll with a ribbon band. And look at you . . . you're crazy! Talkin' so big. Big when you talk, walkin' down an endless road. Do what you must, just what you do. Don't take on an extra load. What have you got? What can you give? What will you eat? Where will you live? Is that how you see Laurie? C'mon, hurry boy–day's a comin'. C'mon, we've got no time . . . Take it from me, kid, and try to forget. Try to forget. Hurry! It'll soon be day.

Martin: Laurie, Laurie, forgive me . . . forgive me . . .

(*Top picks up their bundles and they both leave.*)

101

Daylight is coming as Laurie excitedly descends the steps carrying a small satchel. *(She goes to the shed and knocks lightly.)*

Laurie: Martin, it's daybreak. Are you ready? *(She knocks louder.)* Martin? Martin! Martin! *(Suddenly she throws the door open and falls down weeping. Beth, running out of the house, rushes to her.)*

Beth: Laurie, Laurie, Sister! Oh Laurie, what's wrong? What have I done? Mother!

Laurie: Sh, Beth! Can it end this way? No, I must leave now!

Beth: Oh, Sister, what is wrong? Have you forgotten what day this is?

Laurie: *(to herself)* I must leave now.

Beth: *(pulling away)* You scare me, Laurie.

Ma Moss: *(coming down the steps)* Laurie, Beth, what has happened?

Beth: *(rushing to her mother)* They've gone, they've gone, and Laurie says she's going too!

Ma Moss: What? Is it true they've left? Is this our Laurie?

Laurie: *(calmly)* Yes, Mother, they have left, and I must also leave.

Ma Moss: What are you saying, Laurie? It's graduation day!

Laurie: *(firmly)* I mean it, Mother; I am leaving, too.

Ma Moss: All the things we've planned . . . What do you mean? You promised me . . . Believe I understand. You may think you loved that boy, but Laurie . . .

Laurie: I know, Mother, but try to see . . . how changed this day must seem for me. How changed I, too, have come to be. Goodbye, Beth. Sister, goodbye.

Ma Moss: You are strange to me. I cannot understand. I cannot even recognize your face.

Laurie: Goodbye, Mother, and please ask Grandpa to forgive me that I go.

Ma Moss: I can ask no question, I can hear no answer.

Laurie: Goodbye to all the other things that I have loved. *(She exits slowly.)*

Ma Moss thinks sadly of all the plans that were laid and all the dreams that were made for graduation day. ("What love we put into each thought, each plan . . . ") Her regret takes a more hopeful turn when she thinks, "This love and care we put into each thought, each plan, each making . . . is just beginning . . . "

102

Is just be - gin - ning, be - gin - ning. _____

As Laurie goes to find her own life, Ma Moss turns to her younger daughter, knowing that although one responsibility has ended, another has begun.

103

Lesson Focus

Expression: Musical elements are combined into a whole to express a musical or extramusical idea. *(D–E)*

Materials

○ **Record Information**
- Overture to *Les Indes Galantes* by Jean–Phillipe Rameau (rah-**moe**), 1685-1764
  Record 5 Side B Band 2
  La Grande Ecurie et la Chambre du Roy
  Jean–Claude Malgoire, conductor
- Rondo from *Concerto No. 2 for Horn in E♭ Major,* K. 417 by Wolfgang Amadeus Mozart (**moet**-sahrt), 1756-1791
  Record 6 Side A Band 1
  Mason Jones, French horn
  Philadelphia Orchestra
  Eugene Ormandy, conductor
- Prelude to Act III from *Lohengrin*
  (Record 2 Side B Band1)
- *Symphony in D major,* ("Classical") by Sergei Prokofiev (pruh-**kaw**-fee-yef), 1891-1953
  Record 6 Side B Band 2
  New York Philharmonic
  Leonard Bernstein, conductor

○ **Teacher's Resource Binder:**
  Activity Sheets
- **Activity Sheet 18**, page A31
- Optional—
  Biography 6, pages B11-B12

Use Your Listening Skills In the Audience

The audience is an essential element of any musical performance. A good audience must have . . .

Attending Skills

- Arrive at the concert hall or theater in time to be seated and read the program notes before the curtain rises.
- Be considerate of others: talk only during the times for applause and intermissions.

Listening Skills

- Listen for important themes. Notice how they are repeated, altered, and varied.
- Listen for music of various historical periods. Is the music all the same, or do you hear music of different times and places?

Responding Skills

Show your appreciation by applauding

- when the conductor reaches the podium
- when the soloists walk on stage
- at the end of a scene, at the theater
- at the end of a composition, at a concert

The Chickawa Symphony Orchestra
Harvey Higgenbottom, Music Director
and Principal Conductor

Overture to *Les Indes Galentes* ....Jean Philippe Rameau
(1683-1764)

Rondo from the *Concerto for Horn in E♭ Major*.......Wolfgang Amadeau Mozart
(1759-1791)

Jane Doe, soloist

Prelude to Act III of *Lohengrin* ....Richard Wagner
(1830-1883)

Intermission

Symphony in D major, ...Sergei Prokofiev
Op.25 ("Classical") (1891-1953)

Allegro
Larghetto
Gavotte (Allegro non troppo)
Finale (Molto vivace)

104

The Lesson

1. Use the illustrations and "stream of consciousness" prose on pupil page 105 to initiate a discussion about feelings the students may have had when attending a formal concert.

2. Have a "practice session" for concert attendance, reviewing the skills described on page 104. If possible, time this lesson to coincide with an upcoming youth concert or other concert appropriate for class attendance. Activities could include:

- a field trip to purchase tickets or a letter-writing activity for ordering by mail
- setting up the classroom or auditorium for a class concert. Assign some students to be ticket-takers and ushers. Then listen to the "recorded concert" as given in the book as if it were live. Review appropriate times to talk, applaud, leave seats, and so on.

Precede and follow the formal concert with a study of each composition on the program. Use the call chart for "Prelude to Act III" from *Lohengrin* (pages 58-59) and Activity Sheet 18 (*Listening Guide—Classical Symphony*). Then read the program notes for the concert on page 105.

3. **OPTIONAL** After the students have participated in a concert, they may wish to plan a classroom concert of their own. Develop the program by selecting music from the repertoires of class performers or other performing school ensembles. Assign roles, such as program note writers, publicity committee, ticket sellers, ushers, engineers to record the performance, and a critic to review the concert. When the concert is over, evaluate the behavior of the audience.

"Tonight's the night! The most famous symphony orchestra in the county is in our town. I'm going to be in the audience . . . What should I wear? How will I know where to sit . . . what to do . . . Wonder if I'll have to be absolutely quiet the whole evening . . . What if I clap at the wrong time . . . will people laugh at me? get mad? How will I know what to listen for?"

Hmmm—I wonder if I look at the program, will that help me know what to do? Just three pieces; gosh, program shouldn't be too long . . . uh-oh, wonder what those extra lines of words under the "Class-i-cal Sym-pho-ny" mean???

What's on the back? "Program notes." Well, maybe that will be a little help. . . . might as well read it. . . . .

Program Notes

Overture to Les Indes Galantes by J.P. Rameau (1683-1764)

Jean Phillipe Rameau wrote many opera-ballets, of which *Les Indes Galantes* was probably the most popular. The overture to *Les Indes Galantes* does not actually use any melodies from the opera-ballet that follows, nor is there any attempt to set the mood for the opening scene. Instead, the overture provides the audience with a beautiful "appetizer" to stimulate the musical appetite for the "banquet" to come.

Concerto for Horn in E♭ Major, K. 417

This concerto is one of the four horn concertos written during Mozart's Viennese years. The work was written for an acquaintance who was not a professional musician, but played the instrument exceptionally well. The rondo is the last movement of the concerto. The opening theme is a sprightly tune announced by the horn, which begins with a motive built on the pitches of the tonic triad.

Prelude to Act III of Lohengrin · Richard Wagner (1813-1883)

Richard Wagner is considered the leading composer of German Romantic opera. His aim was to unify all components of music theater (music, libretto, lighting, staging, set design) to create a total art work. Wagner's works include "The Ring Cycle" (a series of four operas), *Tristan and Isolde, The Flying Dutchman,* and *Lohengrin.* This prelude precedes the moment when Lohengrin and his bride Elsa are escorted to the wedding chamber.

Symphony in D major, Op. 25 ("Classical") · Sergei Prokofiev (1891-1953)

Sergei Prokofiev was one of the most prominent Russian composers of the twentieth century. His works include such well known compositions as *Peter and the Wolf, The Love of Three Oranges,* and the ballet *Romeo and Juliet.* Prokofiev composed this work because he wanted to write a symphony "as Mozart or Haydn may have written if they lived in our day." The *Classical Symphony* is in four movements, and while its instrumentation and musical forms are common to the classical era, its harmonies and rhythms are more at home in the early twentieth century.

105

Lesson Focus

Evaluation: Review concepts and skills studied in Unit 2. *(D–S)*

Materials

○ **Record Information:**
- *Basse Danse "Mon Desir"*
  Record 6   Side B   Band 1
  Ancient Instrument Ensemble of Zurich
- Overture to *Hansel and Gretel* (excerpt) by Engelbert Humperdinck (**hum**-puhr-dingk), 1854–1921
  Record 6   Side B   Band 2
  Gurzenich Orchestra
- Third movement from *Divertimento No. 17 in D* by Wolfgang Amadeus Mozart (**moet**-sahrt), 1756–1791
  Record 6   Side B   Band 3
  N.Y. Philomusica Ensemble
- *Two-part Invention in D minor* by J.S. Bach (**bahk**), 1685–1750
  Record 6   Side B   Band 4
  Walter Carlos, Moog synthesizer
- *Ave Maris Stella* by Paul Winter, 1939
  Record 6   Side B   Band 5
  Paul Winter Consort

○ **Other:** Prepare sheets previously used— Activity Sheets 11, 13, 15, 16

○ **Teacher's Resource Binder:**

Evaluation   Review 2, page Ev9
   Musical Progress Report 2, page Ev10

Clues to Musical Style—Putting It All Together

In this unit you have learned that there are many clues to musical style. Clues may be heard in

- the choices of timbre
- the way rhythm and melody are organized
- the kind of texture selected

Listen to compositions that you have not heard before. Which of these clues will help you to identify the origin of each work? You may find that in some music the choice of instruments is the most helpful clue. For other music, it may be the kind of texture used. As you listen, look again at your "Musical Clue" charts to help you recall the characteristics of each musical element.

Composers sometimes borrow ideas from the music of earlier times. This is what the composers did for the two pieces you are about to hear. Can you decide

- when the music was composed?
- where the composer may have found his or her ideas?
- which earlier period is suggested by the music?

Portrait of Mlle. Riviere (1805)
by Jean-Auguste-Dominique Ingres

I Like Ingres, a copy (1962)
by Larry Rivers

106

The Lesson

1. Ask the students to read the information on page 106. Distribute a copy of *Review 2* and each activity sheet and a pencil to each student. (See **Materials**.) Explain that they are to
   - use the Musical Clue sheets to recall different characteristics of each historical period
   - circle the historical period
   - circle the musical characteristics

2. Play the recorded examples.

   Basse Danse "Mon Desir": Renaissance; timbre—original instruments; rhythm—steady beat and melodic line moving evenly in relation to the beat; melody—moving mostly by steps or small skips; central pitch—apparent; texture—quite thin

   Overture to *Hansel and Gretel*: Romantic; timbre—varied due to large orchestra; melody—range sometimes restricted, sometimes very wide; texture—dense with many lines moving simultaneously

   Third Movement from *Divertimento No. 17*: Classical; timbre—limited contrast due to small orchestra; rhythm—steady beat, accented, all melodic lines moving evenly in relation to the steady beat; melody—strong sense of central pitch

   Two-part Invention in D minor: Baroque, but in a twentieth-century transcription; timbre—synthesizer; rhythm—steady beats; texture—two-part polyphony; melody—alternating between moving by steps and skips; central pitch—strongly present

   Ave Maris Stella: Medieval, but in a twentieth-century arrangement; timbre—saxophone, percussion; rhythm—jazz style after opening solo; melody—limited range, moving mostly by steps—some students may recognize this as a Gregorian chant; texture—mostly monophonic

Unit 3

The Musician Performs and Creates

Unit Overview

Unit 3 focuses on the performance and creation of music. Students sing in various ensembles and learn to play the guitar, percussion instruments, and the dulcimer. Finally, the students learn skills to create their own music, using classical, rap, and jazz ideas.

Texas Essential Elements for Unit 3

1A: PE (pages 108; 110; 115; 119; 122–123; 125; 129; 131; 138; 140–141; 143; 145; 149; 151–153; 155; 157–158)

 TE (pages 110–112; 115–116; 118–120; 122–123; 126; 129–130; 138; 140–142; 144; 150–152; 154; 156–157; 162)

 TRB (pages K2; K5; K8; K17; O2; O4; O6; O8; O9; O13; O18; O20; O22; O26; O28; M4; M19; E23; AS33; AS36; AS37; AS38; AS40; I11; EV11; EV14; EV16)

1B: PE (pages 108; 110; 115; 119; 121; 122–123; 125–129; 131; 132–135; 137; 138; 140–141; 143; 145–147; 149–158; 160–161)

 TE (pages 110–112; 115–116; 118–120; 122–123; 126; 129–130; 132–135; 138; 140–142; 144; 146; 150–152; 154; 156–157; 162)

(continued on top of page)

TRB (pages K2; K5; K8; K11; K17; O2; O4; O6; O8; O9; O13; O18; O20; O22; O26; O28; E23; M4; M19; M24; AS33; AS34; AS35; AS36; AS37; AS38; AS39; AS40; AS42; I11; EV11; EV14; EV16)

1C: PE (pages 108; 115; 123; 125–128; 131; 132; 138–143; 144–147; 149–154; 156–157; 159–161)

 TE (pages 112; 115–116; 118; 122; 124; 126; 128–129; 131; 132; 138; 140–142; 144; 146–148; 150–152; 154; 156–157; 162)

 TRB (pages K17; O2; O4; O6; O8; O9; O13; O18; O20; O22; O26; O28; E23; M24; AS32; AS33; AS42; I11; EV11; EV14; EV16)

1D: PE (pages 108; 110; 115; 119; 122; 125; 129; 131; 145–146; 149–155; 157; 160–161)

 TE (pages 111–112; 115–116; 118; 120; 122–123; 126; 129–130; 138; 142; 144; 146; 150–152; 154; 160; 162)

 TRB (pages K2; O2; O4; O6; O8; O9; O13; O18; O20; O22; O26; O28; E23; AS33; AS36; AS37; AS38; AS40; I11; EV11; EV14; EV16)

1A: TE (page 154)
 TRB (page AS42)

1F: PE (pages 156–157)
 PE (pages 108; 115; 119; 122; 135; 145; 149; 151–152)
 TE (pages 108–112; 115–116; 118–119; 122–123; 127–130; 135–136; 138; 142; 144; 148; 162)
 TRB (pages K2; K5; K8; K11; O2; O4; O6; O8; O9; O13; O18; O20; O22; O26; O28; M4; M19; E23; AS40; EV11; EV14; EV16)

3A: PE (page 136)
 TE (page 139)

3B: PE (pages 121; 123; 124–129; 131; 132–135; 137; 145; 149; 154; 160–161)
 TE (pages 111; 120; 122–123; 124; 126; 128; 130–131; 132–136; 144–146; 151; 155; 160; 162)
 TRB (pages O2; O4; O6; O8; O9; O13; O18; O20; O22; O26; O28; E23; M19; M24; AS32; AS34; AS35; AS36; AS37; AS38; AS39; AS40; AS41; AS42; I11; EV14; EV16)

4A: PE (pages 119; 121–123; 131; 137; 138; 142–143; 145; 149; 151–155; 157; 160–161)
 TE (pages 118; 120–122; 130–131; 135; 137; 138; 142; 144–145; 147; 154; 157; 160; 162)
 TRB (pages AS32; AS42; EV14; EV16)

4B: PE (pages 122; 145; 157)
 TE (pages 144–145)

5A: PE (pages 115; 119; 125; 127–129; 131; 133–135; 137; 140–142; 145–147; 149–154; 158; 160–161)
 TE (pages 108–112; 115–116; 118–120; 122–123; 124; 126–131; 132–136; 138; 140–142; 144; 146–148; 150–152; 155; 160; 162)
 TRB (pages K5; K8; K11; K17; O2; O4; O6; O8; O9; O13; O18; O20; O22; O26; O28; M19; M24; E23; AS34; AS35; AS36; AS38; AS39; AS40; I11; EV14; EV16)

Lesson Focus

Melody: A melody may be relatively high or low. *(P–E)*

Materials

○ **Record Information:**
  • Peace on Earth
    Record 6   Side B   Band 6
    Voices: mixed voices

The Musician Sings

Most people participate in some form of musical performance throughout their lives.

Some individuals may choose performance as a career. They perform as professional musicians, earning their living as performers, conductors, or teachers.

Others may become amateur performers. They enjoy playing in community bands, choirs, and orchestras, or perhaps just "jamming" with friends.

Still others find performance a satisfying form of recreation. Perhaps they strum the guitar while sitting in the park, pick out a tune on the electric organ, or "whistle while they work"!

The purpose of this unit is to provide you with some of the musical skills that will allow you to continue to perform music in a variety of ways throughout your life.

Begin by finding your best singing range. Experiment by singing "America" in three different keys. Which is your most comfortable singing range? Use the following beginning pitches.

Tr. I / Tr. II (F)   C.V. (B♭)   Bar. (E♭)

108

The Lesson

1. Discuss different ways in which the students have participated in performance: church or community choirs, instrumental groups such as drum and bugle corps or orchestras, making music informally with friends or family. Ask the students to talk about family members who make music.

2. Discuss possible hardships involved when choosing music as a career. There are many hours of practice and rehearsal, stiff competition, and few jobs. Finally, speak of the satisfaction that comes from sharing one's music with others.

3. Invite the students to explore their performing skills by first determining their best singing range. (See **For Your Information.**) To determine their appropriate ranges, ask all students to sing "America" ("My country, 'tis of thee

. . .") in three different keys: F, B♭, and E♭. Use the piano to accompany. Ask the students to decide which key is the most comfortable.

4. *OPTIONAL* Check their decisions again by repeating the song in these three keys. Ask the students to sing only when their "chosen" key is played. **Did you choose the correct range for your voice?**

5. Designate those who chose the first example as Treble I and II, those who chose the second example as Changing Voices, and those who chose the third example as Baritones. Some students may be able to sing in more than one key. Help these students to choose their correct parts as needed. (Changing Voices and Baritones should be boys only.)

6. **Follow the score on page 109 and learn to sing the round "Peace on Earth."** Any one of the

 Texas Essential Elements, The Musician Sings, pp. 108–123: 1A, 1B, 1C, 1D, 2, 3B, 4A, 4B, 5A (Please see Unit 3 opener, page 107, for component and page references.)

Peace on Earth

Words by Lee Hays

Music by Hans Eisler

For Your Information

Many students' voices at this stage are in the process of change. Range may be shifting, and usable pitches may become limited for a time. Boys may be singing in any of these four vocal ranges: Treble I and II, Changing Voice, or Baritone. They will find that melodies often involve a wider range than they are able to sing and that they will need to perform special parts.

Note the following vocal ranges with their extensions:

Treble I

Treble II

Changing Voice
(actual pitch)

Baritone

four parts to this round may be sung as a repeated ostinato if needed to accommodate voice ranges. Use the syllable "loo" when accompanying the round. Changing Voices may decide to sing Line 4 only while others sing the complete round. Note that Changing Voices will need to sing Line 4 at the notated pitch (not an octave lower).

Lesson Focus

Texture: Musical quality is affected by the degree of rhythmic contrast between musical lines occurring simultaneously. *(P—S)*

Materials

○ **Piano Accompaniment:** page 278

○ **Record Information:**
- Rufus Rustus and Chicken
  Record 6 Side B Band 7
  Voices: mixed voices
  Accompaniment: clarinet, trumpet, trombone, tuba, piano, banjo, percussion

○ **Instruments:** autoharp, guitar, or ukulele

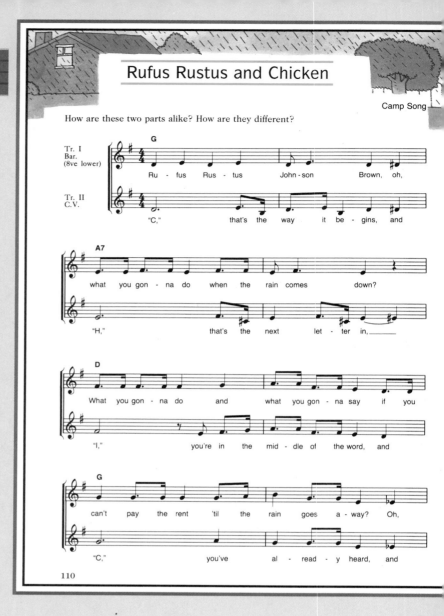

Rufus Rustus and Chicken

Camp Song

How are these two parts alike? How are they different?

110

The Lesson

1. Begin the session with Vocal Warm-up 1. Help the students understand that producing a good vocal sound involves sensing where your voice is "inside" you. Ask the students to stand up straight and sing the "Yoo-hoo" sequence given below.

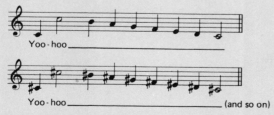

Now ask the students to sing this sequence using the following movements: place hands on both sides of head, bend over singing the first two pitches in the pattern, and slowly move back to standing position while singing the descending pitches. **What happens to your voice when you move this way?** The students will discover that they feel a change of voice placement from throat to head. Soaring to a higher pitch becomes easier now and is executed with better tone quality. Repeat this several times. Now ask the students to remain standing and sing in the same manner. They will discover that the tone placement feels the same as when moving.

2. Divide the students into four groups. Assign each pitch in the following chord sequence to a separate group. Ask the students of these three groups to sing this sequence as a continuous harmonic accompaniment. The students in the fourth group should freely improvise melodies simultaneously over this ground. All the students should use their new "inside" way of singing. Vary this activity until most of the students have had the opportunity to improvise their own melodies.

G
you know and I know and ev-'ry-bod-y knows that you

"K," now you're near-ing the end, and

A7
can't pay the rent if you ain't got the dough.

"E," now you're round-ing the bend.

D
Ru - fus Rus - tus John - son Brown, oh,

C - H - I - C - K - E - N, oh,

G   D   G
what you gon - na do when the rain comes down?

that's the way you spell (clap,   clap) chick - en.

111

Doo, doo, doo, doo...

struments such as autoharp, guitar, or ukulele. **Which chords will be needed to play this
accompaniment?** (G, D, and A7)

3. Open books to "Rufus Rustus and Chicken" on
   pages 110–111. Ask the students to look for
   the same pitches in Part 1 that are sung at the
   same time in Part 2. (This occurs throughout
   the arrangement.) **We have discovered there
   are many pitches that are the same in both
   parts. What is the major difference between
   the parts?** (The rhythm of Part 2 has mostly
   sustained sounds, whereas Part 1 moves in
   short sounds. Both parts have many syncopated patterns.)

4. Divide the song into two parts as written. Sing
   the song with the recording or with the piano
   accompaniment.

5. Encourage the students to play their own accompaniment while singing this song. Use in-

OPTIONAL

Lesson Focus

Harmony: Two or more musical lines may occur simultaneously. *(P–S)*

Materials

○ **Piano Accompaniment:** page 280
○ **Record Information:**
  • When You and I Were Young, Maggie, Blues
  Record 6   Side B   Band 8
  Voices: mixed voices
  Accompaniment: piccolo, saxophone, trumpet, trombone, piano

When You and I Were Young Maggie Blues

Words by Jack Frost

Music by Timmy McHugh

112

The Lesson

1. List several familiar children's songs on the chalkboard. Ask the students if they have ever sung these before. (Most will have.) Invite the students to sing the songs as one continuous melody (medley).

Song	Beginning Pitch
Skip to My Lou	G
Lazy Mary, Will You Get Up?	E♭
Ten Little Indians	E♭
London Bridge	G
Oh, Dear, What Can the Matter Be?	B♭
Paw Paw Patch	E♭
Sandy Land	G
Mary Had a Little Lamb	G

2. Ask each student to choose one song from the list to sing while others are singing their own choices. They will discover that all these songs can be sung at the same time. **How is it possi-** ble that these songs can be sung at the same time? (When songs have the same chord sequence, they can be sung together as "partner songs.") **Let's test this out.** Write the following chord sequence on the chalkboard: E♭-E♭ -B♭-B♭-E♭-E♭ B♭-E♭. Play these chords on the piano on the first beat of every measure in sequence. Sing all the songs as one student points to each chord in correct time. **Do all these songs fit this sequence?** (yes)

3. Open books to page 112. Introduce a new partner song. Learn to sing each song separately by listening to the recording, then divide into two groups and sing both songs at the same time. (Changing Voices and Baritones sing Part 2 in bass clef, and Treble I's and II's sing Part 1.)

113

and when you lis - ten just christ - en it and say I've got these

old, Mag - gie, when

"When you and I were young, Mag-gie," blues.

you and ____ I were ____ young. ____

114

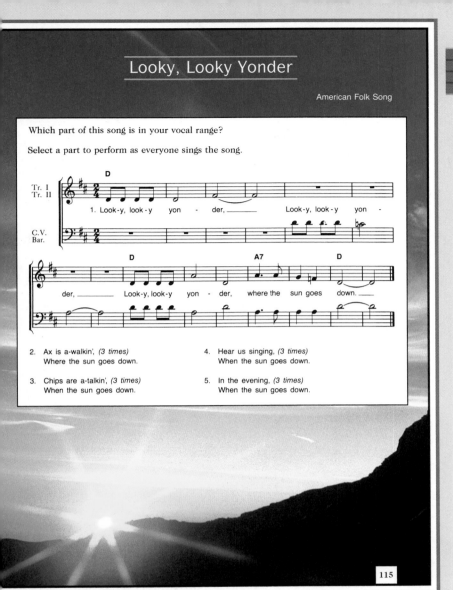

Looky, Looky Yonder

American Folk Song

Which part of this song is in your vocal range?

Select a part to perform as everyone sings the song.

Tr. I
Tr. II

1. Look-y, look-y yon - der, _____ Look-y, look-y yon -

C.V.
Bar.

der, _____ Look-y, look-y yon - der, where the sun goes down. _____

2. Ax is a-walkin', *(3 times)*
   Where the sun goes down.

3. Chips are a-talkin', *(3 times)*
   When the sun goes down.

4. Hear us singing, *(3 times)*
   When the sun goes down.

5. In the evening, *(3 times)*
   When the sun goes down.

115

Lesson Focus

Harmony: Two or more musical lines may occur simultaneously. *(P–S)*

Materials

○ **Piano Accompaniment:** page 285
○ **Record Information:**
  • Looky, Looky Yonder
    Record 6   Side B   Band 9
    Voices: mixed voices
    Accompaniment: dobro guitar, acoustic guitar, double bass
○ **Teacher's Resource Binder:**
  • Optional—
    Orff Activity 3, page O6

The Lesson

1. Review Vocal Warm-up 1 (page 110). Introduce a new melodic idea of ascending and descending scale patterns: Vocal Warm-up 2.

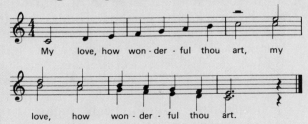

My love, how won-der-ful thou art, my

love, how won-der-ful thou art.

Use this scale song to help the students develop more resonance in the voice. Sing vowel sounds with a relaxed jaw. Help the students become aware that an open mouth creates space for the voice to resonate.

2. Ask the students to scan the score of "Looky, Looky Yonder," page 115. **Decide which part of the song is in your vocal range.** Learn to sing the song. Ask Changing Voices and Baritones to determine when they are singing the melody or a harmony part. (harmony on the last phrase)

3. **Look at the score. Is there any other part in your vocal range?** (Changing Voices can also sing the Treble I or II parts.) Ask the students to decide how many people should perform each part to achieve the best vocal balance.

115

Lesson Focus

Harmony: Two or more musical lines may occur simultaneously. *(P–S)*

Materials

○ **Piano Accompaniments:** pages 286, 288
○ **Record Information:**
  • The Water Is Wide
  Record 7   Side A   Band 1
  Voices: mixed voices
  Accompaniment: recorder, acoustic guitar, double bass, percussion
  • Hand Me Down My Walkin' Cane
  Record 7   Side A   Band 2
  Voices: mixed voices
  Accompaniment: banjo, acoustic guitar, double bass, percussion
○ **Teacher's Resource Binder:**
  • Optional—
  Instrumental Accompaniment 5, page I11
  Orff Activities 8, 10, pages O18, O22

The Lesson

1. Ask the students to perform Vocal Warm-up 3. Draw attention to the importance of enunciating words when singing. Explain that precise enunciation of consonants is needed to shape the words of a song. Write the words of "Sergeant Pepper" on the chalkboard. (See **For Your Information**.) Ask the students to use lots of "lip action" when chanting or singing this song. Sing this song several times, increasing the tempo with each repetition. **Can your words still be understood when you're singing faster?**

2. Apply enunciation skills when singing the songs on pages 116–117. First ask the students to follow the score of "The Water Is Wide" as the recording is played. **How are the two parts alike? How are they different?** (Part 2 echoes Part 1 in the beginning and closing phrases but uses a harmonic echo for the other phrases.) Divide the students into two groups and have them sing this song.

3. Introduce "Hand Me Down My Walkin' Cane" and begin learning this song. Know that the students will need additional practice time to become secure singing the parts. Play the recording. The students will recognize that this song is similar to "The Water Is Wide" as both begin in an echo arrangement. **Where do the groups stop the echo and begin singing simultaneously?** (Measure 9) Divide into two groups as indicated on the score and sing the song. Assign some Treble I and Baritone singers to sing the special harmony part (lower notes on the Treble I staff) in the last four measures of the song.

Hand Me Down My Walkin' Cane

Southern Mountain Song

2. Oh, if I die in Tennessee, *(3 times)*
   Just ship me back, C.O.D.
   All my sins been taken away,
      taken away.

117

For Your Information

"Sergeant Pepper":

Lesson Focus

Harmony: Chords and melody may move simultaneously in relation to each other. *(P–S)*

Materials

○ **Piano Accompaniment:** page 290

○ **Record Information:**
  • Rock Around the Clock
    Record 7   Side A   Band 3
    Voices: mixed voices
    Accompaniment: saxophone, electric guitar, double bass, percussion

○ **Teacher's Resource Binder:**
  • Optional—
    Mainstreaming Suggestion 9, page M19

Rock Around the Clock

Words and Music by Max Freedman and Jimmy De Knight

118

The Lesson

1. Help the students "tune" their ears in preparation for harmonizing this song by singing a chord sequence, Vocal Warm-up 4. Write the following chord sequence on the chalkboard.

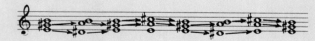

Divide the class into three groups: Changing Voices and Baritones on lowest pitches, Treble II's on middle pitches, Treble I's on the highest pitches. **Sing the first chord.** Discuss how the parts should move up, move down, or remain the same to create the next chord.

Follow this sequence until the students can change chords with relative ease. Encourage the students to listen to one another for good intonation and blend.

2. Ask the students to open their books to page 118 and follow the music for "Rock Around the Clock" as the recording is played. Discuss the time period in which this music was popular. (Mid- and late 1950s ; early rock featured such stars as Elvis Presley and Little Richard; music had a hard-driving rhythm and a fairly simple harmonic structure.) Invite the students to sing the melody in unison. Pay particular attention to the syncopated rhythms. (Tied eighth notes create the syncopations here.)

3. When the students are familiar with the melody, invite them to create a harmony part. Ask the students to read from the score on page 119 singing only the chord changes using the syllable "loo." (The students will discover that this is the same sequence as was used in the optional vocal warm-up.)

Improvise a three-part harmonic accompaniment to go with this rock tune from the Fifties. Divide into three groups to sing the changes in pitch. You may wish to hum, sing words on the harmony pitches, or create your own ideas.

One, two, three o'-clock, four o'-clock, rock,

Five, six, sev-en o'-clock, eight o'-clock, rock.

Nine, ten, e-lev-en o'-clock, twelve o'-clock, rock,

We're gon-na rock a-round the clock to-night.

Put your glad rags on and join me, hon',
We'll have some fun when the clock strikes one.

We're gon-na rock a-round the clock to-night,

We're gon-na rock, rock, rock till broad day-light,

We're gon-na rock, gon-na rock a-round____ the clock to - night.

119

4. Ask the students to chant the rhythm of the words (Verse 1 only). Then divide into vocal parts and sing the rhythm of the words in harmony as shown on page 119. When the students can sing this with ease, choose a soloist (or group) to sing the melody. Perform both verses in four parts.

Lesson Focus

Form: A musical whole is a combination of smaller segments. *(D–S)*

Materials

○ **Piano Accompaniment:** page 292

○ **Record Information:**
  • Mango Walk
    Record 7   Side A   Band 4
    Voices: mixed voices
    Accompaniment: tin whistle, acoustic guitar, double bass, percussion
  • *Jamaican Rumba*
    by Arthur Benjamin, 1938–1960
    Record 7   Side A   Band 5
    Philadelphia Orchestra
    Eugene Ormandy, conductor

○ **Instruments:** mallet instruments with high A; electronic keyboards; pianos; soprano recorders (enough for each student to have an instrument)

○ **Other:** a pencil for each student

○ **Teacher's Resource Binder:**
  Activity Sheets
    • **Activity Sheet 19,** page A32
    • Optional—
      Orff Activity 7, page O13

Mango Walk

Traditional

The Lesson

1. Ask the students to examine the upper part of "Mango Walk" (Treble I and Baritone part). **What is the shortest sound that occurs in the melody line?** (eighth note) Establish a tempo for the eighth note, and ask the students to speak the words of this part in rhythm. Use the same technique to speak the lower part. When both parts have been performed accurately, play the recording of "Mango Walk." The students should follow the upper part first, then the lower part. Play the recording again and invite the students to sing the part indicated for their voice range.

2. Compare Themes A and B for *Jamaican Rumba* (see page 121) with the upper and lower parts of "Mango Walk." Help the students discover that Theme A is similar to the upper part of "Mango Walk" and the first two measures of Theme B are similar to the lower part.

3. **OPTIONAL** Divide the class into two groups. Each group should practice playing either Theme A or Theme B of *Jamaican Rumba*. Use recorders, keyboards, or mallet instruments until the themes can be played accurately. Then combine groups to create a two-part texture. (If there are not enough instruments available to create this texture, play one theme while one student plays the other.)

4. Listen to *Jamaican Rumba*. Identify the sound of marimba and vibraphone, orchestral bells, and strings for the students as they follow Theme A and Theme B from the recording. (See **For Your Information**.) The students should focus their attention on the pictures of these instruments shown on the bottom of page 121 as they listen.

5. Distribute a copy of Activity Sheet 19 (*Jamaican Rumba*) and a pencil to each student. Ask

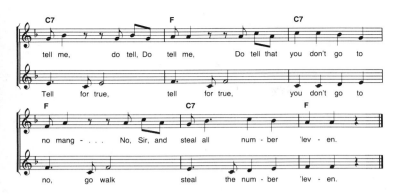

tell me, do tell, Do tell me, Do tell that you don't go to

Tell for true, tell for true, you don't go to

no mang - ... No, Sir, and steal all num-ber 'lev-en.

no, go walk steal the num-ber 'lev-en.

LISTENING

Jamaican Rumba

by Arthur Benjamin

"Jamaican Rumba" is based on musical ideas found in "Mango Walk." Two main melodies are heard in the piece.

Melody A

Melody B

Which of these melodies is like the upper part of "Mango Walk"? Which one is similar to the lower part?

These two melodies are heard both alone and together as partners in "Jamaican Rumba." Can you determine which melody each of these instruments is playing?

121

For Your Information

Form of *Jamaican Rumba:*

1. **Introduction**
2. **A** (marimba and vibraphone)
3. **A** (strings)
4. **B** (marimba and vibraphone)
5. **Bridge**
6. **A** (orchestral bells and vibraphone)
7. **Bridge**
8. **B** (strings)
9. **A** (orchestral bells) and **B** (marimba and vibraphone)
10. **Coda**

the students to complete the activity sheet as they listen again. Play the recording as many times as needed to determine the correct answers.

6. Invite the students to discuss their findings and to correct their papers. (See **For Your Information** for the correct answers.) Listen again to verify the answers.

PERFORM/ CREATE 8

Lesson Focus

Harmony: Two or more musical lines may occur simultaneously. *(E–S)*

Materials

○ **Record Information:**
- *Canon in D*
  by Johann Pachelbel
  (**pahk**-uhl-bel),
  1653–1706
  Record 7 Side A Band 6
  Collegium Aurem
- *Bells and Pachelbels*
  by Buryl Red, 1936–
  Record 7 Side B Band 1

○ **Teacher's Resource Binder:**

Activity Sheets
- **Activity Sheet 20**, page A33 (one for each student)
- Optional—
  Kodaly Activities 2, 3 pages K2, K5
  Orff Activity 9, page O20

Canon in D
by Johann Pachelbel

Johann Pachelbel (1653–1706) was a German composer of the Baroque era. Although he was primarily an organist, Pachelbel composed many works for chorus and instrumental ensembles.

Listen to this composition. It is based on a series of melodic ideas, each of which is eight beats long. All of the ideas are based on the same chord sequence.

The ground bass shown below is repeated many times. Sing along with it using the syllable "doo" or "loo" until you are very sure of the chord sequence. Try each new melodic idea as it is introduced.

After you have heard all the melodic ideas, close your eyes and improvise a melody that "feels right" to you.

122

The Lesson

1. Listen to *Canon in D.* Help the students discover that this music consists of a series of continuous melodic ideas (each eight beats long) and is based on a repeated chord sequence over a ground bass. These melodic ideas are introduced consecutively by the first violins, repeated by the second violins, and finally played by the third violins. The students should follow the notation (on page 122) as they listen.

2. **Listen again! The ground bass on page 122 is repeated many times. Sing along until you are very familiar with the chord sequence. Then close your eyes and improvise a melody that seems right to you.** Encourage the students not to worry about what others are singing. **Listen carefully to the recording!** Some students will improvise, but others may sing a harmony part or one of the melodic ideas.

3. Listen to the recording of *Bells and Pachelbels*. **How is this composition like the *Canon in D*?** (The ground bass melody and the chord sequence are the same.) **How are they different?** (The rhythmic structure, instrumentation, and style are all different.)

4. Invite the students to follow the call chart on page 123 as the recording is played again. Then ask them to listen for melodic ideas on which they might base an improvisation. **Can you add melodic ideas to this piece? Can you hold some pitches longer so that they fit with more than one chord?** Ask the students to practice softly singing their improvised melodies with the recording.

Bells and Pachelbels

by Buryl Red

Listen to the recording. How is this piece different from Pachelbel's
Canon in D? Listen again and improvise your own melodic ideas.

Introduction   Measures 1-8

The introduction begins with a sustained chime sound on D, continues with an ostinato of steady sixteenth notes, and closes with a single statement of the main theme (Pachelbel's ground bass) in eighth notes.

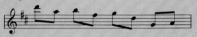

Section A (synthesized sounds) Measures 9-32

The main theme is repeated three times as part of the chord sequence from the *Canon in D.* These chords move in whole notes using bell sounds; a background ostinato moves in steady sixteenth notes.

Section B (acoustic sounds) Measures 33-48

The background ostinato now moves in steady sixteenth note triplets. The main theme is heard in half notes using piano and harp sounds. In the last measures of this section, the entrance of bell sounds creates a brief canon.

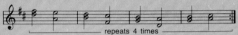

Transition (synthesized and acoustic sounds) Measures 49-51

The main theme and chord sequence from Section A are heard using synthesized vocal sounds moving in quarter notes. (The chord sequence is stated here in two different keys at the same time!) A fanfare of trumpet sounds moving in eighth notes quickly follows, leading us into the coda.

   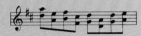

Coda   Measures 52-60

The trumpet fanfare from the transition is transformed into a sixteenth note ostinato. This ostinato consists of the main theme played forward and then backward. (See the example above.) The remaining music is based on an extended D major chord and includes references to all the musical materials heard in the piece.

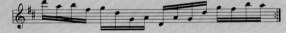

123

5. Distribute Activity Sheet 20 (*Music Manuscript Paper)* for the students to notate their melodic ideas. Invite the students to share these melodic ideas so that several may be sung with the recorded accompaniment by the class. These ideas may also be sung together to create partner songs with accompaniment.

PERFORM/CREATE 9

Lesson Focus

Harmony: Chords and melody may move simultaneously in relation to each other. *(P–S)*

Materials

○ **Piano Accompaniment:** page 294
○ **Record Information:**
  • Buffalo Gals
    Record 7 Side B Band 2
    Voices: male solo
    Accompaniment: guitar, accordion, percussion
○ **Instruments:** guitars
○ **Teacher's Resource Binder:**
  [Activity Sheets] • **Activity Sheet 21,** page A34
  • Optional—
    Kodaly Activity 4, page K5
    Mainstreaming Suggestion 10, page M19, M22

The Musician Performs: Guitar

Learn how to "pick" folk tunes on the guitar.

Playing Position
Hold the guitar comfortably and securely. Rest your left foot on a foot rest or a small coffee can. Place the guitar so that there are four points of contact with the body:
1. Underneath the right forearm
2. Against the chest
3. Inside the right knee
4. On the left knee
If you are holding the guitar correctly, your right hand will fall directly in front of you.

Your body should be vertically aligned, and your shoulders level. Slant the guitar so that the head is slightly higher than your shoulders.

Hand Positions
• Place the thumb on the back of the guitar neck to provide balance and support for fingers pressing down on the strings.
• Press strings with fingertips to avoid touching adjacent strings.
• Fingers on the left hand are numbered in this order:

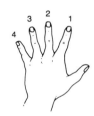

124

The Lesson

1. Review the names of the guitar strings—E, A, D, G, B, E—and the numbering system for frets. (Label the fret nearest the neck of the guitar 1, the next fret 2, and so on.) Read the instructions for the correct playing position on pupil page 124, and ask students to assume this position. Guide the students as they practice finding and plucking a series of pitches. **Play the B string in the first fret. Play the A string in the third fret. . . .**

2. Ask the students to read the instructions for hand positions on pupil page 124. Discuss the classical Spanish labeling of the right-hand fingers (*p, i, m, a*). Identify *p* for *pulgar* or thumb, *i* for *indice* or index, *m* for *mayor* or middle finger, and *a* for *ami* or ring finger. **We will use these labels to refer to the fingers as we learn to play melodies on the guitar.** Invite the stu-

dents to practice playing the following pattern:

  D string (*p*)–G string (*i*)–B string (*m*)–E string (*a*)

Play this pattern repeatedly with steady beats, gradually increasing the tempo.

3. Sing the song "Buffalo Gals." When the students are familiar with the words and melody, invite them to play the open-string accompaniment (D and A) shown on pupil page 125. Instruct the students to use only *p* to pluck these two strings, playing the pattern four times to accompany each verse.

4. Distribute Activity Sheet 21 (*The Upward Trail*). Ask the students to sing and play "The Upward Trail," working independently. Take time to assist individual students in tuning procedures as shown on the activity sheet.

OPTIONAL

  Texas Essential Elements, The Musician Performs: Guitar, pp. 124–131: 1A, 1B, 1C, 1D, 2, 3B, 4A, 5A (Please see Unit 3 opener, page 107, for component and page references.)

Buffalo Gals

Music by Cool White

Place your right hand just behind the sound hole in a relaxed manner. To play single-line melodies or special bass parts, use the thumb (*p*) and fingers (*i, m, a*) to pluck individual strings.

D   A7   D
1. As I was walk-ing down the street, down the street, down the street,
2. I asked her if she'd stop and talk, stop and talk, stop and talk,

D   A7   D
A pret-ty gal I chanced to meet, Oh, she was fair to see.
Her feet took up the whole side-walk and left no room for me.

D   A7   D
Oh, Buf-fa-lo Gals, won't you come out to-night, come out to-night, come out to-night?

D   A7   D
Oh, Buf-fa-lo Gals, won't you come out to-night and dance by the light of the moon?

Use the thumb (*p*) to play an open-string accompaniment to "Buffalo Gals." Repeat the following pattern four times to complete the song.

1. As   I was walking   down the street,   down the street,   down the street,

125

For Your Information

Holt Music, Level 7, includes an introduction to playing guitar chords. In the guitar section of Level 8, students will learn to play melodies. They will begin accompanying their own singing by playing individual pitches of root bass or walking bass patterns. These patterns allow students to concentrate on moving left-hand fingers to specific pitches while plucking strings with the right thumb. As students become more adept at finding pitches, other right-hand plucking patterns are introduced. Tablature notation is introduced as an expeditious method of reading and playing melodies. Tablature is often shown in conjunction with traditional notation so that the transfer of reading skills may be accomplished easily.

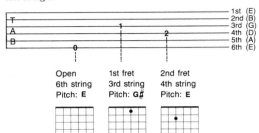

PERFORM/ CREATE 10

Lesson Focus

Harmony: Two or more pitches may be sounded simultaneously. *(P–S)*

Materials

○ **Piano Accompaniments:** pages 296, 297

○ **Record Information:**
  • Down in the Valley
    Record 7 Side B Band 3
    Voices: treble voices
    Accompaniment: harmonica, fiddle, guitar
  • Taps
    Record 7 Side B Band 4
    Voices: mixed voices
    Accompaniment: guitar, celesta

○ **Instruments:** guitars

○ **Teacher's Resource Binder:**
  Activity Sheets • **Activity Sheet 22,** page A35

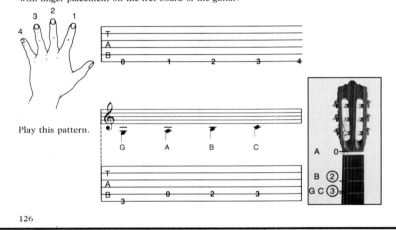

Learn to Read Tablature

Tablature is a form of notation for guitar that directs the fingers to the correct strings and frets. It does not indicate rhythm. When using tablature, the performer must already know the melody.

When playing from tablature, read the fret numbers in sequence from left to right.

Open 6th string Pitch: **E**	1st fret 3rd string Pitch: **G♯**	2nd fret 4th string Pitch: **E**

Read the tablature and pluck these pitches with your thumb on the sixth string. Compare the tablature with traditional notation and with finger placement on the fret board of the guitar.

Play this pattern.

G   A   B   C

126

The Lesson

1. Review "Down in the Valley" and learn "Taps" for this lesson. (See **For Your Information.**)

2. Draw the students' attention to reading tablature on page 126. Discuss limitations of tablature compared to staff notation. The students will note that tablature indicates only pitch and not rhythm.

3. Learn to pluck the four pitches at the bottom of page 126 (G, A, B, C). Now ask the students to play these pitches in the following sequence: **G-A-B-C, C-B-A-G.** When the students can easily play this sequence, ask them to read and play the tablature for "Down in the Valley." The students should sing the melody as they play the walking bass accompaniment. HINT: Gently rest the *i-m-a* fingers on the remaining strings (E, B, G) while the thumb

moves freely between the lower strings. This right-hand position makes it easier to judge distance between strings.

4. Review the *p-i-m-a* practice drill from the previous lesson. When the students have these fingers "working" again, invite them to read the tablature for "Taps." They will find that the melody is played mostly on open strings. Use *i-m-a* as indicated on the page, with one finger to each string. **On which word will you need to place a left-hand finger on the fret board?** (*well*) HINT: Play the melody with the thumb (*p*) resting gently on the low E string. This frees the *i-m-a* fingers to move on the higher strings. (Again, this helps to judge distance between strings.)

5. Provide additional opportunities to practice *p-i-m-a*. Distribute Activity Sheet **22** (*More*

Down in the Valley

Traditional

Use your thumb to play this walking bass accompaniment.

Down in the val - ley, val - ley so low,____

Hang your head o - ver, hear the wind blow.____

Read the tablature. Use *i, m, a* to play this melody. Use one finger on each string: D, G, B.

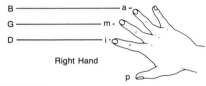

B ——————————— a -
G ——————————— m -
D ——————————— i -

Right Hand

p

Taps

U.S. Army Bugle Call

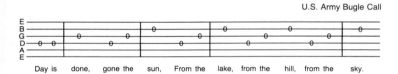

Day is   done,   gone the   sun,   From the   lake,   from the   hill,   from the   sky.

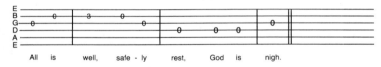

All   is   well,   safe - ly   rest,   God   is   nigh.

127

For Your Information

The following melody for ''Taps'' may be sung by the students before they attempt to play it on the guitar:

Melodies to Play). The students may wish to form trios. Each member supplies a different guitar part for "Down in the Valley." Provide class time for the trios to perform.

Lesson Focus
Melody: A series of pitches may move up or down by steps or skips. *(P–S)*

Materials
○ **Piano Accompaniments:** pages 298, 299

○ **Record Information:**
- Can the Circle Be Unbroken?
  Record 7 Side B Band 5
  Voices: mixed voices
  Accompaniment: guitar, piano, percussion
- The Cruel War
  Record 7 Side B Band 6
  Voices: female solo
  Accompaniment: guitar, harp

○ **Instruments:** guitars

○ **Teacher's Resource Binder:**

Activity Sheets

- **Activity Sheet 23,** page A36
- **Activity Sheet 24,** page A37
- Optional—
  Orff Activities 4, 13, pages O8, O28

The Lesson

1. Play the recording for "Can the Circle Be Unbroken?" and "The Cruel War." Learn to sing these songs. When the students are very familiar with these melodies, they may begin learning to play them on the guitar.

2. Ask the students to open their books to page 128. Demonstrate the "rest stroke" technique. Use fingers *i* and *m*. Make these fingers "walk" slowly on the high E string four times. After each "step," the finger should rest on the B string. Repeat this on the B string with fingers coming to rest on the G string. Invite the students to continue to practice the "rest stroke" by repeating this sequence on the D and A strings.

3. Ask the students to read and play the tablature for "Can the Circle Be Unbroken?" Use the rest stroke technique.

4. Before continuing, instruct the students to practice alternating fingers *i* and *m* again following the notation on page 129.

5. Ask the students to read and play the tablature for "The Cruel War." Alternate singing and playing this melody until all three verses have been completed. All the students may play, or individual guitarists may be selected to play the melody as an instrumental solo between verses.

6. **OPTIONAL** Extend the students' repertoire by distributing Activity Sheet 23 (*Aura Lee*). Encourage the students to learn to play this song on their own. They will find this melody challenging because the ring finger is used to play the third fret. They will need to stretch their fingers farther to reach this fret.

7. **OPTIONAL** Invite the students to transcribe a song from

The Cruel War

Words by Peter Yarrow

Music by Paul Stookey

Practice alternating fingers *i* and *m* as you move among three strings.
Begin on the D string.

i m i m   i m i m   i m i m   i m i m   i m i m   i

Play "The Cruel War."

1. The cruel war is rag-ing, and John-ny has to fight,

I want to be with him from morn-ing till night.

2. I'll go to your captain, get down on my knees,
   Ten thousand gold guineas I'd give for your release.

3. Ten thousand gold guineas, it grieves my heart so;
   Won't you let me go with you? Oh, no, my love, no.

129

notation to tablature. Explain that the purpose of this activity is to help them create their own scores. They might begin transcribing a simple tune such as "Hot Cross Buns." Review the melody by singing this song. **In how many different places can you play this melody on the guitar?** (The melody may be started on many different frets.) Have the students use Activity Sheet 24 (*Create Your Own Tablature for a Song*) to write out at least two different places to begin playing "Hot Cross Buns."

Lesson Focus

Melody: A series of pitches may move up or down by steps or skips. *(P–S)*

Materials

○ **Piano Accompaniment:** page 300
○ **Record Information:**
 • Gotta Travel On
  Record 7 Side B Band 7
  Voices: mixed voices
  Accompaniment: electric guitar, piano, double bass
 • *Carolina Shout*
  James P. Johnson, 1891–1955
  Record 7 Side B Band 8
  First Nashville Guitar Quartet

○ **Instruments:** guitars
○ **Teacher's Resource Binder:**
  Activity Sheets
 • **Activity Sheet 25,** page A38
 • Optional—
  Kodaly Activity 6, page K8
  Orff Activity 12, page O26

Gotta Travel On

Words and Music by Paul Clayton

I've laid a-round and played a-round this old town too

long, Sum-mer's al-most gone, yes,

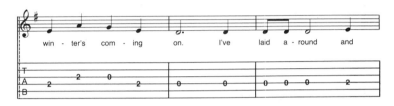

win-ter's com-ing on. I've laid a-round and

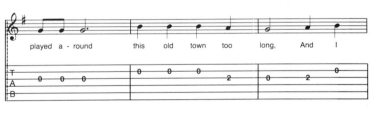

played a-round this old town too long, And I

130

The Lesson

1. To learn the song "Gotta Travel On," ask the students to listen to the recording and follow the score on pages 130–131. When they are familiar with the melody, suggest adding a harmony part. Explain that country songs are often easy to harmonize using mostly thirds and sixths. Teach this part by rote to boys who sing in this range:

2. Add the boys' part to the melody, and sing this song in a two-part arrangement along with the recording.

3. Learn to play the melody using tablature. Create an arrangement of this song by alternately singing and playing the melody.

4. Help the students become familiar with the two themes in *Carolina Shout*. Ask them to play the first few measures of both Theme A and Theme B. They will discover that Theme A requires considerable technique and skill to perform at tempo.

5. Play *Carolina Shout* while the students follow the form of the music at the bottom of page 131. Guide them in assessing this performance. **How would you rate the performing skills of these guitarists?** (The guitarists are skilled musicians and outstanding performers.)

feel like I've got ta tra vel on. _____

LISTENING

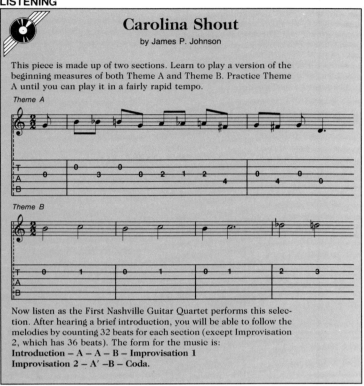

Carolina Shout
by James P. Johnson

This piece is made up of two sections. Learn to play a version of the beginning measures of both Theme A and Theme B. Practice Theme A until you can play it in a fairly rapid tempo.

Theme A

Theme B

Now listen as the First Nashville Guitar Quartet performs this selection. After hearing a brief introduction, you will be able to follow the melodies by counting 32 beats for each section (except Improvisation 2, which has 36 beats). The form for the music is:

Introduction – A – A – B – Improvisation 1
Improvisation 2 – A′ – B – Coda.

131

For Your Information

Carolina Shout is performed by an unusual ensemble comprising four outstanding guitarists: Chet Atkins, John Pell, John Knowles, and Liona Boyd. The first melody, Theme A, is a sprightly tune demonstrating the dexterity and technique required by each performer. The second melody, Theme B, contrasts nicely with Theme A, as it is not as ''busy'' and involves simple syncopations. The improvisations on these two sections move from folk music to jazz. The coda ends on a chord that leaves the listener with the sound of jazz ''ringing in the ears.''

6. Encourage the students to form their own guitar ensemble. Provide each member with Activity Sheet 25 (*Playing in an Ensemble*). Expect members to work independently. The students will discover that one person can play a melody and harmony part while another plays a bass part.

OPTIONAL

Lesson Focus

Rhythm: A series of beats may be organized into regular or irregular groupings by stressing certain beats. *(P–S)*

Materials

○ **Instruments:** miscellaneous classroom percussion instruments: maracas, claves, guiros and scratchers, woodblocks, temple blocks, drums; mallets

○ **Teacher's Resource Binder:**

Activity Sheets • Activity Sheet 26, page A39

For Your Information

The purpose of this section is to introduce students to techniques, vocabulary, and notation needed for playing percussion instruments. Students are given opportunities to read and perform rhythm patterns in a variety of styles, with special attention to African and Latin American percussion styles.

The Musician Performs: Percussion

A percussionist plays many different kinds of instruments. Some of these produce sounds that have **definite pitch,** such as tuned drums, gongs, and marimbas. Other instruments, such as rattles, cymbals, and claves, produce sounds of **indefinite pitch.** These instruments have a high, medium, or low range of pitch.

As with other instruments, different sounds can be made on each one. Rattles, such as maracas, can be played so that a dry, single sound is produced. They can also be shaken to create a continuous sound. The sound of percussion instruments can be varied depending on:

• the part of the instrument struck
• the size, shape, and material of the striker
• the force, angle, and duration of these strikes

Be a percussionist. Create and play rhythm patterns.

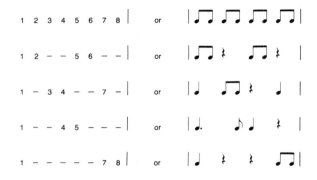

Play a rhythm pattern called **clave:**

132

The Lesson

1. Ask the students to open their books to page 132 and read about the percussionist. Draw the students' attention to the counting patterns and the way each is notated. **Look at the number patterns first; practice clapping on each count, resting on the dashes.** After each number pattern, the students should read and perform the notated version of the pattern.

2. Introduce the rhythm pattern called "clave" (a term used to identify a particular pattern in the Afro-Cuban tradition). This pattern is often played by the claves in percussion ensembles (hence its name), but it may also be played by other instruments.

   The students will discover that this pattern is a combination of two sets of eight counts, created by combining two of the rhythm patterns previously performed.

3. Use rhythmic patterns from this lesson together or in sequence to create interesting rhythmic ideas. Distribute instruments, and have the students perform these ideas to create a percussion ensemble piece See Activity Sheet 26 (*Play Latin American Percussion Instruments*) for performing techniques for these instruments.

Texas Essential Elements, The Musician Performs: Percussion, pp. 132–137: 1A, 1B, 1C, 2, 3A, 3B, 4A, 5A (Please see Unit 3 opener, page 107, for component and page references.)

Learn to Play Conga Drum

Using the heel of alternate hands, hit the center of the drum and leave your hand on the drumhead. Use the syllable "ta" to describe this sound. (T)

Using the fingertips of alternate hands, hit the center of the drum, and leave fingertips on the drumhead. Use the syllable "ka" to describe this sound. (K)

For a high, cracking sound, use the fingertips of alternate hands to slap the drumhead while the heel of your hand strikes the rim. The syllable "bop" is used to describe this sound. (B)

Using only the fingers of alternate hands, strike the edge of the drumhead and take your fingers off. Use the syllable "de" to describe this sound. (D)

Practice each of the following patterns, then combine and perform them together.

Ex. 1	T K B K T K D D	T K B K T K D D
Ex. 2	1 - - 4 - - 7 -	- - 3 - 5 - - -

Use these patterns to accompany "Comin' Home Baby."

LISTENING

Comin' Home Baby
by Benjamin Tucker and Robert Dorough

133

Lesson Focus
Rhythm: A series of beats may be organized into regular or irregular groupings by stressing certain beats. **(P–S)**

Materials
○ **Record Information:**
  • *Comin' Home Baby*
    Benjamin Tucker, 1930–
    Robert Dorough, 1923–
    Record 8 Side A Band 1
    Ensemble conducted by
    Sergio Mendez
○ **Instruments:** conga drums; tub drums; miscellaneous Latin American percussion instruments; claves, maracas, guiros with scratchers, cowbells with mallets
○ **Other:** Activity Sheet 26 (as prepared for Perform/Create 13, page 132)

The Lesson

1. Ask the students to open their books to page 133. Read about each of the playing positions and techniques and practice them on desktops. Speak patterns such as "bop-rest-bop-rest" or "ta-ka-rest-rest" and have the students echo these patterns on their desktop "conga drums."

2. The students should practice each technique on page 133 several times before attempting to read and play the symbols. Speak and perform the following sequence:

   $\frac{4}{4}$—ta-ka-rest-rest
   $\frac{4}{4}$—ta-ka-bop-rest
   $\frac{6}{4}$—ta-ka-bop-ka-rest-rest
   $\frac{6}{4}$—ta-ka-bop-ka-de-de

3. Draw the students' attention to the percussion patterns shown on page 133.

Example 1: The students are to rhythmically speak the letters as syllables, then perform and speak the pattern together.
Example 2: Speak the syllables of the first pattern and clap the clave pattern.

Ask the students to combine Examples 1 and 2. The students should perform the first pattern and speak the clave pattern.

4. Listen to the recording of *Comin' Home Baby*. Distribute available drums. Invite the students to add their percussion patterns from Step 3 to accompany the music.

5. Refer the students to Activity Sheet 26 (See *OPTIONAL* **Materials**) for additional ideas. After they have explored and practiced these sounds, use them as new accompaniment materials for *Comin' Home Baby*.

Lesson Focus

Rhythm: A series of beats may be organized into regular or irregular groupings by stressing certain beats. *(P–S)*

Materials

○ **Record Information:**
  • Mustapha Tetty Addy—Master Drummer from Ghana
  Record 8   Side A   Band 2

○ **Instruments:** two-tone bell (or high- and low-pitched cowbells) and mallets; guiro and scratcher, rattles or maracas; two conga or tub drums (one high-pitched and one low-pitched) and stick; woodblocks or temple blocks and mallets

Rhythmic Sounds From Ghana

Learn to play the conga drum with master drummer, Mustapha Tetty Addy. Listen to the recording and play along. Add these percussion instruments to create an African percussion ensemble.

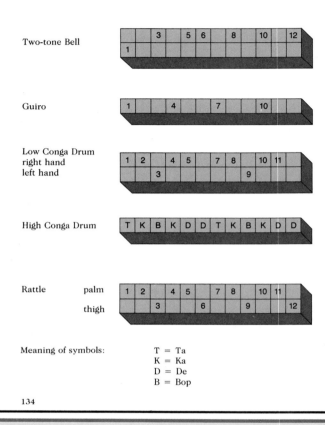

Meaning of symbols:
  T = Ta
  K = Ka
  D = De
  B = Bop

134

The Lesson

1. Ask the students to open their books to page 134 and look at the score. Help students learn each part individually; then combine all parts to create a percussion ensemble with the class.

2. Begin with the two-tone bell part. The students are to play high or low sounds on the beat indicated and maintain silence where there are empty boxes.

3. When the students are familiar with the two-tone bell part, help them learn the guiro part.

4. Invite the students to play the two conga drums. Help the students read and perform the low conga drum part. Use one hand to slap the drum head and a stick to strike the rim or the wood surface.

5. **OPTIONAL** Review the meaning of the symbols used in the part for high conga drum. (See Perform/Create 14, page 133.) The students may also need to refer to the previous lesson to review how the "ta-ka-de-bop" sounds are produced.

6. Help the students learn to play the rattle part. The right hand, holding the rattle, moves between the thigh and the left hand. Hold the left hand above the thigh with palm downward. The students will need to practice this up-and-down movement.

7. Combine the two conga drum patterns and perform them with the recorded sounds of Mustapha Tetty Addy—Master Drummer from Ghana.

8. **OPTIONAL** Combine all percussion parts from this lesson and invite the class to perform as a percussion ensemble.

Percussion in an African Style

Read the score.
Use instruments and voices to perform the music.

	1	2	3	4	5	6	7	8	9	10	11	12
Master Drum	1	•	3	4	•	6	7	•	9	10	•	12
Low Drum	1	•	•	4	•	6	7	•	•	10	•	12
Medium-low Drum	1	•	3	•	5	6	7	•	•	10	•	12
Low Drum	1	•	•	4	•	•	7	•	•	10	•	•
Medium Drum	•	2	•	4	•	6	•	8	•	10	•	12
High Drum	1 D	2 G	3 D	4 D	5 G	6 D	7 D	8 G	9 D	10 D	11 G	12 D
Medium-high Drum	•	2	3	•	5	6	•	8	9	•	11	12
Medium-low Drum	1 G	2 G	3 D	4 G	5 G	6 D	7 G	8 G	9 D	10 G	11 G	12 D
Two-toned Bell	1 L	•	3 H	•	5 H	6 H	•	8 H	•	10 H	•	12 H
Large Woodblock	1	•	3	•	5	•	7	•	9	•	11	•
Rattle	1 U	•	3 D	4 U	5 D	6 D	7 U	8 D	9 U	10 D	11 U	12 D
Sing the 5th of a major scale	•	•	•	•	5 Ya	6 ku	•	•	•	•	11 ku	•
Sing the 3rd of a major scale	•	•	•	•	•	•	7 Ke	8 le	9 le	10 Ya	•	•

135

PERFORM/CREATE 16

Lesson Focus
Rhythm: A series of beats may be organized into regular or irregular groupings by stressing certain beats. *(P–S)*

Materials
○ **Record Information:**
  • Percussion in an African Style
    Record 8   Side A   Band 3
    Voices: mixed voices
    Accompaniment: percussion
○ **Instruments:** conga drum; assorted pitched drums: 2 low, 2 medium-low, 1 medium, 1 medium-high, 1 high; two-tone bell (or low- and high-pitched cowbells) and mallets; large woodblock; rattle (or gourd)

The Lesson

1. Ask the students to open their books to page 135. Discuss symbols that are found in the score:

   Drums: **H**—highest pitch on drum; **L**—lower pitch on same drum
   Two-tone bell: **H**—higher pitch; **L**—lower pitch
   Gourds: **U**—upward to hit left hand; **D**—downward to hit leg (thigh)

2. Distribute instruments and assign parts. Ask one student to play the two-tone bell part, another to be master drummer and lead the instrumental group, and a third to be vocal leader for the singers. Assign other students to the remaining parts in equal numbers. Practice each part separately.

3. Help the singers understand their score. Syllables are indicated below the pulse numbers and are sung on the fifth and third degrees of

any major scale. The words are pronounced: "a" as in father, "u" as in glue, "e" as in hey.

4. When playing in ensemble, the master drummer is responsible for the starting signal. She or he plays 1–2–3–4–5–6 with a stick on the rim of the drum. Other percussion players immediately begin together after this opening sequence establishes the beat. The vocal leader enters after the instrumental parts are established, and the other voices follow. The piece ends when the master drummer plays 7–8–9–10–11–12–1 in the same manner as at the beginning of the piece. The students may wish to stop playing (pause) to prepare for the final sound of the piece, "1," played by all parts together.

5. Play the recording of "Percussion in an African Style." Ask the students to compare their performance to the recorded version. Guide the students to refine their performance.

OPTIONAL

135

PERFORM/ CREATE **17**

Lesson Focus
Expression: Musical elements are combined into a whole to express a musical or extramusical idea. *(P–S)*

Materials
○ **Record Information:**
  • *Talking Drums—traditional music from Ghana*
  Record 8   Side A   Band 4
○ **Instruments:** high- and low-pitched drums or slit-log drums; mallets, beaters, or sticks

Talking Drums

Hundreds of years before Western cultures developed rapid communication systems, some Africans sent messages from village to village over many miles using talking drums. This was possible because many African languages are tonal.

In a tonal language, the meaning of a word depends on the pitch at which each syllable is spoken.

For example, the Lokele people of northern Zaire use the word *lisaka* (lee-sah-kah) to mean three different things:

Higher sound		This means "puddle" or
Lower sound	li-sa-ka	"marsh."
Higher sound	ka	This means "promise."
Lower sound	li-sa-	
Higher sound	sa-ka	This means "poison."
Lower sound	li-	

You can see how very important it is to speak the higher and lower sounds in the correct place!

Drum language uses these higher and lower sounds to communicate messages. The combination of higher and lower sounds makes it possible to actually communicate messages using talking drums.

136

The Lesson

1. Discuss the use of talking drums (see **For Your Information**), and read the information on pupil pages 136–137. Take time to read the words from each example of *lisaka* on page 136 aloud, using low and high vocal sounds.

2. Distribute available drums. Invite the students to chant and play each of the examples for *lisaka* on page 136 using the lower and higher sounds as indicated.

3. Invite the students to listen to the recorded example of talking drums. **In Ghana, talking drums were used to send messages during wartime and peacetime.** Explain that the recorded example carried an important message for all who heard and understood the drum language.

OPTIONAL

4. **Transfer the idea of talking drums to your own language.** Ask the students to create high and low sounds to express spoken phrases from their own language(s). The students should first speak these phrases using high and low vocal sounds, then play the high and low sound patterns on a drum, and finally add improvised rhythms to enhance their drum phrases.

Drum phrases can be very poetic. Drum language often uses vivid word-imagery to make the listener "feel" the message.

For example, in the Lokele language the spoken phrase "don't worry" or "don't be afraid" could be expressed in drum language as "take away the knot of the heart into the air."

Use available drums to produce high and low sounds. Chant and perform the high and low sounds for the word *lisaka* on page 140. Use only steady beats for now.

Create drum phrases using spoken words from your own language:

- speak each phrase using natural pitch inflections
- play these phrases on a drum using high and low sounds
- improvise rhythms to enhance your drum phrase

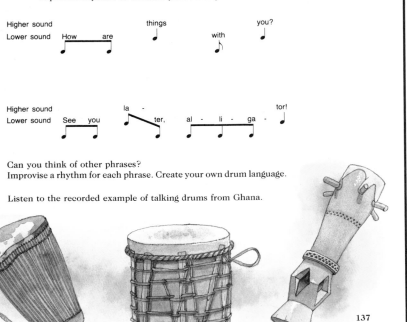

Can you think of other phrases?
Improvise a rhythm for each phrase. Create your own drum language.

Listen to the recorded example of talking drums from Ghana.

137

For Your Information

The people in traditional Central and West Africa developed their own resources for communication hundreds of years ago: "talking" drums. The drums used were two-toned or variably pitched instruments upon which messages were played. The best time to send a message was said to be in the early morning or late evening (probably due to village activity during the middle of the day, as well as the heating effect of the sun on air movement.) Messages were often sent along the banks of rivers because sound carries well over water. The messages could be heard clearly from a distance of five to seven miles. Radio, telephone, and telegraph have replaced talking drums as a means of communication, but drum language can still be heard and understood in some Central and West African villages.

Lesson Focus

Melody: A series of pitches bound by the octave "belong together," forming a tonal set. *(P–S)*

Materials

○ **Piano Accompaniment:** page 301

○ **Record Information:**
- The Keys of Canterbury
  Record 8 Side A Band 5
  Voices: mixed voices
  Accompaniment: recorder, crumhorns, sackbuts, dulcimer, lute, percussion

○ **Instruments:** one dulcimer; pick and noter for each student

○ **Teacher's Resource Binder:**

Activity Sheets
- **Activity Sheet 27,** page A40
- **Activity Sheet 28,** page A41
- Optional—
  Mainstreaming Suggestion 11, page M24

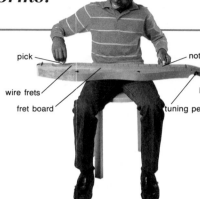

The Musician Performs: Dulcimer

Many folk melodies are based on ancient scales called **modes.** "The Keys to Canterbury" is based on the **Aeolian** mode.

pick   note

wire frets   h

fret board   tuning peg

The Keys of Canterbury

English Folk Song

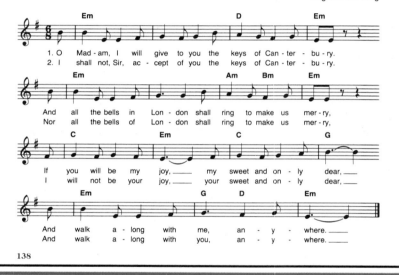

1. O Mad-am, I will give to you the keys of Can-ter-bu-ry.
2. I shall not, Sir, ac-cept of you the keys of Can-ter-bu-ry.

And all the bells in Lon-don shall ring to make us mer-ry,
Nor all the bells of Lon-don shall ring to make us mer-ry,

If you will be my joy,_____ my sweet and on-ly dear,
I will not be your joy,_____ your sweet and on-ly dear,

And walk a-long with me, an-y-where. _____
And walk a-long with you, an-y-where. _____

138

The Lesson

1. Ask the students to open their books to page 138. Play the recording or perform the song "The Keys of Canterbury" as the students follow the music.

2. Discuss the "sound" of the melody. Conclude that the melody has a unique sound that is neither major nor minor but is based on an ancient scale called a mode. This particular melody is based on the Aeolian mode. **Many modal songs were brought to the United States from England. The people of Appalachia preserved these songs in their own folk music in a form very close to the original.**

3. Learn to sing both verses of this Aeolian melody.

4. **The dulcimer is often used to accompany the modal songs of Appalachia.** Demonstrate the sound of the dulcimer by strumming the strings or playing a song. You may use "Are You Sleeping?" on Activity Sheet 27 (*Melodies—Ionian Mode*).

5. Ask the students to read page 139; then distribute dulcimers to the class. Discuss the information on page 139 about playing modes. Ask the students to assume the proper playing position, sliding the noter (a short dowel) from fret to fret to play a major scale. (The scale begins on the third fret of the finger board.) Notice that this fret is labeled number 1 (on the pupil page) because it is the first step of the scale. The major scale is the same as the Ionian mode. The students should strum toward themselves, sounding the lowest string first.

6. Refer the students to Activity Sheet 28 (*How a Dulcimer Is Constructed*). They may read the

OPTIONAL

OPTIONAL

⭐ **Texas Essential Elements, The Musician Performs: Dulcimer, pp. 138–143: 1A, 1B, 1C, 1D, 2, 3A, 3B, 4A, 5A** (Please see Unit 3 opener, page 107, for component and page references.)

Perform a Mode on the Dulcimer

For Your Information

The mountain dulcimer is an instrument that originated in the United States. The dulcimer can produce the distinctive sound of a melody played with a constant accompaniment or drone.

Another unique feature is the instrument's fixed fret board arrangement of whole and half steps. To play a variety of melodies, the student must learn about various modes. When playing melodies using different modes, the first step of the mode is shifted. The student must know how to retune the instrument as well as where to begin each mode in order to accommodate the arrangement of whole and half steps.

Because the dulcimer is a folk instrument, the songs performed on it are often based on modes. Each mode is made up of five whole steps and two half steps. On the dulcimer, the whole-step frets are larger than the half-step frets.

Whole-step frets look like this:

Half-step frets look like this:

Each mode has a distinctive sound because it has a different arrangement of whole and half steps. Between which tones do the half steps occur in this mode?

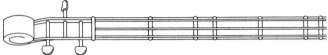

Play this mode on the dulcimer. Hold the dulcimer on your knees with its head to your left. Hold the noter in your left hand so that the thumb is on the top of the stick, pressing down. The noter should touch only the string nearest you. The second knuckle of the index finger should slide along the side of the fret board. To strum, hold the pick in your right hand and move the pick back toward you.

Examine the frets.
On which fret will you begin in order to play the sequence of whole and half steps shown above?
This time, as you move the noter from fret to fret, pluck only the string closest to you.

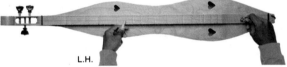

L.H.   R.H. strum

Sound familiar? It should! It's the major scale that you have heard many times. It is also called the **Ionian** mode.

139

directions to understand the process of making their own instrument. If there is interest, students will find that most local music merchants can supply inexpensive dulcimer kits. If you have any construction skills, you may wish to build one or more dulcimers as a class project. Relatively few tools are needed for assembly of the instrument. Experiment with building an instrument before guiding the students in this activity.

Lesson Focus

Melody: A series of pitches bound by the octave "belong together," forming a tonal set. *(P–I)*

Materials

○ **Piano Accompaniment:** page 302
○ **Record Information:**
  • Go Tell Aunt Rhody
  Record 8 Side A Band 6
  Voices: female solo
  Accompaniment: oboe, dulcimer, harp, celesta
○ **Instruments:** dulcimers; picks and noters
○ **Teacher's Resource Binder:**
  • Optional—
  Enrichment Activities 7, 8 page E23
  Kodaly Activity 8, page K11
  Orff Activity 5, page O9
○ **Other:** Activity Sheet 27 (as prepared for Perform/Create 18 page 139)

Go Tell Aunt Rhody

Traditional

Read the song tablature and perform a song in the Ionian mode. To play different pitches, slide the noter up and down the string nearest you while strumming all the strings.

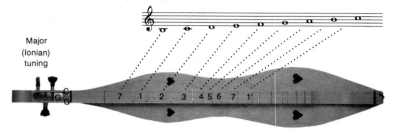

Major (Ionian) tuning

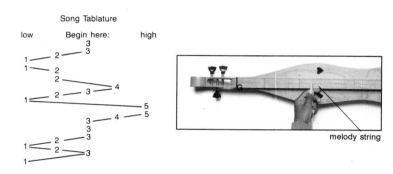

Song Tablature

low   Begin here: high

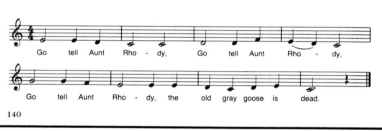

melody string

Go tell Aunt Rho - dy, Go tell Aunt Rho - dy,

Go tell Aunt Rho - dy, the old gray goose is dead.

140

The Lesson

1. Distribute dulcimers to the students. Review the correct playing position, and ask the students to warm up by playing the Ionian mode. (See page 139.) Remind them to begin on the third fret.

2. Vary this warm-up. Divide the students into two groups, and have them play the Ionian mode as a canon.

3. Open books to page 140, and ask the students to read the instructions. First sing "Go Tell Aunt Rhody" several times to be sure the stu-

dents are familiar with the rhythm of the melody. Then direct their attention to the song tablature. Remind students that the numbers indicate scale steps, not fret numbers. Ask them to follow the scale numbers and the lines for the direction the noter will slide to play each pitch of the melody. **Does the song tablature show the rhythm for the melody?** (No. The students will need to remember the rhythm.) Learn to play this melody.

4. Refer the students to Activity Sheet 27 (see **Materials**) for additional songs in this mode. The students may learn to play the melodies on the activity sheet—"Skip to My Lou" and "Are You Sleeping?"—independently or as a class activity.

OPTIONAL

5. Introduce the sound of the Mixolydian mode. Ask the students to read the top half of page

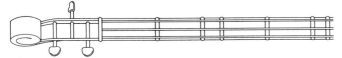

Perform in a New Mode

Perform in the **Mixolydian** mode. Where are the half steps in relation to the whole steps in this mode? Can you decide where "1" will be on the dulcimer by studying this arrangement of frets?

Did you determine that "1" will be played on the open string in this mode?

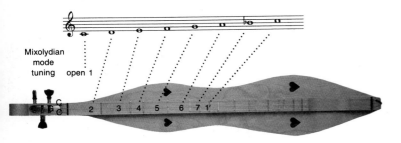

Mixolydian mode tuning   open 1

Experiment with the Mixolydian mode.

1. Retune the dulcimer so that the melody will be in tune with the drone strings. Change the pitch of the melody string from G to C.

2. Use the noter and play the pitches of this mode on the melody string. Begin on the open string, playing up and then down.

3. Read the tablature on the following pages. Learn to play "The Highwayman" and "Old Joe Clark," which are folk melodies in the Mixolydian mode.

141

141 and to discuss the new arrangement of whole and half steps. **Look at the fret board and decide where the first step will begin.** (at the open string) Ask the students to play the pitches in this mode.

6. After the students have played the Mixolydian mode, they may notice that the harmony (or drone) strings do not sound in tune with the mode. (They are correct. The melody string needs to be retuned to match the drone strings.) Instruct the students to read the text at the bottom of pupil page 141 and retune as instructed in the first step. When tuning is completed, ask the students to play the pitches and strum the drone strings again.

Lesson Focus

Melody: A series of pitches bound by the octave "belong together," forming a tonal set. **(P–I)**

Materials

○ **Piano Accompaniments:**
   pages 303, 304

○ **Record Information:**
   • The Highwayman
     Record 8   Side A   Band 7
     Voices: male solo
     Accompaniment: penny whistle, dulcimer, medieval harp, percussion
   • Old Joe Clark
     Record 8   Side A   Band 8
     Voices: mixed voices
     Accompaniment: dulcimer, hammered dulcimer, psaltery, autoharp, Jew's harp, fiddlesticks
   • *Celebration for a Gray Day*
     Richard Farina, 1937–1966
     Record 8   Side B   Band 1
     Mimi Farina, dulcimer
     Richard Farina, guitar

○ **Instruments:** dulcimers with noters

○ **Teacher's Resource Binder:**
   Checkpoint 3, page Ev11

Evaluation	• Optional—
	Kodaly Activity 11, page K17
	Orff Activities 1, 2 pages O2, O4

Perform in the Mixolydian Mode

"The Highwayman" uses all the pitches in the Mixolydian mode. Play the mode. Listen for the unusual sound of the seventh step.

Begin here (open string):

The Highwayman

English Folk Song

1. It's of a jol-ly high-way-man, Like-wise a no-ted rov - er,
2. I rob-bed lords, I rob-bed dukes in a ve-ry rak-ish man-ner,

I drove my par-ents al-most wild, When first I went a rov - ing.
Not on-ly to main-tain my-self, Like-wise my a-ged mo-ther.

142

The Lesson

1. Introduce *Celebration for a Gray Day.* Tell the students that there are two performers—a guitarist and a dulcimer player. The music consists of a medley of tunes that begins with "Are You Sleeping?"; continues with an old fiddle tune called "Bonaparte's Retreat," an old English carol called "Good King Wenceslas," and the traditional songs "Old Joe Clark" and "Good Night, Ladies"; and concludes with the return of "Are You Sleeping?" Play the recording as the students listen for these tunes.

2. Ask the students to open their books to page 142, and direct the students' attention to the melody of "The Highwayman." Learn to sing the song. Notice the uneven galloping rhythm throughout.

3. Distribute dulcimers and have the students tune for the Mixolydian mode. To play "The Highwayman," begin on the open string and follow the song tablature. Point out that all the pitches in the Mixolydian mode are stated in this first phrase.

4. **OPTIONAL** If time allows, learn another tune based on the Mixolydian mode, "Old Joe Clark" on pupil page 143. Follow the same procedure as in Steps 2 and 3; sing the song first to establish the rhythm before playing this melody.

Old Joe Clark

American Folk Song

Compare the melody written in traditional notation with the song tablature shown below.

Verse

1. Old Joe Clark, he   had   a   house   six - teen sto - ries   high;
2. I   went down to   Old Joe's house,   nev-er been there be - fore.

Ev - ery sto - ry   in   that house was filled with chick - en   pie.
He slept on   a   fea - ther bed and   I   slept on the   floor.

Refrain

Round and round,   Old Joe Clark,   Round and round I   say;

Round and round,   Old Joe Clark, I   have - n't long to   stay.

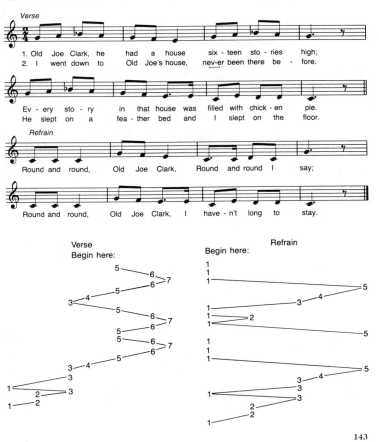

Verse
Begin here:

Refrain
Begin here:

143

Lesson Focus

Harmony: Two or more musical lines may occur simultaneously. *(P–E)*

Materials

○ **Record Information:**
  • *A Ground*
    by George Frederick Handel,
    1685–1759
    Record 8   Side B   Band 2
    orchestra conducted by
    Leopold Stokowski

○ **Instruments:** piano

The Musician Composes, Improvises, and Arranges

Milton Babbitt, American composer

For some of us, the word *composer* conjures up images of round-shouldered individuals, peering out through bent spectacles from under shaggy wigs. We forget sometimes that some of our favorite popular performers are composers.

Composing, improvising, and arranging all involve using original musical ideas to create new musical sounds. There are, however, some differences among the three.

Improvising means creating musical ideas "on the spot." You might be whistling your own tune as you walk down the street, "doodling" on the guitar, or making up a vocal or instrumental part as you listen to a recording.

Composing involves planning ahead. The composer may begin with jotting down ideas for a folk song, writing a score for a symphony orchestra, or developing ideas on an electronic synthesizer.

Arranging is taking existing music and creating special parts for instruments and voices. The result is a new arrangement, not a new composition.

Look through this chapter. Choose ideas that you find most interesting. Improvise, compose, or arrange your own music for
  • voices   • instruments   • computer

144

The Lesson

1. Ask the students to read pupil page 144 and discuss the musician as composer, improviser, and arranger. Make sure these terms are understood by the students; review the definitions as necessary.

2. Invite the students to look through this section. They will discover opportunities to compose, improvise, and arrange music for voice, instruments, and computer. *(OPTIONAL)*

3. Begin with an improvisational activity. Ask one or two students to go to the piano and slowly play the descending bass pattern shown at the top of page 145.

4. Help the students sing the melodic pattern shown on pupil page 145 as the bass pattern is played. When they are very familiar with this melodic pattern, ask them to close their eyes

and improvise their own two-measure endings using the syllable "li," "loo," or "la." They may decide to sustain one pitch or use rapidly moving melodic ideas for their two-measure endings.

Provide ample practice time until the students are comfortable with improvising their own ideas. Share these ideas by asking the entire class to sing the first two measures with individuals performing improvised endings.

5. Play the recording of *A Ground*. The students should listen and compare Handel's ideas to their own. They will discover that the ground bass is repeated throughout. The first two measures of the full orchestra are only slightly different from the melodic pattern on pupil page 145. (The orchestra performs an octave skip on the last eighth note of each measure; the pupil copy remains on the same pitch.)

Be an Improviser

Create an improvisation on this ground bass (repeated bass pattern). Slowly play this descending pattern on the piano.

Continue to play the ground bass and sing this melody. Create your own ending.

Li - li - li - li - li - li - li   (etc. . .)

Repeat this ground bass many times as individuals share their ideas for completing the melody.

LISTENING

A Ground
by George Frederick Handel

George Frederick Handel (1685–1759) was a major composer of the Baroque era. Among his many works is the famous oratorio, *The Messiah*.

Listen to "A Ground" by Handel. How does this compare to the music you have just sung and played?

George Frederick Handel

145

For Your Information

A Ground, by George Frederick Handel, is an example of music in which a bass pattern (ground bass) is continuously repeated throughout the piece. Different melodic ideas are played over this ground bass, providing variety and interest. In this orchestrated excerpt from Handel's original harpsichord composition, the instruments are heard over the ground bass in the following order: full orchestra, woodwinds, strings (echo), brass, strings (echo), full orchestra.

The music that follows consists of various melodies played over the ground bass by different sections of the orchestra. (See **For Your Information**.)

PERFORM/CREATE 22

Lesson Focus

Rhythm: Music may move in relation to the underlying steady beat. *(P–S)*

Materials

○ **Record Information:**
  • Rap, Rhythm, and Scratch
  Record 8 Side B Band 3
  Voices: mixed voices
  Accompaniment: synthesizer, electronic percussion
○ **Instruments:** assorted drums, cymbals, brushes, sticks, beaters; trap drum set
○ **Other:** inexpensive record player (older model); record-sized cardboard disk; old phonograph recording
○ **Teacher's Resource Binder:**
  • Optional—
  Mainstreaming Suggestion 12, page M24

The Lesson

1. Invite the students to perform a "rap." Rhythmically chant the rap shown on pupil pages 146–147. If needed, define the slang expressions for the students:
   boom box—portable cassette recorder and speakers;

   dogs—tennis shoes;
   togs—clothes;
   Mister Cool, ol' Tiny—nicknames;
   break boys—breakdancers;
   biting—stealing another dancer's ideas.

2. Ask the students to create a rhythmic ostinato in 2/2 meter to accompany this rap. They may use classroom instruments such as drums or cymbals with brushes. Invite the students to practice their ostinato with the rap.

3. Discuss the technique of "scratching." Scratching is a sound effect or a pattern produced by "backspinning" a record. Scratching should be done on an inexpensive record player. Using an older, disposable recording is also recommended. A cardboard disk is first placed on the turntable. This allows the turntable to continue in forward motion while the recording is "backspun." The equipment will not be damaged when backspinning is properly executed. The "deejay" backspins, gently placing fingers on the edge of the record. A soft touch is required. Ask a few students to experiment with "scratching."

4. Select a "scratch" that adds interest to the dance idea. Perform the "scratch" sounds where indicated in the rap. Liberties may be taken with the meter if additional beats are

146

Lit - tle ol' Tin - y gon - na go, go, go!

(Drum improvisation with scratch)

Hey, my man, is that all you know?

Here it comes, don't be bit - ing my move,

'Cause I am the best, and this will prove.

(Drum improvisation with scratch)

Look sharp, break boys, cause when I'm done,

You gon - na know I'm Num - ber One!

Create Your Own Rap, Rhythm, and Scratch Music
Learn to create scratch music. Use an inexpensive record player. Place a piece of cardboard on the turntable. (You may want to use an old recording.) The cardboard allows the turntable to maintain its normal speed at all times, even when the recording is stopped or backspun. Control the record by putting your hand on the record's edge while backspinning.

147

For Your Information

Rap music originated on the city streets and became popular in the early 1980s. Rapping is essentially rhythmically "talking" to a taped accompaniment. A classic rap requires original use of slang, unusual rhymes, and strong visual imagery. Performers use recordings as a sound source for taped accompaniments. These taped accompaniments often consist of unique electronic effects created by reversing or stopping the recordings created.

By applying this technique correctly, a talented "deejay" can repeat a drum beat or musical phrase at will. Rap music often accompanies breakdancing: an energetic combination of movements from martial arts, gymnastics, mime, and dance.

needed for these sounds. Invite the students to perform the "Rap, Rhythm, and Scratch."

5. Invite the students to listen to the recording of "Rap, Rhythm, and Scratch." Ask them to compare their ideas to the recorded performance. *OPTIONAL*

6. Encourage the students to create their own rap. They may divide into five groups and follow the instructions on page 147. Provide class time for these groups to share their raps. *OPTIONAL*

Lesson Focus

Expression: The expressiveness of music is affected by the way rhythm and melody contribute to the musical whole. *(P–S)*

Materials

○ **Piano Accompaniment:** page 305
○ **Record Information:**
  • Carry It On
    Record 8 Side B Band 4
    Voices: mixed voices
    Accompaniment: flute, alto flute, acoustic guitar, electric guitar, percussion

The Lesson

1. Listen to "Carry It On," and help the students learn the first verse.

2. Ask the students to read about the skills needed by the soloists on page 149. Discuss these skills; then listen to Verse 1 again from the perspective of the soloists. **Are there places in the song where special parts could be added?** (There are several: the song has many long, sustained notes, allowing for echo patterns.) Suggest that the students try improvising some echo patterns. First, rhythmically chant where they might occur. Caution the students that the longer sounds of the melody are not the same length. The same echo idea will not always fit.

3. Repeat the verse several times, challenging the students to create more complex musical ideas. They might:
   • rhythmically chant an idea
   • rhythmically sing an idea on one pitch
   • rhythmically sing an idea moving around one pitch
   • freely sing ideas as they occur

4. Ask the students to read about the arranger on page 149. Choose an arranger to organize all three verses and conduct the group's performance.

5. **OPTIONAL** After the students have performed their own version, play the entire recording. Ask the students to listen to the improvised ideas on the recording. Discuss how these ideas might be helpful in refining the class's performance.

Be an Arranger

An arranger of music needs skills in

- reading and writing music
- achieving musical balance among different parts
- combining vocal and instrumental parts in interesting ways

Select one or more class arrangers who have these skills to arrange
"Carry It On."

Select soloists to improvise special parts for each verse:

There's a man (There's a man) by my side . . .

Each soloist must

- listen to the accompaniment
- improvise in relation to the chord sequence
- improvise in relation to the underlying beat

Each soloist may

- echo words
- omit words or phrases
- change the rhythm
- stretch one word over several pitches

The arranger should decide

- when the full group will sing
- which soloist will add parts to verses
- whether the ideas of two or more soloists may be combined

Experiment with several ideas; then decide on the arrangement for
the whole piece.

The arranger becomes the conductor, providing signals for the group.
Perform your completed arrangement.

149

Lesson Focus

Rhythm: Music may move in relation to the underlying steady beat. *(P–E)*

Be a Lyricist

A lyricist needs skills in communicating by means of

- words that evoke images
- rhyming phrases
- words that create a natural rhythmic flow

A lyricist may write words that are very metrical or words that move in a freely flowing rhythm. Prepare lyrics that will be metrical and result in even phrases. Begin by feeling the length of the phrase.

Fill in the empty space with a vocal rhythm such as:

ch - ch - ch - ch - ch - ch - ch - ch - ch

List all the words you can think of that rhyme with "blue." (Sue, glue, true, moo, zoo, too, adieu)

Now begin to change your rhythmic filler (ch's) to a talkin' blues. End your rhythm pattern with one of the rhyming words. Replace the "ch" sounds with words to form a sentence ending with the rhyming word.

(Heard a sto-ry 'bout a gal named Sue)

Play a 12-bar blues accompaniment while "talking" six of the blues phrases you have just created.

150

The Lesson

1. Read about the role of a lyricist and help the students experiment with writing lyrics following the instructions on page 150.

2. Use chant and finger snapping to set the accompaniment pattern. The "Da-da-da-dum" chant may be varied by adding the following melodic pattern.

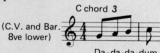

3. Ask the students to fill the empty spaces with the "ch" pattern from pupil page 150.

4. List all the words that rhyme with *blue*. One of these words becomes the final sound in the "ch" pattern.

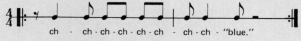

5. Ask the students to replace the "ch" sounds with a sentence that ends with one of the rhyming words:

> Got a gal and her name is Sue.
> Her hair is sticky as glue. . . .
> Wish that I could go to the zoo. . . .

Perform these ideas in a chain.

6. Ask the class to select six statements that seem to fit together topically. The students may perform these statements as "talking" blues while you or a student plays a 12-bar blues accompaniment. (See pupil page 151 for the 12-bar blues in C.) If the "Da-da-da-dum" pattern continues to be used, the students will need to change the pitches accordingly.

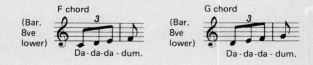

Create Jazz Riffs

Jazz is a musical idiom that evolved from Afro-American roots. Jazz has its own characteristic style, which is highly improvisational in nature. An important part of jazz technique is the ability to improvise melodic ideas on the pitches within a given chord progression.

Liberties are often taken with jazz rhythms. For example, eighth notes are seldom played evenly. Instead of

the performer might play

Some jazz melodies are built on repeated patterns called **riffs.** Read and play some riffs based on a blues chord progression. Use jazz syllables (**scat singing**) to establish the rhythm of each riff. Play each riff on either the root, third, or fifth of the chord.

Basic blues in C

Riff on the root

151

Lesson Focus
Harmony: Chords and melody may move simultaneously in relation to each other. *(P–S)*

Materials
- **Instruments:** pianos or chromatic keyboard instruments
- **Other:** Activity Sheet 20 (as prepared for Perform/Create 8 page 122)

The Lesson

1. Review the pitches in a major chord. Divide the students into three groups. Ask each group to echo the pattern you dictate; then combine the patterns.

2. Discuss which of these pitches were the root, the third, and the fifth of the chord. (Root-C, third-E, fifth-G) Distribute available instruments. Ask the students to begin on C and skip every other key until E and G have been reached. Ask them to echo the Step 1 patterns

again, this time playing the pitches on instruments. After the students have mastered all the patterns, have them use this same process to identify the root, third, and fifth of the chords F and G.

3. Ask the students to open their books to page 151. Read the information about jazz. Follow the examples to learn the riff; then perform each riff on the root, third, fifth, and their combinations. Use piano or guitar accompaniment so that the students can hear the chord changes clearly.

4. Distribute Activity Sheet 20 (see **Materials**) to each student on which to compose and notate their own riffs. Select several of these riffs to be played by the class. The composer decides if his or her riff is to be played on the root, third, or fifth of the chord.

OPTIONAL

151

For Your Information

An important part of jazz technique is the ability to improvise melodic ideas on the pitches within a given chord progression. This lesson provides students with the opportunity to create and arrange melodic ideas based on the root, third, and fifth of the major chord.

Compose your own riff. Base your riff on the pitches of each chord in the basic blues in C (shown on page 151).

152

5. Continue on page 153 at another time. Introduce the students to a distinctive aspect of the jazz sound, the "blue" note or "bent" sound. Ask the students to follow the notation on page 153 to play the major scales with lowered sevenths. When they understand how the seventh is lowered for each scale, ask them to play the riff on the root and lowered seventh.

6. Distribute manuscript paper again. Encourage the students either to compose a riff and write instructions for how it is to be played or to notate their own blues riff using a combination of ideas from these examples.

Blues notes

Jazz melodies sound different to us because some of the notes are
"bent," or sung and played lower or higher in pitch. This bending of
notes can be as little as a quarter tone or as much as a whole tone.
These bent notes are called **blues notes.**

Use blues notes to create jazz riffs. Add a lowered seventh to the harmony. Use this lowered seventh to play a riff on the root.

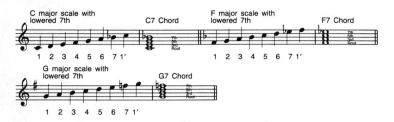

Riff on the root and lowered seventh

Compose your own blues riff on the third of each chord. How can you
lower the third?

Lesson Focus

Time and Place: The way musical elements are combined into a whole reflects the origin of the music. *(D–S)*

Materials

○ **Record Information:**
  • *Joan's Blues*
  by Joan Wildman, 1938
  Record 8   Side B   Band 5
  Accompaniment: piano, string bass, percussion

○ **Instruments:** piano; guitar or autoharp; recorder or glockenspiel; drum, triangle, or cymbal

○ **Teacher's Resource Binder:**
  Activity Sheets • **Activity Sheet 29,** page A42

Improvise in Jazz Style

When improvising jazz, a performer often begins with a basic musical structure and then improvises a series of "choruses" using the following techniques:

Melody	The original melody might be ornamented with added notes. The shape of the original melody might be preserved, even though some notes are changed.
Structure	The original melody might be stretched or compressed, creating phrases of different lengths.
Harmony	The chord progression might be made more complex by adding chords or altering some chords.
Rhythm	The accents could be changed so that they fall on different beats of the measure. The rhythmic units could be varied by alternating groups of eighth notes, quarter notes, and triplet figures or by shifting the placement of rests.

Begin by listening to the original theme of "Joan's Blues" while following the notation on page 155. Then listen to the first chorus and compare it to the original theme.

Keep in mind, as you compare the chorus with the original theme, that the chorus was notated after it was performed, by listening to the recording and writing down the musical ideas. The performers improvised the choruses "on the spot."

As you listen to the complete composition, try to decide:

• What is the function of the bass player during the piano solo?
• What is the function of the drummer?
• How does the 16-bar theme become a "12-bar blues"?

Try developing your own improvisation. Begin by composing a four- or eight-measure musical idea. Plan a chord progression; devise a simple melodic shape to use. Then begin to experiment. Use some of the ideas you learned from listening to "Joan's Blues." Work alone or with others.

154

The Lesson

1. Read the opening discussion on pupil page 154 together (all text except the last paragraph). You may wish to illustrate briefly each improvisational technique by taking a familiar tune (such as "Are You Sleeping?") and altering it according to the description on the pupil page.

2. Play the first 17 measures of *Joan's Blues* (original theme only) while the students follow the score on page 155. (For now, the students should ignore the notation for the first chorus.) Play the theme several times, until you feel that the students will be able to recognize a variation (first chorus) of the original theme.

3. Play the first chorus and help the students compare the original theme with this improvisation. **How is the melodic material ex-** **panded?** (The intervals and the phrase lengths are expanded; the melodic contour of the second phrase is inverted.) **What pitches in the original melody seem most important?** (B♭ and F) **What pitches in the improvisation seem most important?** (D♭ and F) **Do these important pitches occur in the same places in the measure?** (yes, in Measures 2 and 10, but otherwise no, due to the expansion of phrases)

4. Distribute Activity Sheet 29 (*Joan's Blues Call Chart*). Play the entire composition as the students follow the chart.

5. After listening to the recording and discussing *Joan's Blues,* read the final paragraph on page 154. Give the students the opportunity to work individually or in small groups to explore ways of improvising, based on the techniques listed on page 154. The students may wish to begin with a familiar tune such as "Looky,

Joan's Blues

by Joan Wildman

155

Looky Yonder" (page 115) rather than composing their own tune.

If the students are improvising individually, each student will need to use an instrument on which both melody and harmony can be played, such as piano. The students might instead work in groups of three:
- One student provides harmony on guitar, autoharp, or piano.
- One student provides melody on recorder or glockenspiel.
- One student provides rhythm on a drum, triangle, or cymbal.

Lesson Focus

Expression: The expressiveness of music is affected by tempo, melody, and rhythm. *(C–I)*

Materials

○ **Record Information:**
  • *Earth's Magnetic Field* (excerpt)
    Charles Dodge, 1942–
    Record 8   Side B   Band 6

○ **Other:** microcomputer

○ **Teacher's Resource Binder:**
  Activity Sheets • **Activity Sheet 30**, pages A43–45

The Computer as a Composing Tool

The computer has become a valuable tool for the composer. It is capable of

  • choosing and controlling pitch
  • choosing and controlling rhythm
  • choosing and controlling harmony
  • determining form (sequencing sounds and linking them together)
  • choosing and controlling dynamics
  • choosing and controlling sound quality (timbre)
  • choosing and controlling the attack, decay, and sustain time
  • generating musical sounds
  • controlling one or more synthesizers
  • converting sounds played on keyboard into music notation

Each of these capabilities can make the composer's work easier, but it is the composer who must make the final decision about what sounds best and is most musically appropriate.

156

The Lesson

1. Read page 156, and focus the students' attention on ways composers use computers to aid them in their work. Discuss how each of these functions might save time for the composer. Help the students determine that even though the computer can make musical decisions, only the composer is able to listen and make value judgments about whether the computer's decisions sound "right."

2. Briefly discuss the text on page 157 together. Help the students to examine the graph. **How is the graph similar to musical notation?** (It contains symbols that are higher and lower and symbols that appear to show duration.) Listen to *Earth's Magnetic Field* as the students follow the graph. (The recorded excerpt covers only the first portion of the graph.) Explain to the students that the complete composition is based on data gathered over an entire year (1961); these data were used to

create musical events that take up only one side of a record album. (Note that the graph that appears on the pupil page shows only the month of January.)

3. **If you, as the composer, wanted to convert data such as your telephone number into musical sounds, how would you do it?** (A series of pitches might be assigned to each of the numbers 0–9 and then placed on a music staff in the same order as the original telephone number.)

Invite the students to explore the examples on page 153 to see how the resulting melody could be changed by:
  • turning it upside down
  • reversing the order of the notes
  • turning the melody upside down and reversing the order of the notes

4. One student (or several students) should type information from Activity Sheet 30 (*Tele-*

The Earth's Magnetic Field
by Charles Dodge

The earth is a giant magnet. Like other magnets, it has north and south poles and a magnetic field surrounding it. This magnetic field is constantly being altered by a force known as the solar wind (caused by changes in the sun's atmosphere). Scientists are able to record these magnetic field changes on a graph that looks similar to musical notation:

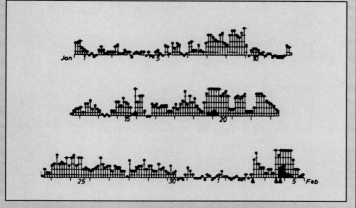

Charles Dodge (1942–) is a twentieth century American composer who specializes in computer music. Dodge converted information about the earth's magnetic field gathered during the year 1961 into a series of notes. Other musical decisions, including tempo, dynamics, and register, were also made with the help of the computer. The resulting music is titled "The Earth's Magnetic Field." Without the aid of a computer, the conversion of this immense amount of information into music would not have been possible.

As you listen to the music, follow the graph above. Can you see a relationship between what you see and what you hear?

157

Music Microcomputer Program) into the microcomputer. Using the procedure outlined in the manual for the computer, store the program on a disk so that it may be recalled and loaded into the computer when needed. Make copies of this disk for each available microcomputer.

5. Allow small groups of students to work with the computer program, supplying the requested information at each prompt on the screen. Discuss the similarities between the resulting melodies and *Earth's Magnetic Field*. (The computer was used to transform raw data into music and to make some musical decisions, leaving other musical decisions to the composer.) In the case of "tele-music," the students choose between the normal, upside-down, backward, or upside-down-and-backward versions.

6. Invite the students to compare the similarities in notation that resulted from "tele-music" and the graph shown on page 157. (Both show pitch and duration.)

Convert Your Telephone Number Into Music

Using a similar method to the one used for "The Earth's Magnetic Field," you can compose a piece of music using your telephone number and the computer. Each of the digits in your telephone number can be converted into a pitch. If you were to make this conversion without a computer, you might do it this way:

Assign one of the following pitches to each digit of your telephone number:

If your telephone number is 314-555-1212, the melody derived from it would be:

To add variety, you might want to turn the melody upside down:

Play it backwards:

Or play it upside down and backwards:

158

Composing With Tele-Music

To make this composition task easier, type the program called Tele-Music into your computer. Save the program on a disk, and use it to create a composition based on your telephone number. The computer will help you by

- converting the number into pitches (a melody)
- turning the melody upside down
- reversing the melody
- randomly adding rhythm to the melody
- changing the tempo of the melody to suit you
- playing the composition for you

159

PERFORM/ CREATE 28

Lesson Focus

Rhythm: A series of beats may be organized into regular or irregular groupings by stressing certain beats. **(D–S)**

Materials

○ **Record Information:**
  • *Javanaise*
    Claude Bolling, 1930–
    Record 9   Side A   Band 1
    Jean Pierre Rampal, flute
    Claude Bolling, piano
○ **Instruments:** assorted drums, brushes, and sticks or trap drum set
○ **Teacher's Resource Binder:**
  • Optional—
    Biography 7, pages B13–B14

LISTENING

Javanaise
by Claude Bolling

Listen to the music. Add a percussion part as indicated on the call chart below.

The music	Your percussion part
Introduction Piano opens with sounds in the middle register, separating quickly into opposite ends of the keyboard.	
Section A The piano introduces a jaunty Theme A in $\frac{5}{4}$ meter, creating an uneven galloping motion.	sock cymbals $\frac{5}{4}$ bass drum
Interlude The flute enters, playing sustained sounds moving stepwise, beginning low and reaching high.	(rub brush on cymbal using a circular motion to produce sustained sounds)
Section A (cont.) Theme A is now played by the flute with piano accompaniment.	s.c. $\frac{5}{4}$ b.d.
Section B Percussion stops. Piano introduces Theme B. Flute and piano echo each other often. Theme A returns briefly as an interlude. Section B closes with rising piano octaves answered by a rapidly descending flute scale. piano flute	s.c. $\frac{5}{4}$ b.d.

160

The Lesson

1. Play a portion of the recording of *Javanaise*. Ask the students to determine the accented and unaccented beats. **Does this music move in twos or threes?** (Neither; this music is in $\frac{5}{4}$ meter and can be felt in groups of five beats or a combination of threes and twos.) Direct the students to tap accented beats with the left hand on the left knee and unaccented beats with the right hand on the right knee. Practice this meter until the pattern of accents is easily felt.

2. Open books to pages 160–161. Play the entire selection. Invite the students to follow the call chart as you indicate the beginning of each section.

3. Draw attention to the percussion part. The students can perform this part as the recorded music is played. They will notice that their part consists of playing the $\frac{5}{4}$ rhythm on various percussion instruments (some percussion sounds they can choose, including the rubbing sound of a brush on a drum head or cymbal).

4. Distribute instruments, or simulate the sound of the percussion instruments needed. Two cymbals struck together and suddenly muted can simulate the sound of sock cymbals (trap set cymbals). Drums struck with a large soft beater or hand can simulate a trap set bass drum. Paper rubbed together can sound like a brush rubbed on a drum head.

5. Play the recording as the students add their accompanying percussion parts. The students should play their parts very softly (never louder than the recording).

160

<u>Section C</u> Percussion returns to stay. Flute plays a flowing melody. Piano and double bass embellish simple harmonies for accompaniment. Flute solo ends with a low trill. tr ~~~~~~~	(select new timbres)
<u>Section C</u> (cont.) Piano takes the lead. Later, the flute returns to close this section. Flute and piano echo each other. A rhythmic sequence on one repeated note ends this section.	(continue timbres or select new ones)
<u>Introduction</u> The original piano music from the beginning is repeated.	
<u>Section A</u> Theme A (piano)	s.c. b.d.
<u>Interlude</u> (flute)	(brush)
<u>Section A</u> Theme A (flute with piano accompaniment)	s.c. b.d.
<u>Coda</u> Flute and piano repeat a two-note figure twice, before a final flourish brings the music to a sudden stop!	

161

For Your Information

Prepare for this lesson by becoming familiar with the call chart for *Javanaise* on pupil pages 160–161 and its correlation with the music.

Lesson Focus

Evaluation: Review concepts and skills studied in Unit 3. *(D–S)*

Materials

○ **Piano Accompaniment**: page 306

○ **Record Information**:
  • Come Join in the Chorus
    Record 9   Side A   Band 2
    Voices: mixed choir
    Accompaniment: string ensemble, celesta, harpsichord
  • Mustapha Tetty Addy—Master Drummer
    Record 8   Side A   Band 2
  • Comin' Home Baby
    Record 8   Side A   Band 1

○ **Instruments**: guitar; dulcimer; Latin-American and African percussion instruments; piano; bass xylophone

○ **Other**: a pencil for each student

○ **Teacher's Resource Binder**:
  | Evaluation | |

  Review 3 page Ev14
  Musical Progress Report 3, page Ev16

Review 3

Come Join in the Chorus

Music by Wolfgang Amadeus Mozart

162

The Lesson

1. Distribute a copy of *Review 3* and a pencil to each student. Explain to the class that they will be evaluating themselves and applying information gained in Unit 3 to the process of learning a new song. Begin by asking the students to follow "Come Join in the Chorus" (page 162) while you play the recording.

2. Discuss the basically homophonic style of the song. Ask the students accurately to speak the words in rhythm, paying close attention to when the rests occur. Adjust the balance of the recording so that only the accompaniment can be heard; ask the Changing Voice and Baritone singers to perform their parts with the recording. Correct any errors in pitch or rhythm. Follow this procedure for the Treble I and II singers; then combine all four parts and perform the song with the recording.

3. Ask the students to evaluate their efforts by completing Part 1 of *Review 3*.

4. Invite the students to select one of the activities from Part 2 of *Review 3*—Special Ways to Perform. Ask them to prepare their chosen assignment either as an individual out-of-class activity or in small groups with others who have chosen the same activity. All students will need to use their books for song references and have access to Latin-American and African recordings, as well as percussion instruments. (See **Materials**.) When the students have completed the assignments and marked their review sheets, invite them to share their performances with the class.

5. Use the information gained through this evaluation as well as observations made throughout the unit to complete *Musical Progress Report 3* for each student.

OPTIONAL

Unit 4

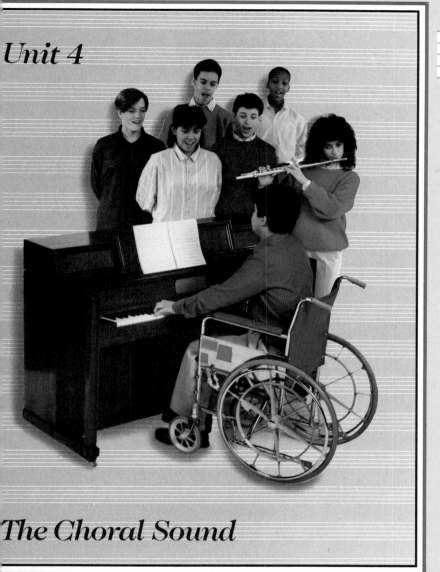

The Choral Sound

Unit Overview

Unit 4 concentrates on choral music and vocal ensemble techniques. A wide variety of choral arrangements reinforces what has been learned in the previous units, with an emphasis on texture, expression, and instrumental accompaniments. All of the songs have from one to five parts, especially selected and arranged for the young teenage voice in transition.

Texas Essential Elements for Unit 4

Texas Essential Elements, The Choral Sound, pp. 163–219: 1A, 1B, 1C, 1D, 1E, 1F, 2, 3B, 4A, 4B, 5A (Please see Unit 4 opener, page 163, for component and page references.)

163

Lesson Focus

Harmony: Two or more musical lines may occur simultaneously. *(P–S)*

Materials

- **Piano Accompaniment:** page 310
- **Record Information:**
  - The Gift of Song
    Record 9   Side A   Band 3
    Voices: mixed choir
    Accompaniment: alto flute, 12-string guitar, rhythm guitar, double bass, drums, percussion
- **Teacher's Resource Binder:**
  - Optional—
    Instrumental Accompaniment 6, page I15
    Kodaly Activity 10, page K14
    Orff Activity 14, page O30

The Vocal Experience

In this unit you will have the opportunity to

- find the best part for your vocal range
- sing your part with a choral ensemble
- develop correct habits for supporting a good vocal sound
- train your ear to sing in tune with others
- develop good diction for singing
- sing within large and small ensembles
- sing in a variety of vocal styles

Begin by performing this song.
Which part will best fit your vocal range?

The Gift of Song

Words and Music by Patti Ingalls
Arranged by Buryl Red

164

The Lesson

1. Prior to each rehearsal, ask the students to perform a vocal warm-up. **Good intonation is essential to a good choral sound. Breathing properly to support the tone will help you stay in tune.** Begin the rehearsal with a review of Vocal Warm-up 1. (See Perform/Create 2, page 110, Step 1.)

2. Ask the students to open their books to pages 164–165. Read and discuss what they will learn in Unit 4, "The Choral Sound."

3. Learn to sing "The Gift of Song" (pages 164–165). As students listen to the recording, ask them to identify which vocal part is the most comfortable for their range. (Treble I's and II's: Part 1; Changing Voices and Baritones: Part 2.) Invite them to sing along while you play the recording again.

4. When the students are familiar with their vocal parts, begin to work toward an expressive performance of the song. First, draw the students' attention to proper support. **Can you use one breath to support your vocal sound for four measures of this song?** Suggest that they crescendo on long notes to keep the pitch from "sagging." **Examine the lyrics.** Help the students discover that the text is organized into sentences lasting eight measures. Make decisions as to where a quick breath may be taken so that the ideas expressed in the lyrics will not be interrupted.

165

Lesson Focus

Harmony: Chords and melody may move simultaneously in relation to each other.
(P–I)

Materials

○ **Piano Accompaniment:** page 309
○ **Record Information:**
  • Who?
    Record 9   Side A   Band 4
    Voices: mixed voices
    Accompaniment: oboe, french horn, cimbalom, harp
○ **Teacher's Resource Binder:**
  • Optional—
    Kodaly Activity 7, page K11
    Orff Activity 6, page O11

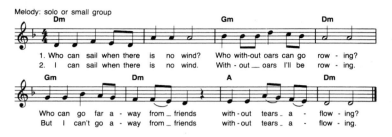

Who?

Scandinavian Folk Song

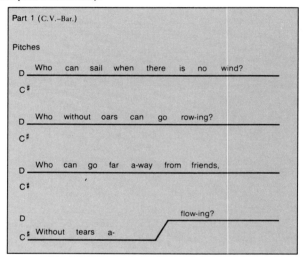

166

The Lesson

1. Use a vocal warm-up to prepare students for performing harmony in a minor key. Divide the class into three groups. Ask the students to sing the following patterns (single pitches in unison and in parts for each chord). Transpose the patterns chromatically by a half step. Stay within a limited range to accommodate the students' vocal ranges.

Repeat the same procedure, using a minor chord.

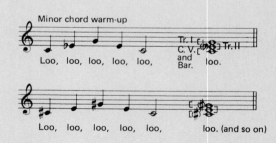

2. Play the recording of "Who?" and challenge the students to determine whether this song is in a major or minor key. (minor) Ask the students to open their books to page 166. Perform this song in unison as follows: Changing Voices and Baritones sing Phrases 1 and 4; Treble I's and II's sing Phrases 2 and 3.

3. When the students know the song, assign the melody to soloists or a small group. The remaining students can follow the ikons (indicating changes of pitch) on the pupil pages to

166

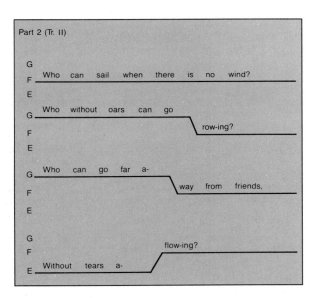

Part 2 (Tr. II)

```
G
F    Who  can  sail  when  there  is  no  wind?
E
G    Who  without  oars  can  go
F                              row-ing?
E
G    Who  can  go  far  a-
F                        way  from  friends,
E
G                   flow-ing?
F
E    Without  tears  a-
```

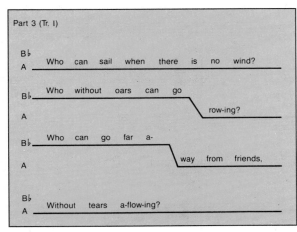

Part 3 (Tr. I)

```
Bb
A    Who  can  sail  when  there  is  no  wind?
Bb   Who  without  oars  can  go
A                             row-ing?
Bb   Who  can  go  far  a-
A                       way  from  friends,
Bb   Without  tears  a-flow-ing?
A
```

create a three-part chordal accompaniment for the song.

4. After the vocal parts have been learned and practiced in ensemble, encourage the students to strive for a balanced choral sound. **Which part should be heard above all the others?** (the melody) Discuss what the students singing harmony will need to do to achieve a good choral balance. (Listen carefully when singing; never sing louder than the melody; balance the volume of the harmony parts with each other.)

Lesson Focus

Harmony: Two or more musical lines may occur simultaneously. *(P–S)*

Materials

○ **Piano Accompaniment:** page 314
○ **Record Information:**
  • Wadaleeacha
    Record 9   Side A   Band 5
    Voices: mixed voices
    Accompaniment: barrel organ, tack piano, percussion

For Your Information

Hand-jive patterns can be created by using the following motions:
  • tapping one fist on top of the other
  • moving hands back and forth over each other
  • pointing over shoulder with thumb
  • touching right and left shoulders with opposite hands at the same time

The Lesson

1. Help the students create four different hand-jive patterns that they can add to each of the four phrases of the song "Wadaleeacha." Play the recording as students explore a variety of hand-jive motions. (See **For Your Information** for suggestions.)

2. Review intervals by writing the following example on the chalkboard.

   Help the students remember that the number of lines and spaces determines the name of the interval.

3. Invite the students to examine the music for "Wadaleeacha" on page 168. **What interval be-** **tween the upper and lower parts occurs most often?** (a sixth) **Why will both parts be fairly easy to sing?** (Both contain many repeated notes and often move by steps rather than skips.)

4. Use the recording to learn both parts of "Wadaleeacha." Assign parts, and have the students follow their own part silently as they listen to the recording again. Then invite the students to sing along with the recording. Correct any errors, and then ask the students to sing with the accompaniment tract of the recording.

5. Invite the students to sing "Wadaleeacha" again and add the hand-jive accompaniment from Step 1.

OPTIONAL

Aura Lee

American Folk Song
Arranged by Buryl Red

Learn to sing this two-part arrangement of a simple folk song.

Part 1: As the black-bird in the spring, 'neath the wil-low tree,
Part 2: Oh, _____ be-neath, be-neath the wil-low

Sat and piped I heard him sing, sing of Au-ra Lee.
tree. Oh _____ I heard, I heard him sing of

Au-ra Lee, Au-ra Lee, maid of gold-en hair.
Au-ra Lee, oh Au-ra Lee, ah. _____

Sun-shine came a-long with thee, and swal-lows in the air.
Sun-shine came a-long with thee, oh. _____

169

Lesson Focus

Time and Place: The way musical elements are combined into a whole reflects the origin of the music. **(P–S)**

Materials

○ **Piano Accompaniment:** page 316
○ **Record Information:**
  • Aura Lee
    Record 9 Side A Band 6a
    Voices: mixed voices
    Accompaniment: acoustic guitar
    Band 6b
    Female voice
    Ensemble conducted by Buryl Red
○ **Teacher's Resource Binder:**
  [Activity Sheets] • **Activity Sheet 31,** page A46
  • Optional—
    Instrumental Accompaniment 7, page 120
    Kodaly Activity 9, page K14

For Your Information

Changing Voices and Baritones should sing Part 2 of the choral arrangement an octave below the pitch notated on pupil page 169. The arrangement should be sung in a simple folk style.

The Lesson

1. Learn to sing the two-part arrangement of "Aura Lee" as shown on page 169. Help the students sing in a simple, *legato* folk style. Listen to the recording of the two-part arrangement of "Aura Lee."

2. Distribute a copy of Activity Sheet 31 (*Listening Guide—Aura Lee*) to each student. Ask the students to listen to the four different versions of "Aura Lee" for solo voice. They may be surprised to learn that the same singer performs in all the versions. Discuss how the singer used the techniques described on the activity sheet to create the different styles heard on the recording.

3. Invite the students to try singing in the different styles along with the recording. The students should concentrate on vocal color, vowel sounds, vibrato, vocal placement, and support. In group singing, embellishments will need to be minimized or eliminated.

The following part assignments are recommended for the recorded keys:

F major (Folk and Country)
Part 1: Tr. I and Tr. II; Part 2: C.V. and Bar.
G major (Jazz)
Part 1: Tr. II and Bar.; Part 2: Tr. I and C.V.
C major (Gospel)
Part 1: Tr. I and C.V.; Part 2: Tr. II and Bar.
D major (Broadway)
Part 2: Tr. I and Bar.; Part 1: C.V.; Tr. II divide *ad lib.*

Lesson Focus

Rhythm: Individual sounds and silences within a rhythmic line may be longer than, shorter than, or the same as the underlying steady beat. *(P–S)*

Materials

○ **Piano Accompaniment:** page 318
○ **Record Information:**
 • Bye, Bye, Blues
 Record 9 Side B Band 1
 Voices: mixed choir
 Accompaniment: clarinet, saxophone, trumpet, trombone, ukulele, double bass, percussion
○ **Instruments:** drumsticks; sand blocks

Bye, Bye, Blues

Words and Music by Fred Hamm, Dave Bennett, Bert Lown, and Chauncey Gray

Clap or use the vocal sound "ch" to perform this "soft-shoe" rhythm:

170

The Lesson

1. Ask the students to open their books to page 170. Play the recording of the refrain (page 172) to "Bye, Bye, Blues." Ask the students to follow the notation at the top of the page that represents the "filler" while the refrain is played. Invite the students to lightly clap along in these rhythms. Help the students to isolate and practice any troublesome rhythms.

2. Ask the students how they could simulate soft-shoe sounds. (vocal "ch's," sliding palms or sand blocks together, tapping toes, clapping hands, clicking drumsticks)

3. Assign vocal parts. Ask the students to examine the score and note which parts have the melody or harmony. (Treble I's and Baritones begin by singing the melody; Treble II's sing an echoing part; Changing Voices sing a harmonic part to the melody. The song is repeated with all the voices moving together in harmony during the refrain.) Use the recording or piano accompaniment to help the students learn their parts. Perform the soft-shoe sounds from Step 2 as an introduction, and sing this song using the rhythmic filler on page 170 for the refrain.

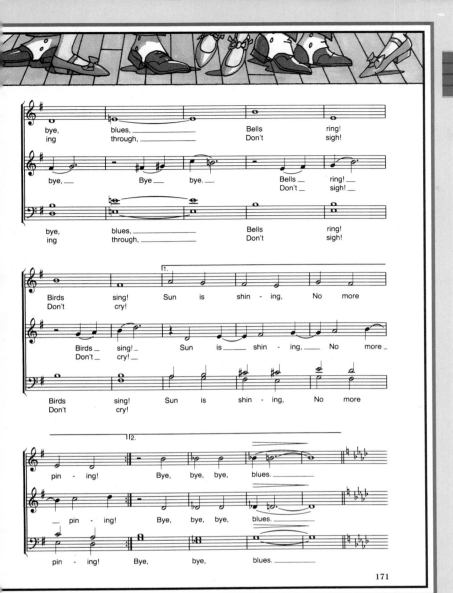

For Your Information

"Bye, Bye, Blues" is a song from the era in which soft-shoe and tap dancing were in vogue. Often the rhythm of a melody was performed so that instead of sustained sounds there were gaps of silence ("stop time"); these gaps were "filled in" with interesting rhythmic sounds performed by a soft-shoe or tap dancer.

171

172

173

CHORAL SOUND 6

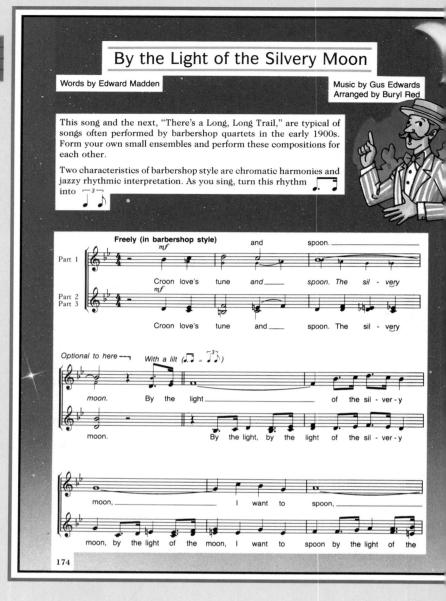

By the Light of the Silvery Moon

Words by Edward Madden

Music by Gus Edwards
Arranged by Buryl Red

This song and the next, "There's a Long, Long Trail," are typical of songs often performed by barbershop quartets in the early 1900s. Form your own small ensembles and perform these compositions for each other.

Two characteristics of barbershop style are chromatic harmonies and jazzy rhythmic interpretation. As you sing, turn this rhythm into...

174

Lesson Focus

Time and Place: The way musical elements are combined into a whole reflects the origin of the music. *(P–S)*

Materials

○ **Piano Accompaniment:** page 322
○ **Record Information:**
  • By the Light of the Silvery Moon
    Record 9 Side B Band 2
    Voices: mixed voices
    Accompaniment: clarinet, ukulele, double bass, percussion

The Lesson

1. Invite the students to explore different methods of creating and controlling vocal timbre (color). Discuss how vocal timbre can be affected by the use of certain sounds. Suggest to the students that a bright sound "feels" like this:

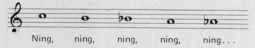

Ning, ning, ning, ning, ning...

Ask the students to sing these bright sounds several times. Suggest that a dark sound "feels" like this:

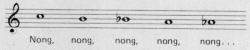

Nong, nong, nong, nong, nong...

Ask the students to compare bright and dark timbres by singing these patterns.

2. Listen to the recording of "By the Light of the Silvery Moon." Read and discuss the information on page 174 about the barbershop quartet arrangement of this music.

3. Invite all students to sing the melody. Discuss whether this song should be performed with bright or dark sounds. (rather dark but not heavy)

4. Assign parts according to vocal range. (See **For Your Information**.) The students will realize that these parts include some imitation, with much of the harmony sung in thirds and sixths. Discuss two characteristics of barbershop style: chromatic harmonies and jazzy rhythmic interpretation. Note the way the dotted eighth and sixteenth notes are to be performed. (See the top of page 174.)

174

For Your Information

Vocal part assignments:

Option 1: C.V. and Bar.: Part 1 an octave lower; Tr. I: Part 2; Tr. II: Part 3

Option 2: Tr. I: Part 1; Tr. II: Part 2; Bar.: Part 1 an octave lower; C.V.: Part 3

5. Encourage students to form their own small ensembles and perform as a barbershop group.

Lesson Focus

Articulation: A series of sounds may move from one to the next in either a smoothly connected or a detached manner. *(P–S)*

Materials

○ **Piano Accompaniment:** page 325
○ **Record Information:**
  • There's a Long, Long Trail
    Record 9 Side B Band 3
    Voices: mixed choir
    Accompaniment: harmonica, acoustic guitar, double bass

There's a Long, Long Trail

Words by Stoddard King

Music by Zo Elliot
Arranged by Buryl Red

Breathe only at the rests to maintain a flowing, *legato* sound.

176

The Lesson

1. Ask the students to practice breath control and support by having them sustain a tone through longer phrases. Provide a beginning pitch. Ask the students to take a breath and sustain this tone as long as they can without the pitch wavering or going flat. Then ask the students to sing as many of the "ABC's" on this one pitch as they can using one breath. **Be sure to sing smoothly!** Students should drop out when their one breath is "used up."

2. Ask the students to repeat the ABC's using one breath. This time ask them to change the articulation and sing each letter *staccato* (shortened and disconnected). Remind the students to drop out again when their one breath is "used up."

3. Ask the students to open their books to page 176. Listen to the recording of "There's a Long, Long Trail." Decide whether this song should be sung *legato* or *staccato*. **Do you think it would be appropriate to sing this song *staccato*?** (probably not)

4. Indicate to the students that in this arrangement breaths should only be taken during the rests. **It is important to maintain the *legato* sound by planning breaths.** Caution the students to conserve breath throughout each four-measure phrase.

5. Assign vocal parts (See **For Your Information**.), and learn to sing "There's a Long, Long Trail." This arrangement emphasizes the simple folk qualities of the song; the performance should not be too sentimental.

176

* Cue size notes in the treble clef may be played on any instrument, in any range, or they may be hummed by a solo voice or whistled.

white moon beams.

sing - ing and a white moon beams. _

_ and a white moon beams, There's a

Oo

long long night of wait - ing un - til my dreams all come

Till the day when I'll be

true 'Till the day when I'll be

go - ing down that long, long trail _ with you.

go - ing down that long, long trail with you.

177

For Your Information

Vocal part assignments:
Option 1: Tr. I: Part 1; Tr. II: Part 2; C.V.: Part 3; Bar. Part 4
Option 2: Tr. 1 and Tr. II: Part 1; C.V. (and Tr. II): Part 2; Bar.: Part 3 or 4

Lesson Focus

Expression: The expressiveness of music is affected by the way timbre, dynamics, articulation, rhythm, melody, harmony, and form contribute to the musical whole. *(P–S)*

Materials

○ **Record Information:**
  • *Factory Fantasia*
  Record 9   Side B   Band 4
  Vocal ensemble conducted by Buryl Red

○ **Other:** tape recorder and microphone; overhead projector

○ **Teacher's Resource Binder:**
  • **Activity Sheets 32a–b,**
    pages A47–A48

LISTENING

Factory Fantasia

by Jay W. Gilbert

Steady ♩ = 120

178

The Lesson

1. Ask the students to turn to page 178 and examine the score for *Factory Fantasia.* **How many musical symbols do you recognize?** (Answers will vary.) Display the transparency prepared from Activity Sheet 32a (*Factory Fantasia: Musical Symbols*). Discuss the function of each symbol and locate at least one place in the score where each symbol is to be used. (Refer to the glossary, page 388, as needed.)

2. **Can you find the symbols that are not familiar to you?** Display the transparency prepared from Activity Sheet 32b (*Factory Fantasia: Special Notation*). Direct the students to practice each of the sounds shown on the transparency.

3. Draw the students' attention to the three possible locations of noteheads in relation to the staff line. Practice Measures 11–26 of Part 3 and Measures 41–44 of Part 1 using the three kinds of sounds shown on the transparency (foot stomp, vocal and nonvocal sounds, and clapping).

4. Listen to the recording of *Factory Fantasia* as the students follow the score; encourage them to observe how these sounds are used to simulate factory sounds. **What kinds of factory sounds do you hear?** (steam or air escaping, both loud and quiet machines operating, liquid bubbling, motors humming, a whistle)

5. Ask the students to choose one of the three parts of the score to follow. Play the recording as they follow the notation for their chosen parts. Repeat this process two more times while the students follow each of the other parts. Finally, listen again to hear the interaction of all three parts.

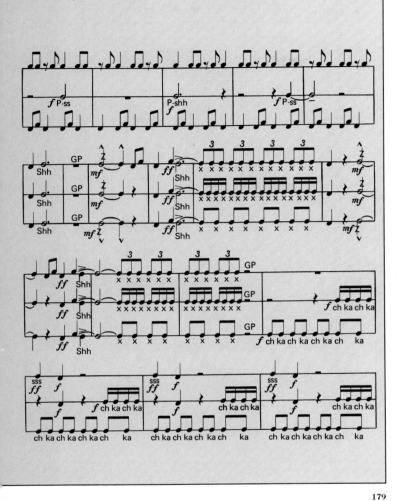

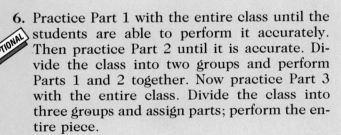

6. Practice Part 1 with the entire class until the students are able to perform it accurately. Then practice Part 2 until it is accurate. Divide the class into two groups and perform Parts 1 and 2 together. Now practice Part 3 with the entire class. Divide the class into three groups and assign parts; perform the entire piece.

7. Refine the dynamics and work to create a more expressive performance. When the performance is accurate and expressive, record it. Play the recording, and ask the students to critique their performance. Help them continue to refine portions of the piece that need additional practice.

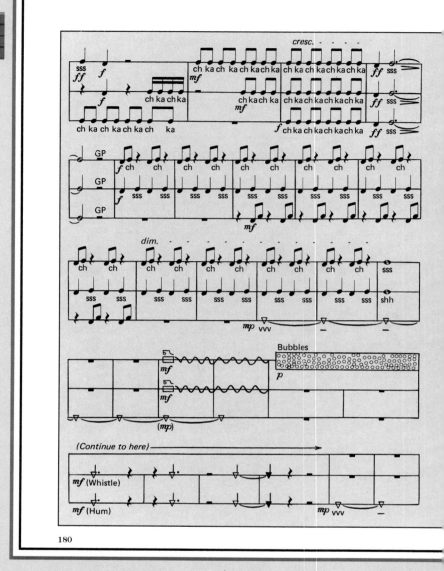

181

CHORAL SOUND 9

Lesson Focus

Rhythm: A series of beats may be organized into regular or irregular groupings by stressing certain beats. *(P–S)*

Materials

○ **Record Information:**
- *Missa*
  Record 9 Side B Band 5
  Voices: mixed choir
  Accompaniment: blown bottles, kalimba

The Lesson

1. Write out the following patterns on the chalkboard. Ask the students to practice each pattern by tapping two fingers against the palm of the opposite hand, observing the indicated accents. When the students can perform each pattern accurately, have them tap the patterns consecutively, keeping the eighth note constant.

2. Ask the students to examine the notation for "*Missa*" shown on pages 182–183. Ask them to note any change in the meter signatures (Measures 5, 6, 7, and so on). Discuss the fermata and its function. Ask the students to lis-

ten to the recording of "*Missa*." **Follow the notation, and observe the use of the fermatas.**

3. Play the recording again, and ask the students to add a steady eighth-note pulse by lightly tapping two fingers against the palm of the opposite hand throughout the song. The students will need to stop tapping and pause at each fermata. The flexible tempo of "*Missa*" will make this exercise challenging. The students must listen carefully and concentrate.

4. Help the students sing "*Missa*" in four parts. Ask them to listen to the recording again, focusing on the style of the sung performance. Guide students to realize that although the music is soft and *legato*, the rhythms should be crisply articulated.

5. Draw the students' attention to the fact that

bu - di - kwen - da - sa - sa ____ (mm)

La - zi - ma - ni   si - che - le - we (mm)   Toh - toa   may - za   li - wa   (mm)

Toh - toa - may - za   li - wa   (mm)   Toh - toa   may - za   li - wa   Kris - to ____

Kris - to   Kris - to   Glo - ri - a. ____

183

For Your Information

The Swahili text is pronounced as follows:

Chrees-too
Nee-tah-koo-tah-nah-nah yay-yay
Ah-tah-koo-tah-nah-mahn-ee
See-nah boo-dee kwen-dah-sah-sah
Lah-zay-mah-nay-see-chay-lay-way
Toe-toe mah-zah lee-wah
Chrees-too Gloe-ree-ah

most syllables in "*Missa*" end in vowels. They should pay special attention to singing these pure vowel sounds but should also clearly articulate the consonants. A few syllables end in *n* or *s*, but these two final consonants should not be overly articulated.

Lesson Focus

Expression: The expressiveness of music is affected by the way dynamics, articulation, and melody contribute to the musical whole. *(P–S)*

Materials

○ **Piano Accompaniment:** page 328
○ **Record Information:**
  • *Hyda*
    Record 9 Side B Band 6
    Voices: mixed voices
  • *Standin' on the Walls of Zion*
    Record 9 Side B Band 7
    Voices: mixed choir
    Accompaniment: dulcimer, hammered dulcimer, psaltery, autoharp, double bass, harmonium, piano, percussion

The Lesson

1. Use the following scales as a vocal warm-up. The students should practice singing the scales at different dynamic levels (*p, mp, mf, f,* and *ff*) and with contrasting articulations (*legato, staccato;* accented, unaccented). Discuss the differences in sound between the minor and major scales.

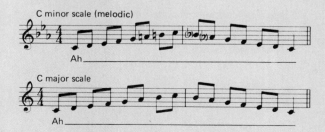

2. Play the recording of "*Hyda.*" Ask the students to follow the score on page 187. **Is this song in a major or minor key?** (minor) **Is it sung legato or staccato?** (legato) **Accented or unaccented?** (accented) Discuss how the dynamics are used. (The unison section begins *p*, and each successive repetition of the melody gets slightly louder—*mp, mf,* and *f*.)

Invite the students to sing the song in unison first, then as a three-part round. Ask the students to experiment with articulation and dynamics on repeated performances: with and without accents, *legato* and *staccato*, and with varying dynamics.

3. Ask the students to turn to page 184. Play the recording of "Standin' on the Walls of Zion." **Follow the notation for this song as you listen for the expressive elements explored in "*Hyda.*"** (Step 2) The students should discover that the song is in a major key, has many accented notes (especially when the word "Zion" is sung), and contains a wide range of dynamics.

185

4. Have the students learn to sing "Standin' on the Walls of Zion" in four parts. **Pay careful attention to all the indicated dynamic changes and accents!**

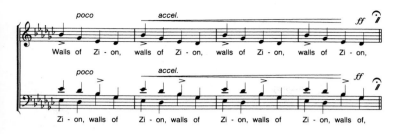

Walls of Zi - on, walls of Zi - on, walls of Zi - on, walls of Zi - on,

Zi - on, walls of Zi - on, walls of Zi - on, walls of Zi - on, walls of,

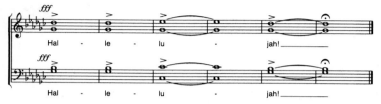

Hal - le - lu - jah! _____

Hal - le - lu - jah! _____

Hyda

Israeli Round

1. Hy - da, hy - da, hy - da-da hy - da, Hy - da, Hy - da, hy - da;

2. Hy - da, hy - da-da hy - da, hy - da, hy - da, hy - da.

3. Hy - da, hy - da-da hy - da, Hy - da, hy - da, hy - da.

187

Lesson Focus

Melody: A series of pitches may move up or down by steps or skips. *(P–S)*

Materials

○ **Piano Accompaniment:** page 336

○ **Record Information:**
  • Roll On, Columbia
    Record 9   Side B   Band 8
    Voices: male solo, female solo, mixed voices
    Accompaniment: flute, acoustic guitar, double bass, electric piano

Roll On, Columbia

Words and Music by Woody Guthrie

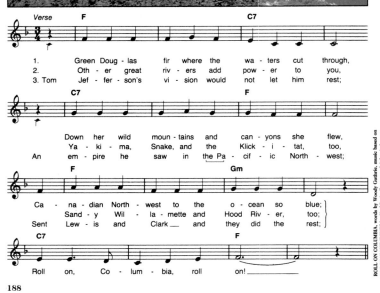

1. Green Doug - las fir where the wa - ters cut through,
2. Oth - er great riv - ers add pow - er to you,
3. Tom Jef - fer - son's vi - sion would not let him rest;

Down her wild moun - tains and can - yons she flew,
Ya - ki - ma, Snake, and the Klick - i - tat, too,
An em - pire he saw in the Pa - cif - ic North - west;

Ca - na - dian North - west to the o - cean so blue;
Sand - y Wil - la - mette and Hood Riv - er, too;
Sent Lew - is and Clark and they did the rest;

Roll on, Co - lum - bia, roll on!

188

ROLL ON COLUMBIA, words by Woody Guthrie, music based on "GOODNIGHT IRENE" by Huddie Ledbetter and John A. Lomax

The Lesson

1. Challenge the students to sight read the melody of a patriotic folk song. Ask them to open their books to page 188 and first tap the rhythm of the melody. (The students should follow the lower staff for the refrain.) Explain that you will strum the written chords on the first beat of each measure while they tap.

2. Return to the beginning of the song and point out that the melody usually moves stepwise or with small skips. Explain to the class that you will again strum the chords and also hum the beginning pitch of each phrase of the melody. Challenge individual students to sight read each phrase of Verse 1 as you strum and hum. Explain to the class that if the student sight reads the phrase correctly, they are to echo it; if the student sight reads incorrectly, they are to remain silent. (Another student is then

given a chance to sight read the phrase.) Follow this procedure phrase by phrase until the melody of the entire song has been sight read.

3. Have the class perform "Roll On, Columbia" in two parts as shown on the pupil pages. Note that the verse is sung in unison and the refrain is sung with Treble I and Baritone (an octave lower than written) voices on Part 1, and Treble II and Changing Voice singers on Part 2.

4. Explain to the students that this song about the Pacific Northwest might be called a "composed" folk song. Folk song lyrics often describe ideas and events of a local nature. Guide the students to realize that although a folk song was probably composed by one person, a song was rarely written down at the time of composition. Through the years, each folk song is transmitted by "ear," and as it

Tr. I
Bar. (8ve lower)

Refrain
Roll on, roll on, _____

Tr. II
C.V.

(melody) Roll on, Co - lum - bia, roll on!

Roll on, roll on, _____

Roll on, Co - lum - bia, roll on, Your

Roll on, roll on, _____

pow - er is turn - ing the dark - ness to dawn;

Roll on, Co - lum - bia, roll on! _____

4. At Bonneville now there are ships in the locks;
The waters have risen and cleared all the rocks.
Shiploads of plenty will steam past the docks;
Roll on, Columbia, roll on!
Refrain

5. And on up the river is Grand Coulee Dam,
The mightiest thing ever built by a man,
To run the great fact'ries and water the land;
Roll on, Columbia, roll on!
Refrain

189

continues to be sung by different singers, the song is changed. Woody Guthrie's songs were written down, but their style and message make them true folk songs.

Lesson Focus

Expression: Musical elements are combined into a whole to express a musical or extramusical idea. *(P–S)*

Materials

○ **Piano Accompaniment:** page 339

○ **Record Information:**
  • Freedom
  Record 10   Side A   Band 1
  Voices: mixed choir
  Accompaniment: banjo, electric bass, piano, percussion

Freedom

Words by Peter Udell

Music by Gary Geld

The Lesson

1. Help the students learn the song "Freedom" (pages 190–192) by singing only the melody with piano accompaniment. Guide the students to consider an appropriate vocal style for the performance of this song. (Suggest that the vocal sound be full, vibrant, and well projected with a touch of "country" style.) After the students have experimented on their own, play the recording as one possible model for performance.

2. **This song has many words to be sung quickly.** Stress using clear diction so that the words can be understood. Ask the students to practice chanting the words in rhythm. **Exaggerate consonants, such as *t, k,* and *f*.** Suggest that they should feel as if they are "chewing" the words!

3. Provide ample time for the students to practice "Freedom." When the parts have been learned, add the fun of singing in "country" style.

For Your Information

This arrangement can be sung in four parts, in two parts, or in unison. (To sing this song as a two-part arrangement, omit the parts notated in bass clef.) Changing Voices will be able to sing the Treble I part an octave below notated pitch for the refrain and coda, but the verse will be out of range. Baritones can sing the Treble II part an octave below notated pitch throughout.

Lesson Focus

Harmony: Chords and melody may move simultaneously in relation to each other. *(P–S)*

Materials

○ **Piano Accompaniment:** page 342

○ **Record Information:**
  • One of Those Songs
  Record 10 Side A Band 2
  Voices: mixed voices
  Accompaniment: small show orchestra

○ **Teacher's Resource Binder:**
  Evaluation • **Checkpoint 4,** page Ev17

For Your Information

The range and the use of few pitches makes "One of Those Songs" easy for students to learn. Baritones may choose to sing the first half of the song as notated or the entire song an octave below.

One of Those Songs

Words by Will Holt   Music by Gregoire Krettly

The first four phrases of this melody are the same.
How does the composer keep these same repeated ideas from becoming dull and monotonous?

192

The Lesson

1. Ask students to follow the score on page 192 as you play only the melody line of "One of Those Songs" on the piano. Ask the students to examine the first five phrases of the song (Measures 1–20). **How does the composer keep these same repeated ideas from becoming dull and monotonous?** (Answers may vary; students may suggest that the syncopated rhythm creates interest.) Guide the students to discover that the changing harmony is a key factor in maintaining musical interest in the repeated phrases.

2. When the students are familiar with the song, invite them to sing along in unison with the recording. Then discuss the challenge of singing well in unison. **The group needs to sing as though they were one voice. Strive for rhythmic and melodic precision. Enunciate your words clearly!** Invite the students to refine their vocal performance of "One of Those Songs."

Follow

Words and Music by Jack Noble White
Arranged by Buryl Red

193

Lesson Focus

Expression: The expressiveness of music is affected by the way dynamics contribute to the musical whole. *(P–S)*

Materials

○ **Piano Accompaniment:** page 344
○ **Record Information:**
   • Follow
     Record 10   Side A   Band 3
     Voices: mixed choir
     Accompaniment: flute, synthesizer, electric piano, electric bass, percussion

The Lesson

1. Prepare students for singing three-part harmony with a warm-up exercise that uses a major chord. Divide the students into three groups. Each group sings one pitch of a major chord using the syllable "loo" (1, 3, 5). Instead of building the chord from the root, a conductor (teacher or student) dictates the fifth step to the first group. This group is to sustain this pitch while the second group, cued by the conductor, sings the third step. The third group then sings the root on cue. When all pitches are in tune, the conductor signals for a cutoff and a breath, then gives a cue for the complete chord to be sung together using the syllable "loo."

   Change the fifth step to create a new major chord. Dictate the fifth step to a different first group, and then proceed in the manner just described.

2. Ask the students to open their books to the song "Follow" (page 197). **Listen to the recording while following the score. Can you hear your own part being sung?** Play the recording again as the students sing along softly with their own part.

3. Practice the parts by isolating each vocal line for the students. Play a single line on the piano while the appropriate group sings along. When each group is familiar with its part, combine the four parts and sing the song.

4. Complete the lesson by asking students to locate the various dynamic markings in the score. **Can you follow the dynamic markings to sing this song expressively? When will you sing softer? Louder?**

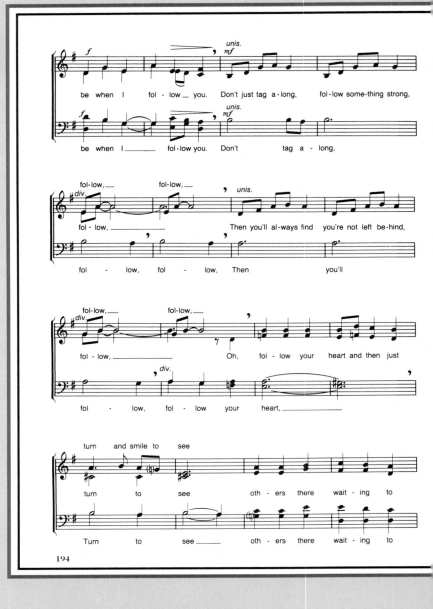

194

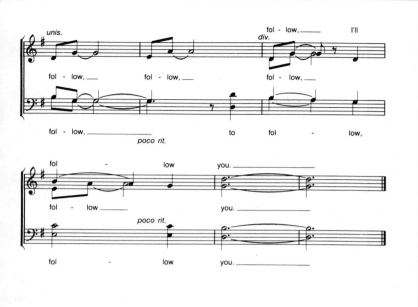

Canción de La Luna

Traditional Mexican Folk Song

195

Lesson Focus

Expression: The expressiveness of music is affected by the way dynamics contribute to the whole. *(P–S)*

Materials

○ **Piano Accompaniment:** page 343
○ **Record Information:**
  • *Canción de la Luna*
    Record 10   Side A   Band 4
    Voices: mixed voices
    Accompaniment: violin, guitars, double bass, accordion, harp, percussion

For Your Information

The translation of "*Canción de la Luna*" follows:
(*Verses*) At two o'clock in the morning, I have come to wake you, my dear,
With guitars and violins I come and salute you with good cheer.
(*Refrain*) Awake, my sweet; wake up quickly; the dawn is coming soon,
The birds are all singing and down has gone the moon.

The Lesson

1. Challenge the students to learn quickly to sing a song in Spanish. Ask the students to examine the melody of "*Canción de la Luna*." **What is unusual about this melody?** (The same melody is used for both the verse and the refrain. This one melodic phrase is repeated six times.) Help the students learn the song by singing the basic melodic phrase on the syllable "loo."

2. Play the recording of "*Canción de la Luna*" and ask the students to listen carefully to the pronunciation of the Spanish words. (The Spanish lyrics are pronounced as follows:
Verse 1—Ah lahs dohs day lah mah-nyah-nah Kay lay **beng**-oe ah deh-spee-**air**-tah
Verse 2—Kohn byo-**lee**-nes ee gee **tahr**-rras Yoe tay **bee**-nay ah sahl-oo **dahr.**
Refrain—Deh spee-**air**-tah, mee byen, Deh-spee-**air**-tah yah ah-mah-nay-see-oe; Yah lohs **pah**-hah-rohs kahn-**tah**-rohn Ee lah **loo**-nah say meh-tee-**oe**.)

3. Have the students perform "*Canción de la Luna*" as shown on pupil page 195. (Treble I and II sing the verses, Changing Voices and Baritones sing the refrain. Note that Changing Voices sing the first note of the refrain an octave higher to accommodate their vocal range.)

Lesson Focus

Harmony: Two or more pitches may be sounded simultaneously. *(P–S)*

Materials

○ **Piano Accompaniment:** page 348
○ **Record Information:**
  • *El Cumbanchero*
    Record 10   Side A   Band 5
    Voices: mixed choir
    Accompaniment: saxophones, trumpets, trombones, piano, double bass, percussion
○ **Instruments:** Latin American percussion instruments such as guiros, claves, bongos, maracas, and conga drums

El Cumbanchero

Words and Music by Rafael Hernandez

196

The Lesson

1. Help the students to hear and perform chords that contain five different pitches. Divide the students into five groups and vocally "stack" the following chord. (Begin with the Baritones singing the lowest note and continue upward. Divide Treble I's and II's into three groups.)

When the chord is complete, have students take a breath, sing the chord again, and then resolve to a C major seventh chord. Practice this warm-up several times.

2. Play the recording of *"El Cumbanchero."* After listening to the recording, ask the students to describe any familiar sounds or musical ideas they just have heard. (The students

should discover that Section A begins with a canon; Section B contains the chord they learned in the warm-up activity.)

3. Assign vocal parts. (See **For Your Information**.) Ask the students to sing along with the recording several times. As the students gain confidence, gradually turn the volume down on the record player to test how well they can carry the parts on their own.

4. Invite the students to accompany *"El Cumbanchero"* with Latin American percussion instruments. Ask the students to create rhythmic ideas that enhance the song. (See pupil page 132 for suggested rhythmic patterns.)

196

For Your Information

Vocal part assignments for "*El Cumbanchero*":
  Section A (Measures 1–16):
    Tr. I and II sing treble clef.
    C.V. and Bar. sing bass clef.
  Section B (beginning at Measure 17):
    Divide into five parts.
    Tr. I and II divide to sing the three treble parts.
    C.V. and Bar. sing bass clef.

The Spanish text is pronounced as follows:
  ah **coom**-bah, **coom**-bahn-**chay**-rroe
  ah **bong**-goe, **bong**-goe-**say**-rroe.
  pree-kee-**tee** kay **vah**-soe-**ahn**-doe
  el **coom**-bahn-**chay**-rroe
  bong-goe-**say**-roe **kay**-say-**va**.
  ee **sway**-nyah ah-see el tam-**bor**,
  bee-ree-**kee**-tee,
  boom-boom-bah.
  ee-**vuel**-vah ah **ray**-pee-**kahr**,
  bee-ree-**kee**-tee,
  boom-boom-bah.

197

Matilda

Traditional
Adapted by Massie Patterson and Sammy Heyward

Lesson Focus

Expression: The expressiveness of music is affected by the way rhythm, melody, and harmony contribute to the musical whole. *(P–S)*

Materials

○ **Piano Accompaniment:** page 353
○ **Record Information:**
  • Matilda
  Record 10   Side A   Band 6
  Voices: mixed choir
  Accompaniment: penny whistle, electric guitar, electric bass, steel drums, percussion
○ **Instruments:** claves, maracas, bongos, conga drums, low-pitched drum
○ **Teacher's Resource Binder:**
  • Optional—
  Orff Activity 11, page O24

The Lesson

1. Review "Wadaleeacha" (page 168). **What special rhythmic idea do you hear throughout the melody?** (dotted eighth and sixteenth patterns and syncopation created by the use of tied notes) **Here's another song in a different style that also makes use of syncopation. Play the recording of "Matilda." Can you tell me which part of the world this song comes from? What is this style of music called?** Guide the students to conclude that this style is called calypso, from the Caribbean.

2. **Which voice or voices sing the melody of "Matilda"?** (Treble I sings the melody throughout.) **In which voice or voices does the syncopation occur?** (Treble I—melody; other voices sing unsyncopated parts, except in Measure 2 of the verse, when they sing the same syncopated rhythms as the melody.)

3. Learn the four-part arrangement on page 199. When the students have learned their parts, add the following accompaniment patterns.

Help the students discover that the claves part is derived from the first measure of the refrain and the bongo part from the second measure of the verse. Help them notice also that the conga drum part is syncopated.

199

Lesson Focus

Rhythm: A series of beats may be organized into regular or irregular groupings by stressing certain beats. *(P–S)*

Materials

○ **Piano Accompaniment:** page 356

○ **Record Information:**
   • *Laredo*
   Record 10   Side A   Band 7
   Voices: mixed voices
   Accompaniment: guitar, double bass, harp, accordion, percussion
   • *El Salón México*
   Record 10   Side A   Band 8
   New York Philharmonic
   Leonard Bernstein, conductor

○ **Instruments:** maracas, claves, bongos, guiro and scratcher, cowbell, or other Mexican percussion instruments

The Lesson

1. Have the students listen to the recording of "*Laredo*" and ask them to tap the underlying short sound (eighth notes). **Look at the melody for "*Laredo*" on pages 200-201. Notice that the melody is notated in the bass clef. How does the melody move?** (mostly by steps; with; movement by half steps creating some chromaticism) Invite the class to sing the melody of "*Laredo*." The Treble I and II singers will need to sing the melody an octave higher than written.

2. Ask the students to examine the Treble I and II part. **How does this part move in relation to the melody?** (The rhythms are identical, and the notes move in parallel motion to each other at the interval of a sixth, creating a basically homophonic texture.) **Which phrases of the song are the same?** (Phrases 1 and 4, 2

and 5, and 3 and 6) **Which phrases of the song are similar to each other?** Phrases 1 and 3 and 4 and 6) **Which phrases of the song are not alike?** (Phrases 2 and 5)

3. Assign vocal parts and teach the class to sing "*Laredo*." **Be sure to sing the 3 + 2 + 2 pattern—$\frac{7}{8}$ meter—correctly in a *legato* style.**

4. Ask the students to clap the rhythm examples at the bottom of pupil page 201. **How are these patterns different?** (The $\frac{7}{8}$ meter example is made up of 3 + 2 + 2 beats, but the $\frac{4}{4}$ meter example is made up of 2 + 3 + 3 beats.) Divide the class into two groups. Ask the class to perform the first example as a round by repeating the example many times. Group 2 begins clapping Measure 1 when Group 1 has finished Measure 1 and begun Measure 2. Help the students to hear the displacement of accents that results.

LISTENING

El Salón México
(excerpt)

Music by Aaron Copland

Clap these patterns.

Which of these patterns is most like "Laredo"?
Which of these patterns is most like the "Laredo"
melody heard in *El Salón México?*

201

For Your Information:

The Spanish text for "*Laredo*" is pronounced as follows:

Yah may boy **pah**-rah el Lah-**ray**-doe, mee byen, Tay **beng**-oe ah day-**seer** ah-dee-**ohs**. Day ah-**yah** tay **mahn**-doe day-**seer**, mee byen, **koe**-moe say mahn-**kwair**-nahn dohs.

Toe-mah **ay**-sah yah-**vee**-tah day **ohr**-roh, mee byen, **ah**-bray mee **pay**-choe ee bair-**ahs**: Loh **moo**-choe kay yoh tay **k'yair**-roe, mee byen, ee el mahl **pah**-goe kay may dahs.

Toe-mah **ay**-sah kah-**hay**-tah day ohr-roh, mee byen, **mee**-rah loh kay **yay**-vah **den**-troe. **Yay**-vah ah-**moh**-rays **yay**-vah **say**-lohs, mee byen, ee oon **poe**-coe day sehn-tee-**myen**-toe. (repeat the first two lines)

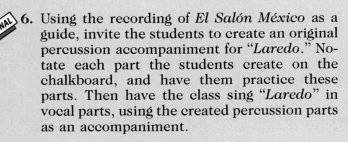

5. Ask the students to listen for the melody of "*Laredo*" as you play the recorded excerpt from *El Salón México*. (The "*Laredo*" melody is performed by a solo bassoon.) **Can you decide which of these examples is performed on the recording of *El Salón México*?** (the $\frac{4}{4}$ meter pattern) **Which example is from the song "*Laredo*"?** (the $\frac{7}{8}$ meter pattern)

6. Using the recording of *El Salón México* as a guide, invite the students to create an original percussion accompaniment for "*Laredo*." Notate each part the students create on the chalkboard, and have them practice these parts. Then have the class sing "*Laredo*" in vocal parts, using the created percussion parts as an accompaniment.

Lesson Focus

Expression: The expressiveness of music is affected by the way dynamics, rhythm, melody, harmony, and form contribute to the musical whole. *(P–S)*

Materials

○ **Piano Accompaniment:** page 359
○ **Record Information:**
  • Sigh No More, Ladies, Sigh No More!
  Record 10 Side B Band 1
  Voices: mixed choir
  Accompaniment: piano
○ **Teacher's Resource Binder:**
  • Optional—
  Biography 8, page B15

The Lesson

1. Write out the following patterns on the chalkboard:

Prepare the students for reading the ⁶⁄₈ meter rhythms in the song by having them tap each of the patterns on their thighs. Challenge the students to perform the patterns in a new order—randomly point to patterns and ask the students to continue to tap without pausing.

2. Look at the score of "Sigh No More, Ladies, Sigh No More!" Ask the students to read the rhythms for each vocal part (Treble I's first, followed by Treble II's, Changing Voices and Baritones), chanting the words and tapping in rhythm on their thighs. When all four parts have been performed, combine all parts, with each student chanting and tapping his or her own part.

3. Ask the students to listen to the recording while following the score for "Sigh No More, Ladies, Sigh No More!" Listen to the recording as needed until the students have learned their individual vocal parts. (The vocal parts are very imitative and will be easy to learn.)

4. Invite the students to examine the score for expressive markings. (The students should discover a variety of dynamic markings including *crescendos, decrescendos,* and accents.) Have the students divide into four

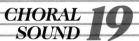

one — on shore, and one — on shore; To one — thing con - stant

one — on shore, and one — on shore; To one — thing con - stant

shore, and one — on shore, and one — on shore;

nev - er. But let — them go, And be — you blithe — and

nev - er.

Then sigh — not so, And be — you blithe — and

bon - ny, Con - vert - ing your sounds of woe — In - to

bon - ny, Con - vert - ing your sounds of woe — In - to

203

parts and perform the song, paying special attention to dynamics and accents.

5. Discuss the form of the music. (The song is essentially in a repeated two-part or **A B** form.
Section A begins with "Sigh no more, ladies";
Section B begins with the refrain "Hey
nonny . . . " The second verse, Section A repeated, begins with "Sing no more . . . " and is
followed by the refrain, Section B, "Hey
nonny . . . ")

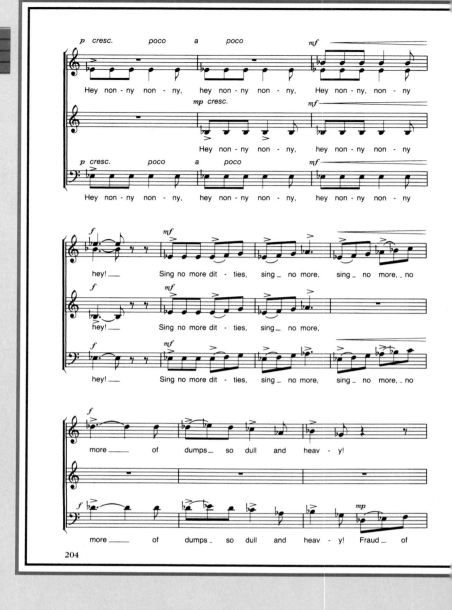

204

mp cresc. poco a poco mf
Fraud _ of men, the fraud _ of men, the fraud _ of men was
mp cresc. poco a poco mf
Fraud _ of men, the fraud _ of men, the fraud _ of men was
cresc. mf
men, the fraud _ of men, the fraud _ of men was ev - er
ev - er so, was ev - er so, Since sum - mer first was leav - y.
ev - er so, was ev - er so, Since sum - mer first was leav - y.
mp
so, was ev - er so, was ev - er so, then
mp
But let _ them go, And be _ you blithe _ and bon - ny, Con -
sigh _ not so, And be _ you blithe _ and bon - ny, Con -

205

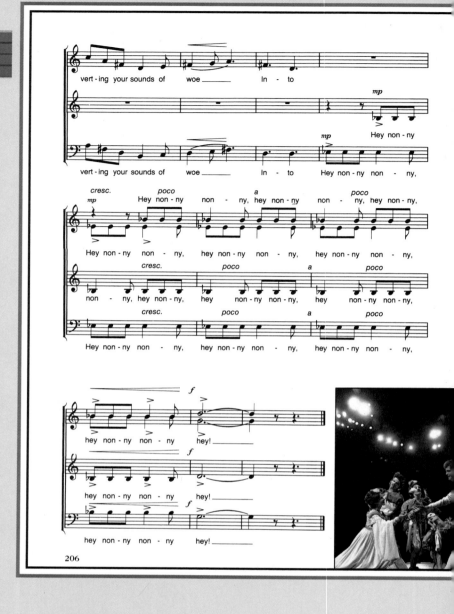

206

Sheep Safely Graze

...ds by Eloise Williams

Music by Johann Sebastian Bach

Sheep safe-ly graze a - mid ver-dant pas-tures; The shep-herd keeps a care-ful watch o'er his flock. Sheep safe-ly graze a - mid ver-dant pas-tures; Se - rene-ly they graze in safe-ty, While tend-ed by the shep-herd. 'Midst the ver-dant fields they safe-ly graze; Ten-der-ly the shep - herd guards his flock. Ten-der-ly he guards his flock.

207

Tr. I
Bar.
(8ve below)

Tr. II
C.V.

Lesson Focus

Harmony: Two or more musical lines may occur simultaneously. *(P—S)*

Materials

○ **Piano Accompaniment:** page 366
○ **Record Information:**
  • Sheep Safely Graze
  Record 10 Side B Band 2
  Voices: mixed voices
  Accompaniment: flute, harpsichord, organ, violincello
○ **Instruments:** flute and piano

The Lesson

1. Ask the students to examine the notation for "Sheep Safely Graze" (page 207). **Based on what you see, what kind of music would you expect to hear on the recording of this song?** (Answers may vary. Guide the students to discover that the harmonic structure is basically homophonic—the same rhythms are used in each part—and that the melody and the text suggest a *legato* style.) Listen to the recording of "Sheep Safely Graze" to reinforce the discussion.

2. Assign vocal parts and learn the song. Emphasize singing in a *legato* style throughout this song. Students should be particularly aware of singing words such as "verdant," "shepherd," "amid," and "tended," in a smoothly connected manner. Work on the phrasing by having the students trace this pattern in the air as they sing each phrase.

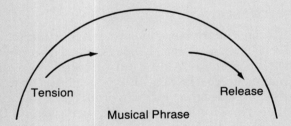

Tension   Release
Musical Phrase

Help them understand where the tension and release occur in each phrase.

3. If appropriate, invite a flutist (to play the upper notes) and a pianist to play the piano accompaniment (page *366*). **OPTIONAL**

4. Invite the students to sing "Sheep Safely Graze" again, using the flute and piano accompaniment (either live or recorded).

Lesson Focus

Expression: The expressiveness of music is affected by the way articulation, harmony, and dynamics contribute to the musical whole. *(P–S)*

Materials

○ **Piano Accompaniment:** page 370
○ **Record Information:**
  • The Sleigh
    Record 10   Side B   Band 3
    Voices: mixed choir
    Accompaniment: violin, balalaika, cimbalom, accordion, double bass, percussion
○ **Instruments:** sleigh bells (or jingle bells); tambourine
○ **Other:** overhead projector
○ **Teacher's Resource Binder:**
  Activity Sheets • **Activity Sheet 33,** page A49

The Sleigh

Music by Richard Kountz
Arranged by W. Riegger

208

The Lesson

1. Display the transparency prepared from Activity Sheet 33 (*Velvet Shoes*). Read the poem with the class. **What kind of mood does the poem suggest?** (peaceful and calm) **How is this mood achieved?** (by the use of words such as *soundless, tranquil, veils, windless peace,* and *silence.*)

2. Read the text for "The Sleigh" (pages 208–211). Guide the students through discussion to compare the song and poem texts. Discover that the texts describe snow in contrasting ways: "Velvet Shoes" describes the beauty and peacefulness of snow, while "The Sleigh" describes the joy and excitement of a ride through the snow. **How might a composer treat the song text?** (Answers will vary but should include the use of fast, accented, and *staccato* sounds.)

3. Listen to the recording of "The Sleigh." **Is the musical setting of the text what you expected?** (Answers will vary.) **What other compositional techniques were used?** (dynamic contrasts; repeated sections; voice imitation between vocal parts)

4. Have the students learn to sing "The Sleigh" in four parts. When they can sing their parts securely, work on the dynamic contrasts. Be sure to emphasize the need for clean diction, especially initial consonants and final *t*'s. Sleigh bells (or jingle bells) may be added to accompany the song, using this rhythm:

208

Mer-ri-ly we go. Ho, hah, We are go-ing on-ward through the night,

Mer-ri-ly we go. Hah, ho, hah, on-ward through the night,

Mer-ri-ly we go. sharp winds blow-ing, Ho, hah, on-ward through the night,

Mer - ri-ly we snow, We are go - ing on-ward through the night,

Hey - a - o - la! Light-ly fly - ing

Hey - a - o - la! Light-ly fly - ing o'er the snow, With a

Hey - a - o - la! Light-ly fly - ing

Hey, hey - a - o - la! Light-ly fly - ing

209

Tambourine — Play 8 times — (Tap) (Shake) — Play 10 times — (Tap)

(Shake) (Tap)

Lesson Focus

Expression: The expressiveness of music is affected by the way dynamics contribute to the musical whole. *(P–S)*

Materials

○ **Piano Accompaniment:** page 376
○ **Record Information:**
  • A Christmas Happening
    Record 10   Side B   Band 4
    Voices: mixed choir
    Accompaniment: electric guitar, electric piano, electric bass, bells, chimes, tambourine, drums

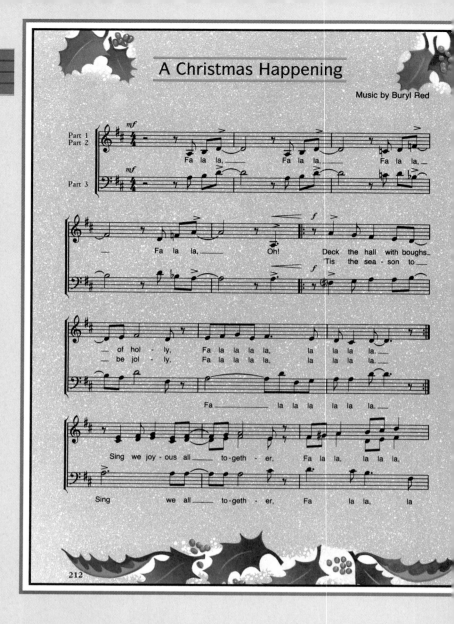

A Christmas Happening

Music by Buryl Red

212

The Lesson

1. Assist the students in learning the song "A Christmas Happening" (pages 212–214). Focus attention on the dynamic markings in the score, and challenge the students to follow all changes carefully.

2. *OPTIONAL* Discuss how other performance considerations will enhance this song. In the first section, the "fa la la" sound should be bright, with a flipped *l*. Ask the students to practice flipping *l* off the tip of the tongue by singing up and down scales and arpeggios. Stress the importance of singing pitches accurately.

3. In the second section (after the change of key, bottom of page 213), the music is more *legato* and needs a smoother vocal sound. For the melismas (many pitches on one syllable), the notes should be clearly articulated, but stu-

dents should avoid making a "ho" sound on each new pitch.

4. Pay attention to the choral balance at the words "Angels we have heard on high." (The melody is in the bass clef. Part 2 doubles the melody at the sixth and should be the softest part. Part 1 is a countermelody and should be heard clearly.) At the words "Gloria in excelsis Deo," all vocal parts should be heard equally.

5. The last part of the piece should sound like a "free-for-all." Different voices, one at a time, speak at random in various languages. (See **For Your Information**.) The dynamic level increases as the phrases are spoken by more and more voices. Some students can sing the melody as notated or an octave lower; others can shout the foreign phrases. (Add foreign phrases other than those in **For Your Infor-**

212

For Your Information

Vocal part assignments for "A Christmas Happening":

Part 1: Tr. I; Part 2: Tr. II; Part 3: C.V. and Bar. (Part 2 may be omitted.)

The ending of the piece includes the phrase "peace on earth" spoken at random in various foreign languages.

The following phrases may be used:

French: *Paix sur la terre!* (pay syur lah tehr)

Spanish: *Paz en la tierra!* (pahss en lah tee-**ayr**-rrah)

Italian: *Pace in terra!* (**pah**-chay een **teh**-rrah)

Swahili: *Amani iwe duniani!* (ah-**mah**-nee **ee**-way doon-**yah**-nee)

German: *Friede auf Erden!* (**frree**-duh ouf **air**-den)

Russian: *Mir na zemle!* (meer nah **zehm**-yeh)

mation, if possible.) The shouting should become louder and louder until, at the end, it overcomes the sung phrases.

214

By the Waters Babylon

Traditional Round

Divide into groups. Sing all the parts of this song in canon, or sing only the part suitable for your voice range as an ostinato.

Can the ground bass shown above be used to accompany this canon? How do you know?

1. By the _ wa - ters, by the _ wa - ters, by the _ wa - ters Ba - by - lon,

2. We sat down and wept, _ we wept, _ we wept, _ When

3. we re - mem - bered, we re - mem - bered. we re - mem - bered Zi - on.

215

Lesson Focus

Harmony: Chords and melody may move simultaneously in relation to each other. *(P–S)*

Materials

○ **Record Information:**
  • By the Waters Babylon
    Record 10   Side B   Band 5
    Voices: treble voices
    Accompaniment: recorders, harmonium

○ **Instruments:** guitar or piano

For Your Information

The round "By the Waters Babylon" is within the range of all vocal parts. Changing Voice singers may sing the first and third phrases of the canon as written; they will need to sing the second phrase an octave lower than notated.

The Lesson

1. Play the recorded accompaniment (instrumental channel only) for "By the Waters Babylon" or play the accompaniment on the piano (pupil page 215). Ask students to listen to the repeated ground bass pattern several times. Then ask them to
   • hum a pitch that sounds in tune with the harmony of each measure. (Allow time for students to explore the sounds of several pitches by playing the pattern many times.)
   • use their chosen pitch as a base to create a melodic idea for each measure of the ground bass or freely improvise melodies for the complete ground bass pattern.

2. Ask the students to open their books to page 215 and learn to sing "By the Waters Babylon." Divide the class into three groups and have them perform the song as a three-part round.

3. Ask the students to consider what might be an appropriate accompaniment for this song. **Can the ground bass be used to accompany this round?** (yes) **How do you know?** (The chord symbols for the ground bass and the round are the same.) Invite the students to create their own arrangement using the following plan:

   Perform the ground bass on a guitar or piano.
   Improvise a vocal introduction.
   Sing the round in unison.
   Sing the round in parts.

CHORAL SOUND 24

Lesson Focus

Harmony: Chords and melody may move simultaneously in relation to each other. *(P–S)*

Materials

○ **Piano Accompaniment:** page 382
○ **Record Information:**
  • Grab Another Hand
  Record 10 Side B Band 6
  Voices: mixed choir
  Accompaniment: flute, trumpet, acoustic guitar, electric guitar, electric piano, electric bass, percussion
○ **Instruments:** claves, maracas, bongos, low-pitched drum

The Lesson

1. Ask the students to open their books to page 216, and play the recording of "Grab Another Hand." **As you listen, can you decide which voice part is singing the melody?** (Baritones sing the melody throughout; other voices join in and sing the melody from the words "Sing this song. . . .")

2. Invite all students to sing the melody. Treble I's and II's should sing the Baritone line one octave higher than written. (Changing Voices may begin to sing this melody starting with the pickups to Measure 10.)

3. When the melody has been learned, Treble I's, Treble II's, and Changing Voices should learn their own parts. Help Treble I's and II's discover that their parts are frequently a third apart. Changing Voices should discover that their part consists of only four pitches (A, B,

C, and D) except when they are singing the melody. Direct attention to the chord structure of the song. **Why are the harmonizing vocal parts fairly repetitive?** (The same chord progression is repeated throughout the song.)

4. Write out the following percussion patterns on the chalkboard. Invite students to accompany the song using these rhythms as they sing.

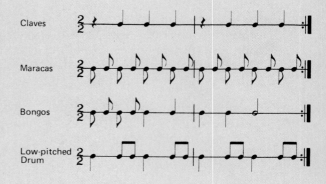

216

2. Shake another hand, shake a hand next to ya, etc.

3. Clap another hand, clap a hand next to ya, etc.

4. Raise another hand, raise a hand next to ya, etc.

5. Hug another friend, hug a friend next to ya, etc.

217

5. Divide the class into small groups of five or six students. Ask each group to create simple choreography to go with the song. After each group shares its original choreography with the class, invite the class to choose its favorite for each verse. Invite the class to practice the selected choreography and perform "Grab Another Hand" with singing, dancing, and instrumental accompaniment.

Lesson Focus

Harmony: Two or more musical lines may occur simultaneously. *(P–S)*

Materials

○ **Record Information:**
  • Now Comes the Hour
    Record 10   Side B   Band 7
    Voices: mixed voices
    Accompaniment: handbell choir
○ **Instruments:** alto or bass metallophone

For Your Information

The canon "Now Comes the Hour" is within the range of all vocal parts. Changing Voice singers will need to sing the first and third phrases of the canon an octave lower than written; the second phrase can be sung at the notated pitch.

Now Comes the Hour

Music by Ludwig van Beethoven

Ludwig van Beethoven was born in the city of Bonn, Germany, in 1770. From 1792 Beethoven's artistic fame never stopped growing, despite the fact that during this time he became totally deaf. When he died in 1827, Beethoven was esteemed as the world's greatest composer. His genius brought the Classical tradition to its height and opened the door to the Romantic era. Among his many works are nine symphonies, 18 string quartets, 32 piano sonatas, and numerous other pieces for piano and for various vocal and instrumental ensembles.

218

The Lesson

1. Draw the following graph on the chalkboard.

   Ask the students to sing and clap the scale numbers in rhythm.

2. *(OPTIONAL)* Invite one or more students to perform the chalkboard example on the alto or bass metallophone and accompany the class as they sing the scale numbers.

3. Ask the students to open their books to page 218. **Can you find the part you have just sung and played?** (the first line of the canon) Suggest to the students that this phrase may be used as an accompaniment for the canon. Play the recording of "Now Comes the Hour" and ask the students to perform this phrase as an ostinato.

4. Ask the students to learn the second and third phrases of "Now Comes the Hour." Assign vocal parts and have the students sing the entire canon.

Let the Sun Shine In

Words by James Rado and Jerome Ragni

Music by Galt MacDermot

219

CHORAL SOUND **29**

Lesson Focus

Evaluation: Review concepts and skills studied in Unit 4. **(D–S)**

Materials

○ **Piano Accompaniment:** page 386

○ **Record Information:**
  • Let the Sun Shine In
    Record 10 Side B Band 8
    Voices: mixed choir
    Accompaniment: tenor saxophone, trumpet, snythesizer, electric guitar, electric bass, electric piano, percussion

○ **Instruments:** tambourines; resonator bells B♭,, C, D, F, F♯, G, A, B♭, C′, D′, E♭′ (or keyboard)

○ **Teacher's Resource Binder:**

  Evaluation
  • **Review 4** page Ev20
  • **Musical Progress Report 4,** page Ev22

For Your Information

Vocal part assignments for "Let the Sun Shine In":
  Tr. I: Parts 1 and 2, Tr. II: Parts 2 and 3, C.V.: Part 3 or 4, and Bar.: Part 4

The Lesson

1. Culminate activities for Unit 4 by challenging the students to demonstrate their musicianship skills; they will be reading and performing a song independently. Distribute *Review 4* to each student. Provide the opportunity for students to work together in special groups determined by their vocal range. Each group is to read and practice its individually assigned part. Explain that students will be checked for rhythmic and melodic accuracy. They may wish to select one member of their group to serve as the conductor.

2. Ask the students to read and perform *Review 4*, Part 2. They are to clap the rhythm part and then play this part on a tambourine.

3. Give the students class time to prepare their parts. Once they are well prepared, have each group perform for the class. Students who are not performing should follow the parts on the *Review 4* sheets to determine if the other groups have executed their parts accurately.

4. After all the groups have performed, ask the students to rate their individual and group performances.

5. Read the final question on the evaluation sheet. Discuss whether students followed carefully the dynamic markings indicated on their scores.

6. Ask the students to open their books to page 219. They will discover that the parts they have been learning are those used in the song "Let the Sun Shine In." **Add words to your part!** Assign several students to play the tambourine part and perform with the recording.

Glossary

A cappella sung without instrumental accompaniment

Accelerando becoming faster

Accidental a written sign (sharp or flat) indicating that a given pitch is to be raised or lowered a half step within a measure

Adagio at moderately slow speed

Aeolian a mode of seven pitches whose scale (by whole and half steps) is W W H W H W W

Allegro at a fast speed

Andante at a medium (walking) speed

Arpeggio notes of a given chord that are performed one after another rather than at the same time

Arranging taking existing music and creating special parts for instruments and voices

Articulation how sounds begin and end when they are performed

Atonal having no central pitch or key; literally, "without tonality"

Beat the steady pulse that underlies most music

Canon a form of imitation in which each part plays or sings the same melody at different times; a round

Central pitch scale step 1, or the pitch to which all other pitches appear to return

Chord three or more pitches occurring at the same time

Choreographer someone who creates dance movements, usually to musical accompaniment

Chromaticism the use of pitches that would not usually be used in a given key or scale

Composing the act of creating and notating new and original music

Concerto a composition for solo instrument(s) and orchestra

Contrary motion the movement of two voice parts in opposite directions

Counterpoint (contrapuntal, *adj.):* the musical combination of two or more melodic lines, each of which is distinct and independent

Diatonic having no chromatic pitches (notes that do not belong in a given key)

Dissonance a combination of pitches that creates a feeling of tension

Dominant the fifth scale tone above the tonic; or ch_ of a given key

Dorian a mode of seven pitches whose scale, in term whole and half steps, is W H W W W H W

Dynamics the degrees of loudness and softnes_ music

Embellishments ornamental notes that decorate a _ ody

Fermata a sign indicating that a note is to be held lo_ than its written value

Harmony a series of chords in a given piece of mu_

Homophony music in which a melody is accompa_ by other voices, generally moving in the s_ rhythm

Imitation the repeating of a melody in one voice _ has already been performed by another, as in a ro_ or canon

Improvising the act of performing music "on the s_ without the aid of notation

Interval the distance (in pitch) between two mu_ tones

Ionian a mode of seven pitches whose scale, in term whole and half steps, is W W H W W W H

Jazz a distinctive style of American music develo_ from ragtime and blues

Key signature the sharps or flats at the beginnin_ each staff that indicate the key of a composition

Largo at a very slow speed

Legato performed in a smooth, connected manner

Major scale a scale of seven pitches ordered, in term whole and half steps, as W W H W W W H

Marcato a heavy, marked articulation

Measure a group of beats, with the first normally re_ ing an accent; the number of beats is determine_ the meter signature

Melody a series of pitches arranged rhythmically to _ ate a musical line

Meter signature a sign consisting of two numbers fo_ at the beginning of a piece of music or section; _ cates the number and type of beat found in each _ sure

Minor scale a scale of seven pitches ordered, in term whole and half steps, as W H W W H W W

220

olydian a mode of seven pitches whose scale, in rms of whole and half steps, is W W H W W H W

le a specific arrangement of pitches to form a scale; sually refers to medieval church modes

lerato at a moderate speed

dulation the change in harmony from one key to an- ther in a musical composition

lophony a single musical line

ive (motif) the smallest rhythmic, melodic, or har- onic unit of a musical theme that can be identified

ement a complete and independent section of a mu- cal composition

e a sign that shows the pitch and the length of a tone

ament a standard type of melodic embellishment uch as a trill, etc.)

nato a musical pattern or figure repeated over and ver

allel motion the same or a similar musical line per- rmed simultaneously at a different pitch

tatonic a scale of five pitches with no half steps be- ween any two pitches; occurs when only the black eys on the piano are used

ase a grouping of notes that forms a musical sen- ence

h the highness or lowness of a musical pitch

phony music in which two or more independent elody lines occur at the same time

Presto at a very fast speed

Ritardando a gradual slowing of the tempo

Scale an arrangement of tones by pitch according to the order of whole steps and half steps

Staccato performed in a short, separated manner

Syncopation a shift of accent from the strong beat to the weak beat in music

Tablature a system of instrumental notation indicating the string, fret, key, or finger to be used, instead of the pitch to be played

Tempo the speed at which the beat moves in music

Texture the consistency of the "fabric" of music; such as thickness, thinness, etc.

Theme a melody or phrase used as basic material for a musical composition

Timbre the quality or color of a sound

Tonal center usually the central pitch in a given key

Tone color see **timbre**

Tonic the first pitch of a scale; or chord of a given key

Transcribe (transcription n.) to transfer from one per- forming medium to another; for example, a piano tran- scription made of an orchestral composition

Variation a musical idea that is repeated with some change

Vibrato a quality of sound produced by small, rapid var- iations in pitch; executed in string instruments by a rapid movement of the left hand

7. My Lord

Words and Music by Joyce Elaine Eiler

Verse
(Tr. tacet)   *mp C. V. and Bar.*

1. Shad - rach, Me - shach, A - bed - ne - go___ in the
2. Mo - ses led the___ chil-dren of Is - ra - el
3. Lit - tle Da - vid___ flung a stone___ and

fier - y fur - nace were tossed.___ Ev - ery-bod - y thought their end___ was
down to the Red___ Sea shore,___ Phar - oah and___ his ar - my close___ be -
made Go - li - ath fall.___ Man, you should have seen his ar - my

near.___ But___ they had faith___ that the Lord a - bove___ would
hind.___ Then the wa - ters part - ed, let Mo - ses through,___ but
run.___ Then the chil-dren of Is - ra - el gave a shout___ and

come and save the day,___ And I could swear I heard those fel - lows
Phar - oah's ar-my was drowned, And from the shore came Mo - ses' thank - ful
fol - lowed them a - way,___ And ev - ery - bod - y heard their he - ro

cresc.

1. 2.

3.

cresc.

say,_____
sound,_____

say,_____

cresc.

cresc.

Coda

My Lord,   My Lord,   ev-ery-thing's gon-na be   all right!

My Lord's gon - na watch o - ver me, and ev-ery-thing's gon-na be   all right!

My Lord,_____   ev-ery-thing's gon-na be   all right!

11. You'll Never Walk Alone

Words by Oscar Hammerstein II

Music by Richard Rodgers

dark._____ At the end of the storm is a

dark._____ At the end of the storm is a

gold - en sky And the sweet sil - ver song of a

gold - en sky And the sweet sil - ver song of a

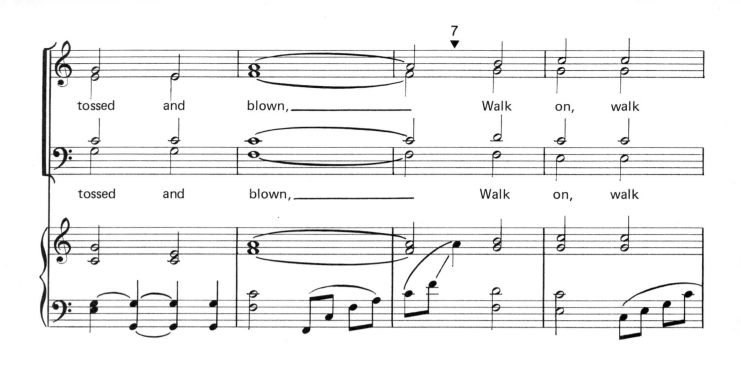

tossed and blown, _____ Walk on, walk

tossed and blown, _____ Walk on, walk

on, with hope in your heart, And you'll

on, with hope in your heart, And you'll

nev - er walk a - lone,_____ You'll

nev - er walk a - lone,_____ You'll

nev - er walk a - lone._____

nev - er walk a - lone._____

14. Good Night, Ladies/Pick a Little, Talk a Little

Words and Music by Meredith Willson

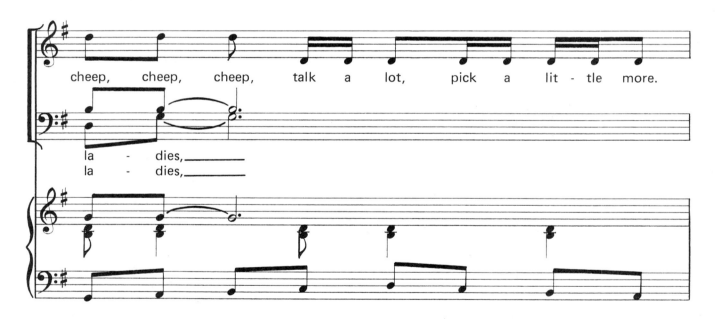

234

cheep, cheep, cheep, cheep, cheep, cheep, cheep, cheep!

Pick a lit - tle, talk a lit - tle, cheep!

16. Let the Rafters Ring

Words and Music by Dick Smith

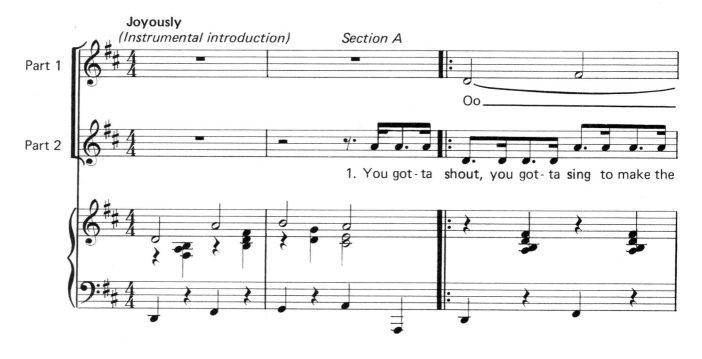

shout, you got-ta sing to make the raf - ters ring,__ You got-ta show ev-er-y-one that you care.__

1.2.

Section B

1. Now the **world needs a** man__ to lend a hand, So let's
2. Now__ we__ ain't great,__ we just con - cen - trate_____ On

all join to - geth - er and make our stand.__
how to free the world from man's greed and hate.__

You got - ta

3.7

3. Now we've

25. Mississippi Boatman's Song

Traditional

1. Oh, the boat - man dance, the ___ boat - man sing, The ___ boat - man good for ev - ery - thing. When the boat - man
2. The ___ oy - ster boat should ___ keep to shore, The ___ fish - ing smack should ven - ture more The ___ schoo - ner sails be -

comes on shore, He spends his mon-ey and he works for more.
fore the wind, The steam-boat leaves___ a___ streak be-hind.

Tr. I

Yo - ho! The boat-man row Up and down the ri-ver in his old ba - teau.

Tr. II

Yo - ho! The boat-man row Up and down the ri-ver in his old ba - teau.

C. V.

Yo - ho! The boat-man row Up and down the ri-ver in his old ba - teau.

Bar.

Yo - ho! The boat-man row Up and down the ri-ver in his old ba - teau.

26. Amen

Spiritual

24. Kol Dodi

Israeli Folk Song

Kol do - di, kol do - di, kol do - di, hi - ne ze ba.

M' - da - leg al he - ha - rim, ___ m' - ka - pets al ___ ha - g'va - ot.   ha - g'va - ot.

32. Fame

Lyrics by Dean Pitchford

Music by Michael Gore

Fame! I'm gon-na live___ for-ev - er.

I'm gon-na learn___how to fly___ high! I feel it com - in' to-geth-

er. Peo-ple will see___ me and die.___ Fame! I'm___

Repeat and fade

40. Waitin' for the Light to Shine

Words and Music by Roger Miller

I have lived in the dark-ness for so long, I'm wait-ing for the light to shine. Far be-yond horizons, I have seen be-yond the things I've been, be-yond the dreams I've dreamed, are the things I've done, In fact each and ev-ery one are the way that I was taught to

run. I am wait-ing for the light to shine,＿ I am

wait-ing for the light to shine. I have lived in the

dark-ness for so long, I'm wait-ing for the light to shine.

46. Leavin's Not the Only Way to Go

Words and Music by Roger Miller

Did the morn-ing come too ear - ly? Was the
lay and let your feel - ings grow ac-

night not long e - nough?__ Does a tear of hes - i - ta - tion fall____ on
cus-tomed to the dark ___ And by morn-ing's light you just_ might solve___ the

ev - ery-thing you touch? Well, it might be just a les - son for the
prob-lems of the heart. And it all might be a les - son for the

has - ty heart to know.___ May-be leav-in's not the on - ly way___ to go.___
has - ty heart to know.___ May-be leav-in's not the on - ly way___ to go.___

1. **2.**

___ 2. May-be ___ Peo-ple

reach new___ un - der-stand - ings all___ the time. They take a sec-ond

look, may-be change their mind. Peo-ple

reach new un-der-stand-ings ev-ery day.___ Tell me not to

reach, I'll just go a - way.___ Did the

morn-ing come too ear - ly? Was the night not long e-nough?___ Does a

tear of hes-i-ta - tion fall___ on ev-ery-thing___ you touch? Well, it

might be just a les - son   for the has - ty heart to know,___   May-be

leav - in's   not the on - ly way___ to go.___   And a

heart with-out__ a home__   is such a lone - ly row to hoe.   May-be

leav - in's   not the on - ly way___   to go.___

42. Muddy Water

Words and Music by Roger Miller

Look out for me, oh, mud-dy wa - ter, your mys-ter-ies____ are deep and wide,____ And I got a need for go - in' some - place, and I____ got a

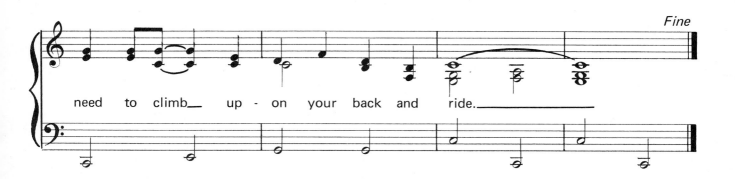

need to climb___ up-on your back and ride.___

Verses

You can look for me
Well___ I been me down

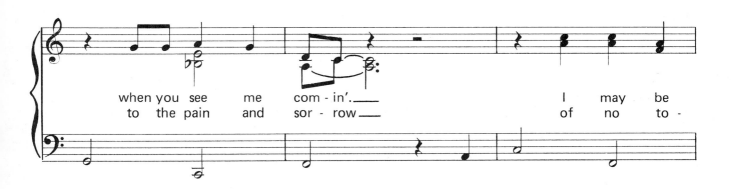

when you see me com-in'.___   I may be
to the pain and sor-row___   of no to-

Refrain   D. S. al Fine

run - nin', I don't know.   I may be
mor - rows com - in' in,   But I put my

tired _____ and run - nin' fe - ver,   but I'll be
pole _____ to the riv - er bot - tom   and I got - ta

head - in' south _ for the mouth of the O - hi - o.   So look out for
hide some - place _ to _ find my - self a - gain.   So look out for

50. When I'm on My Journey

Afro-American Song

69. Procession from *A Ceremony of Carols*

Music by Benjamin Britten

ho - di - e_____ ex - sul - tant jus - ti_____

di - cen - tes:___ glo - ri - a in ex - cel - sis___ De - o. Al - le - lu - ia!

Al - le - lu - ia! Al - le - lu - ia!

70. Morning Has Broken

Words by Eleanor Farjean

Gaelic Melody
Arranged by Buryl Red

1. Morn - ing has bro - ken   Like the first
2. Sweet the rain's new fall   Sun - lit from
3. Mine is the sun - light;   Mine is the

morn - ing,   Black-bird has spo - ken   Like the first
heav - en,   Like the first dew - fall   On the first
morn - ing   Born of the one light   E - den saw

oh _____

bird._____ Praise for the sing - ing; Praise for the
grass. Praise,__ oh praise for the sweet - ness of the wet
play._____Praise,__ oh praise with e - la - tion, Praise ev - ery

Praise__ oh praise,_____ Praise__ oh praise the

morn - ing; Praise for them spring - ing Fresh from the Word._____
gar - den, Sprung in com - plete - ness Where his feet pass._____
morn - ing, God's re - cre - a - tion Of the new day._____

oh__

72. *So Ben Mi Ch'a Bon Tempo*

Words of unknown authorship

Music by Orazio Vecchi

tem - po, Fa la la la, la la la la la la la;
i - to, Fa la la la, la la la la la la la;
di - re, Fa la la la, la la la la la la la;

tem - po, Fa la la la, la la la la la la;
i - to, Fa la la la, la la la la la la;
di - re, Fa la la la, la la la la la la;

tem - po, Fa la la la, la la la la la la;
i - to, Fa la la la, la la la la la la;
di - re, Fa la la la, la la la la la la;

tem - po, Fa la la la, la la la la la la;
i - to, Fa la la la, la la la la la la;
di - re, Fa la la la, la la la la la la;

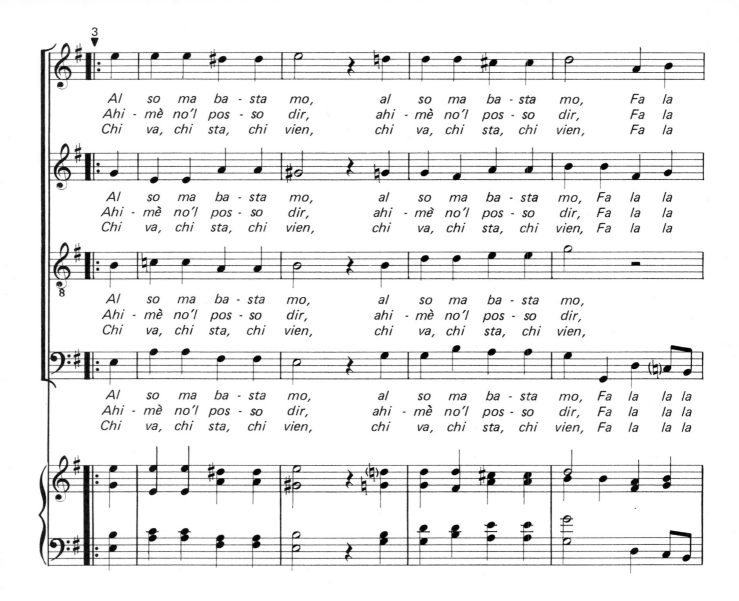

Al so ma ba - sta mo, al so ma ba - sta mo, Fa la
Ahi - mè no'l pos - so dir, ahi - mè no'l pos - so dir, Fa la
Chi va, chi sta, chi vien, chi va, chi sta, chi vien, Fa la

Al so ma ba - sta mo, al so ma ba - sta mo, Fa la la
Ahi - mè no'l pos - so dir, ahi - mè no'l pos - so dir, Fa la la
Chi va, chi sta, chi vien, chi va, chi sta, chi vien, Fa la la

Al so ma ba - sta mo, al so ma ba - sta mo,
Ahi - mè no'l pos - so dir, ahi - mè no'l pos - so dir,
Chi va, chi sta, chi vien, chi va, chi sta, chi vien,

Al so ma ba - sta mo, al so ma ba - sta mo, Fa la la la
Ahi - mè no'l pos - so dir, ahi - mè no'l pos - so dir, Fa la la la
Chi va, chi sta, chi vien, chi va, chi sta, chi vien, Fa la la la

la   la   la,   la   la   la   la   la   la   la.
la   la   la,   la   la   la   la   la   la   la.
la   la   la,   la   la   la   la   la   la   la.

la la la la,   Fa___   la   la   la   la   la   la   la   la.
la la la la,   Fa___   la   la   la   la   la   la   la   la.
la la la la,   Fa___   la   la   la   la   la   la   la   la.

Fa la la   la   la,   la   la   la   la   la.
Fa la la   la   la,   la   la   la   la   la.
Fa la la   la   la,   la   la   la   la   la.

la la la, Fa la   la   la   la   la   la   la   la   la.
la la la, Fa la   la   la   la   la   la   la   la   la.
la la la, Fa la   la   la   la   la   la   la   la   la.

95. A Stranger May Seem Strange

Words by Horace Everett

Music by Aaron Copland

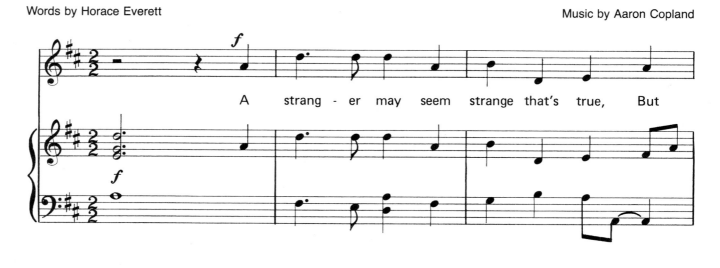

A strang - er may seem strange that's true, But

did it ev - er oc - cur to you that You seem strange to a

strang - er, seem strange to a strang - er seem strange to a

strang - er too. We've come,＿＿＿＿＿＿

We've come,＿＿＿＿＿＿ We've

98. Stomp Your Foot Upon the Floor

Words by Horace Everett

Music by Aaron Copland

Stomp your foot up-on the floor. Throw the win-dows op - en.

Take a breath of fresh June air, and dance a-round the room, and

dance a-round the room.

99. The Plains So Green

Words by Horace Everett

Music by Aaron Copland

in each o - ther's heart._____

in each o - ther's heart._____

mp
The fields of love,

mp
The ten - der grain,

we'll gath - er in

from au - tumn

We'll reap the tears, and gath-er in each rain.

We've wept a -part, and gath-er

oth - er's heart.

in each oth - er's heart.

110. Rufus Rustus and Chicken

Camp Song

ev-ery-bod-y knows that you can't pay the rent if you ain't got the dough.

near-ing the end, and "E," now you're round-ing the bend.

Ru-fus Rus-tus John-son Brown, oh, what you gon-na do when the rain comes down?

C-H-I-C-K-E-N, oh, that's the way you spell *(clap, clap)* chick - en.

112. When You and I Were Young Maggie Blues

Words by Jack Frost

Music by Timmy McHugh

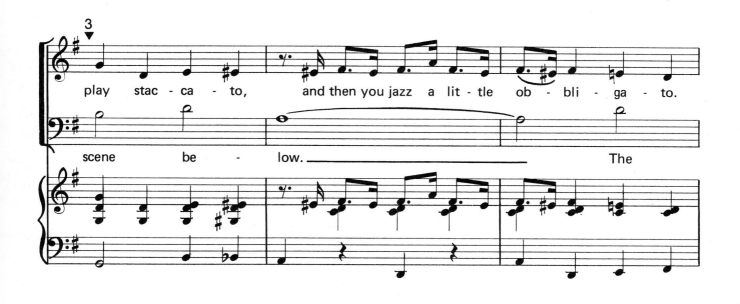

play stac-ca-to, and then you jazz a lit-tle ob-bli-ga-to.

scene be - low. _____ The

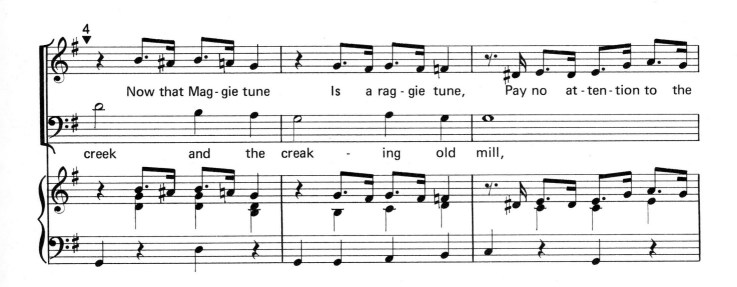

Now that Mag-gie tune Is a rag-gie tune, Pay no at-ten-tion to the

creek and the creak - ing old mill,

282

Ev-ery lov-in' note is a lov-in' boat, just full of mus-ic that you once the dai-sies sprung.

can't re-fuse. Now you know the way tell the band to play, But I love you the same as of

and when you lis-ten just christ-en it and say I've got these old, Mag-gie, when

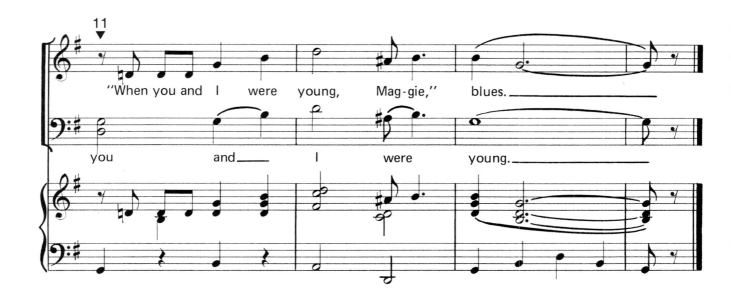

"When you and I were young, Mag-gie," blues._____

you and____ I were young._____

115. Looky, Looky Yonder

American Folk Song

2. Ax is a-walkin', *(3 times)*
   Where the sun goes down.

3. Chips are a-talkin', *(3 times)*
   When the sun goes down.

4. Hear us singing, *(3 times)*
   When the sun goes down.

5. In the evening, *(3 times)*
   When the sun goes down.

116. The Water Is Wide

American Folk Song

2. I once leaned against a young oak tree,
   It seemed as strong as my love seemed,
   It bended and then it broke, you see,
   My love was not the dream I dreamed.

3. The water is wide, I cannot get over,
   There's no true love, at least not for me,
   My love was untrue but I can't complain,
   Someday I hope to love again.

117. Hand Me Down My Walkin' Cane

Southern Mountain Song

Oh, hand me down my walk-in' cane, Gon-na leave on the mid-night cane, Oh, hand me down my walk-in' cane, leave on that

train. All my sins been tak-en a-way, tak-en a-way.____

train. Sins been tak-en a-way, a-way.____

2. Oh, if I die in Tennessee, (*3 times*)
   Just ship me back, C.O.D.
   All my sins been taken away,
       taken away.

118. Rock Around the Clock

Words and Music by Max Freedman and
Jimmy De Knight

One, two, three o'-clock, four o'-clock, rock, Five, six, sev-en o'-clock,

Eight o'-clock, rock. Nine, ten, e-lev-en o'-clock,

twelve o'-clock, rock. We're gon-na rock a-round the clock to-night.— 1. Put your

glad rags on and join me, hon',— We'll have some fun when the
2. clock strikes two and three and four,— If the band slows down we'll—

clock strikes one,
ask for more, } We're gon-na rock a-round the clock to-night,— We're gon-na

rock rock rock till broad day-light,__ We're gon-na rock, gon-na rock a - round__ the clock__ to - night!__

1.

2. When__ the

120. Mango Walk

Traditional

125. Buffalo Gals

Music by Cool White

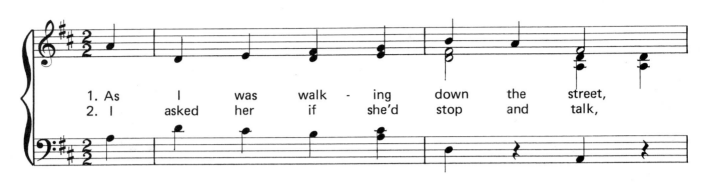

1. As I was walk - ing down the street,
2. I asked her if she'd stop and talk,

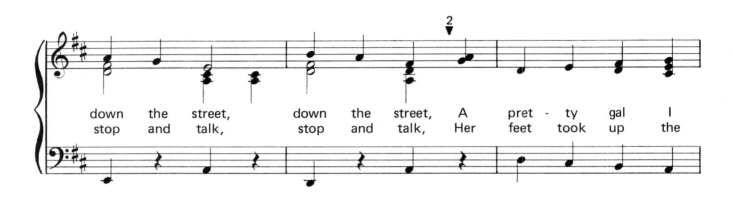

down the street, down the street, A pret - ty gal I
stop and talk, down and stop talk, Her feet took up the

chanced to meet, Oh, she was fair to see.
whole side - walk and left no room for me.

Oh, Buf-fa-lo Gals, won't you come out to-night,

come out to-night, come out to-night? Oh, Buf-fa-lo Gals, won't you

come out to-night and dance by the light of the moon?

127. Down in the Valley

Traditional

Down in the val - ley, val - ley so low, _____

Hang your head o - ver, hear the wind blow. _____

127. Taps

U.S. Army Bugle Call

Day is done, gone the sun, From the

lake, from the hill, from the sky. All is

well, safe - ly rest, God is nigh.

128. Can the Circle Be Unbroken?

Adapted and Arranged by Dan Fox

Can the cir - cle_____ be un - bro - ken?_____ By and by, Lord,

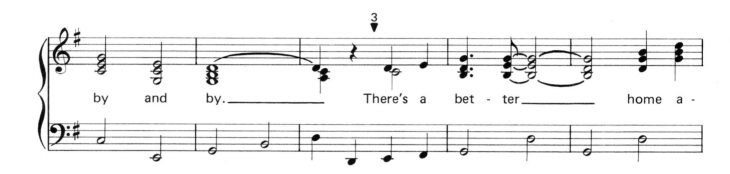

by and by._____ There's a bet - ter_____ home a -

wait - ing_____ in the sky, Lord, in the sky._____

129. The Cruel War

Words by Peter Yarrow

Music by Paul Stookey

1. The cruel war is rag - ing and John - ny has to fight, I
2. I'll go to your cap - tain, get down___ on my knees, Ten
3. Ten thou - sand gold guin - eas, it grieves___ my heart so; Won't you

want to be with him from morn - ing till night.
thou - sand gold guin - eas I'd give for your re - lease.
let me go with you? Oh, no, my love, no.

130. Gotta Travel On

Words and Music by Paul Clayton

I've laid a-round and played a-round this old town too long,

Sum-mer's al-most gone, yes, win-ter's com-ing on. I've

laid a-round and played a-round this old town too long, And I

feel like I've got-ta tra-vel on._____

138. The Keys of Canterbury

English Folk Song

1. Oh Ma - dam, I will give to you the keys of Can - ter -
2. I shall not, Sir, ac - cept of you the keys of Can - ter -

bu - ry. And all the bells in Lon - don shall ring to make us
bu - ry. Nor all the bells of Lon - don shall ring to make us

mer - ry, If you will be my joy,_____ my sweet and on - ly
mer - ry, I will not be your joy,_____ your sweet and on - ly

dear,_____ And walk a - long with me, a - ny - where._____
dear,_____ And walk a - long with you, a - ny - where._____

140. Go Tell Aunt Rhody

Traditional

Go tell Aunt Rho - dy,

Go tell Aunt Rho - dy, Go tell Aunt

Rho - dy, the old gray goose is dead.

142. The Highwayman

English Folk Song

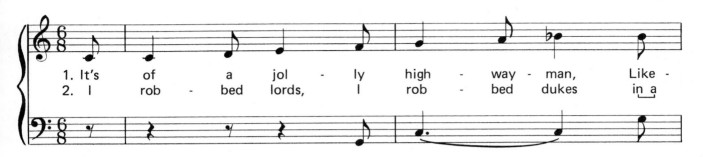

1. It's of a jol - ly high - way - man, Like -
2. I rob - bed lords, I rob - bed dukes in a

wise a no - ted rov - er, I drove my par - ents
ve - ry rak - ish man - ner, Not on - ly to main -

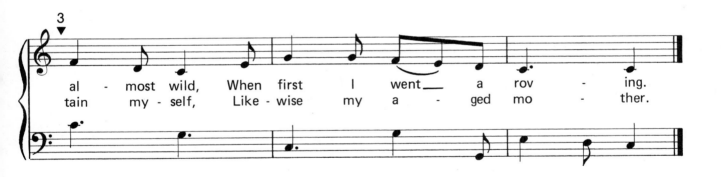

al - most wild, When first I went a rov - ing.
tain my - self, Like - wise my a - ged mo - ther.

143. Old Joe Clark

American Folk Song

Verse

1. Old Joe Clark, he had a house   six - teen sto - ries high;
2. I went down to Old Joe's house,   nev-er been there be - fore.

2

Ev - ery sto - ry in that house was filled with chick - en pie.
He slept on a feath - er bed and I slept on the floor.

Refrain

3

Round and round, Old Joe Clark,   Round and round I say;

4

Round and round, Old Joe Clark,   I have - n't long to stay.

148. Carry It On

Words by Marion Wade

Music by Gil Turner

Theres a man by my side walk-in'. Theres a voice in-side me talk-in'. Theres a word needs a say-in': Carry it on, carry it on. Carry it on, carry it on.

162. Come Join in the Chorus

Music by Wolfgang Amadeus Mozart

Introduction not accounted for on pupil page.

Come __

charm-ing, so joy-ful, so bright to the ear! La-ra-la la la

la-ra-la la la la-ra-la! So___ la!

166. Who?

Scandinavian Folk Song

1. Who can sail when there is no wind? Who with-out oars can go row - ing?
2. I can sail when there is no wind. With - out __ oars I'll be row - ing.

Who can go far a - way from __ friends with-out tears __ a - flow-ing?
But I can't go a - way from __ friends with-out tears __ a - flow - ing.

164. The Gift of Song

Words and Music by Patti Ingalls
Arranged by Buryl Red

way. _____ As I re - ceive _____ so may I
share. _____ As I re - ceive _____ so let me

way. _____ As I re - ceive _____ so may I
share. _____ As I re - ceive _____ so let me

give, _____ And live with joy through - out my life. _____
give, _____ And live with joy my whole life through. _____

give, _____ And live with joy through - out my life. _____
give, _____ And live with joy my whole life through. _____

The gift of song   is a gift of love,
The gift of song   is a gift of love,

The gift of song is a gift of love,
The gift of song is a gift of love,

My heart has heard   it   in   the   night.
And now I've sung   my   song   to   you.

My heart has heard   it   in   the   night.
And now I've sung   my   song   to   you.

168. Wadaleeacha

Traditional

Wa - da-lee - a - cha, wa - da-lee - a - cha, Doo - dle-dee-doo,__

doo - dle-dee - doo.__ Wa - da-lee - a - cha, wa - da-lee - a - cha,

Doo-dle-dee-doo,__ doo-dle-dee-doo.__ Sim-plest thing, there is-n't much to__ it,

All you got-ta do is doo-dle-dee-doo__ it. I like the rest of it, but

what I like best__ is Doo-dle-dee, doo-dle-dee-doo. Yeah!

169. Aura Lee

American Folk Song

170. Bye, Bye, Blues

Words and Music by Fred Hamm, Dave
Bennett, Bert Lown, and Chauncey Gray

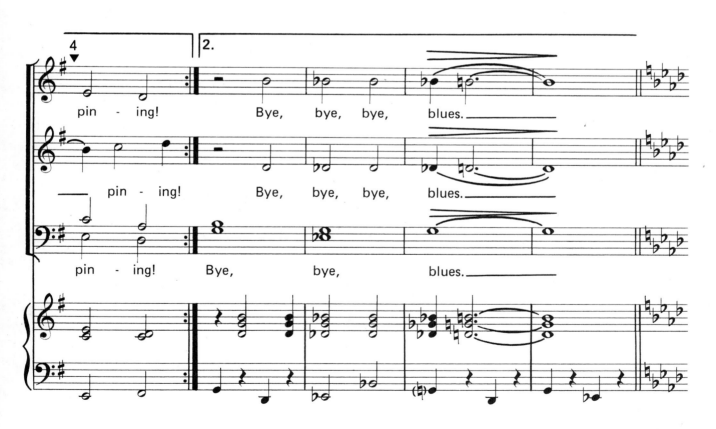

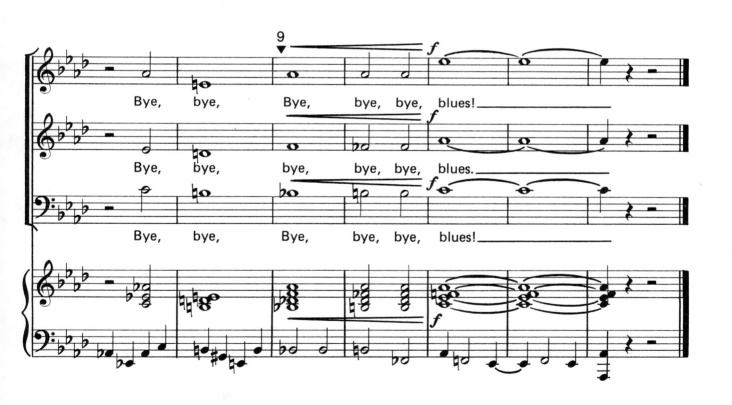

174. By the Light of the Silvery Moon

Words by Edward Madden

Music by Gus Edwards
Arranged by Buryl Red

176. There's a Long, Long, Trail

Words by Stoddard King

Music by Zo Elliot
Arranged by Buryl Red

Cue size notes in the treble clef may be played on any instrument, in any range, or they may be hummed by a solo voice, or whistled.

Till the day when I'll be
dreams all come true Till the day when I'll be
go - ing down that long, long trail___ with you.
go - ing down that long, long trail with you.

184. Standin' on the Walls of Zion

Music by Maurice Gardner

stand-in' on the walls of Zi-on, Zi - on, Zi - on,

stand-in' on the walls of Zi-on, Zi - on, Zi - on,

Saw my ship a-sail-in' home,— Zi - on, Zi - on.

Saw my ship a-sail-in' home,— Zi - on, Zi - on.

1. See that ship a-sail-in' to the Prom-ised Land.____
2. Sails like she's a-heav-y load-ed, Zi - on, Zi - on.

1. See that ship a-sail-in' to the Prom-ised Land.____
2. Sails like she's a-heav-y load-ed, Zi - on, Zi - on.

See that ship a-sail-in' to the Prom-ised Land.____
Sails like she's a-heav-y load-ed, Zi - on, Zi - on.

See that ship a-sail-in' to the Prom-ised Land.____
Sails like she's a-heav-y load-ed, Zi - on, Zi - on.

Shall I be on that ship when she sails?

Shall I be on that ship when she sails?

Shall I be on that ship when she sails? Yes I'm a -

Shall I be on that ship when she sails? Yes I'm a -

188. Roll On, Columbia

Words and Music by Woody Guthrie

1. Green Doug-las fir where the wa-ters cut through, Down her wild
2. Oth - er great riv - ers add pow - er to you, Ya - ki - ma,
3. Tom Jef - fer - son's vi - sion would not let him rest; An em - pire he
4. At Bon - ne - ville now there are ships in the locks; The wat - ers have
5. And on up the riv - er is Grand Cou - lee Dam, The might - i - est

moun - tains and can - yons she flew, Ca - na - dian North - west to the
Snake, and the Klick - i - tat, too, Sand - y Wil - la - mette and
saw in the Pa - cif - ic North - west; Sent Lew - is and Clark and
ris - en and cleared all the rocks. Ship - loads of plen - ty will
thing ev - er built by a man, To run the great fact - 'ries and

ROLL ON COLUMBIA, words by Woody Guthrie, music based on
"GOODNIGHT IRENE" by Huddie Ledbetter and John A. Lomax
TRO—© Copyright 1936 (renewed 1964), 1950 (renewed 1978), 1957
(renewed 1985) and 1963 Ludlow Music, Inc., New York, NY   Used by
Permission

o - cean so blue;
Hood Riv - er too;
they did the rest;
steam past the docks;
wat - er the land;

Roll on, Co - lum - bia, roll on! _____

Refrain

Tr. I
Bar.
(8ve lower)

Roll on, roll on, _____ Roll

Tr. II
C. V.

Roll on, Co - lum - bia, roll on! Roll

(melody)

on, roll on, _____ Roll on, roll

on, Co-lum-bia, roll on, Your pow-er is turn-ing the

on, _____ Roll on, Co-lum-bia, roll on! _____

dark-ness to dawn; Roll on, Co-lum-bia, roll on! _____

190. Freedom

Words by Peter Udell

Music By Gary Geld

train._____ The on-ly way to free-dom is right on through your brain._____

train._____ Go - in'

CODA

D. S. % al Coda ⊕

⊕

Wo-wo - wo - wo-wo.

of mind! Free-dom!

D. S. % al Coda ⊕

gliss.

192. One of Those Songs

Words by Will Holt

Music by Gregoire Krettly

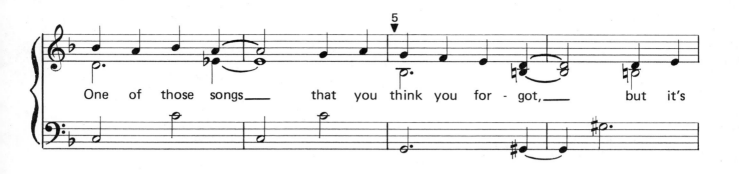

One of those songs___ that you think you for-got,___ but it's

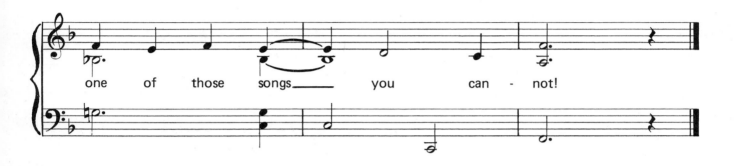

one of those songs___ you can - not!

195. Canción de la Luna

Mexican Folk Song

Verse (Tr. I and II, unison)

A las dos de la ma-ña-na Que le ven-go a des-per-tas,
Con vio-li-nes y gui-tar-ras Yo te vi-ne a sal-u-dar.

Refrain (C. V. and Bar. 8ve lower, unison)

Des-pier-ta, mi bien, des-pier-ta, Des-pier-ta ya aman-e-ció;
Ya los pa-ja-ros can-tar-ón Y la lu-na se me-tió.

343

193. Follow

Words and Music by Jack Noble White
Arranged by Buryl Red

196. *El Cumbanchero*

Words and Music by Rafael Hernandez

199. Matilda

Traditional

Adapted by Massie Patterson and
Sammy Heyward

When that Ma- til -da, she take me mon - ey an' run Ve - ne - zue - la.

Oi, oi Ma - til - da run a - way.

D. C.

{ Sing de cho - rus!
{ To de last time!

Coda

5

run Ve - ne - zue - la.____

200. *Laredo*

Mexican Folk Song

I leave now to go to La-re-do, my love, I come here to say fare- well.___ While I'm
Ya me voy pa-ra el La-re-do, mi bien, Te ven-go a de-cir a-diós.___ De a-

there, I will sore-ly miss you, my love, how much I can nev-er tell._____
llá te man-do de-cir,___ mi bien, co-mo se man-cuer-nan dos._____

202. Sigh No More, Ladies, Sigh No More

Words by William Shakespeare

Music by Emma Lou Diemer

Sigh no more, la - dies, sigh no more, Sigh no more, no

Sigh no more, la - dies, sigh no more,

Sigh no more, la - dies, sigh no more, Sigh no more, no

more! Men were de - cei - vers ev - er,

more!

more! Men were de - cei - vers ev - er, one foot in

207. Sheep Safely Graze

Words by Eloise Williams

Music by J.S. Bach

Introduction not accounted for in Pupil's Book.

Sheep safe-ly graze a-mid ver-dant pas-tures; The shep-herd keeps a care - ful

watch o'er his flock. Sheep safe-ly graze a-mid ver-dant pas-tures; Se-

rene - ly they graze in safe - ty, While tend - ed by the shep - herd.

'Midst the ver-dant fields they safe - ly graze; Ten-der-ly the

shep - herd guards his flock.

Ten-der-ly he guards_____ his flock.

208. The Sleigh

Music by Richard Kountz
Arranged by Wallingford Riegger

Mer - ri - ly we go, Ho, hal - lo! Mer-ri - ly on we go.

Mer - ri - ly we go, Ho, hal - lo! Mer-ri - ly on we go.

Mer - ri - ly we go, Ho, hal - lo! Mer-ri - ly on we go.

Mer - ri - ly we go, Ho, hal - lo! Mer-ri - ly on we go.

Ho, hal - lo! Mer-ri - ly on we go. Hah - hah - hah -

Ho, hal - lo! Mer-ri - ly on we go.

Ho, hal - lo! Mer-ri - ly on we go.

Ho, hal - lo! Mer-ri - ly on we go.

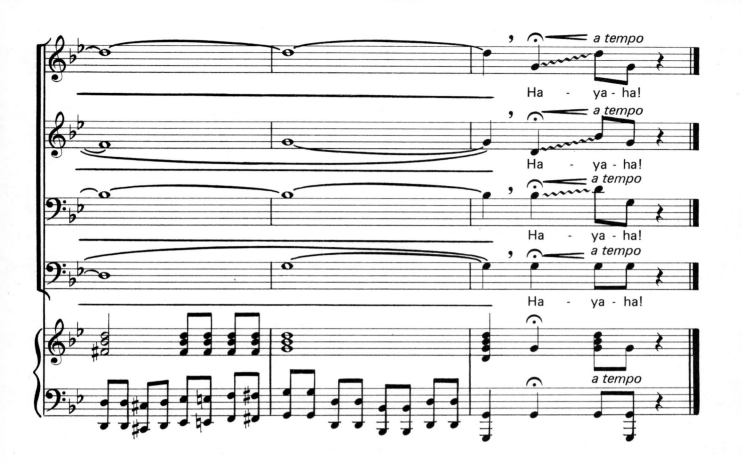

Ha - ya - ha!

Ha - ya - ha!

Ha - ya - ha!

Ha - ya - ha!

212. A Christmas Happening

Music by Buryl Red

Introduction not accounted for in Pupil's Book.

Bright rock tempo

Fa la la,

Fa la la, _____ Fa la la, _____ Fa la la, _____ Oh!

Deck the hall with boughs of hol - ly, Fa la la la la, la la la la.___
'Tis the sea - son to___ be jol - ly, Fa la la la la, la la la la.___

Fa___ la la la la la la.___

Sing we joy - ous all___ to - geth - er, Fa la la, la la la, la la la la___ la,

Sing we all___ to - geth - er, Fa la la, la la la la___ la,

*Play an octave lower on repeat.

Glo -

ri - a   in ex - cel - sis De - o,   in ex - cel - sis

* *Play as is.*

* *The last section is done in this manner: different voices, one at a time, speak at random in the various languages.*
This builds as the phrases are spoken by more and more voices until the speaking eventually overpowers the music.

216. Grab Another Hand

Traditional

lu - ya. Al - le -
lu - ya. Al - le -

hand next to ya, Grab_____ an - oth - er hand and
hand next to ya, Shake_____ an - oth - er hand and
hand next to ya, Clap_____ an - oth - er hand and
hand next to ya, Raise_____ an - oth - er hand and
friend next to ya, Hug_____ an - oth - er friend and

lu - ya. Sing this song Al - la, la, la, la, la____
lu - ya. Sing this song Al - la, la, la, la, la____

sing._____ Sing this song Al - la, la, la, la, la____

la, le - lu - ya, Al - la, la, la, la, la, la, ____ la, le - lu,

la, le - lu - ya, Al - la, la, la, la, la, la, ____ la, le - lu,

____ la, le - lu - ya, Al - la, la, la, la, la, la, ____ la, le - lu,

Al - le - lu - ya, Al - le -

Al - le - lu - ya, Al - le -

Al - la, la, la, la, la, la, ____ la, la - lu - ya, Al - la, la, la, la, la, le -

lu - ya, Al - le - lu - ya.

lu - ya, Al - le - lu - ya.

lu - ya, Al - le - lu - ya.

219. Let the Sun Shine In

Words by James Rado and
Jerome Ragni

Music by Galt MacDermot

shine in,___ the sun shine in.

shine in,___ the sun shine in._____

repeat ad lib. until fade-out

Teacher's Glossary

Blues a style of popular music emerging from the Afro-American work songs and spirituals of the first decade of the 20th century; often follows a 12-bar chord sequence

Blues notes in jazz, refers to lowering the pitch a half step for scale steps 3, 7, and (occasionally) 5

Bongo drums a pair of single head drums that are usually tunable and of the same height, but different diameters; normally played with the hands

Broken chord the pattern produced by the successive execution of the notes of a chord; an arpeggio

Cadence the part of a melodic line or chord sequence that moves to a point of rest

Cadenza A florid passage that usually serves as a technical display for a solo performer

Changing Voice (C.V.) the transitional stage of the male voice

Chord progression see chord sequence

Chord root the note of a triad that determines the remaining pitches, regardless of their relative position

Chord sequence a given succession of harmonies in a piece of music; chord progression

Chord symbols the signs that label the names of chords, and often their inversions (the relative position of the lowest note in a chord)

Chromatic scale in Western music, the twelve half steps of the octave played one after the other

Chromatic tone a pitch that is not part of a given diatonic scale or key signature

Claves a Latin-American percussion instrument consisting of a pair of hard wooden sticks which are struck together

Cocktail shaker a covered metal can filled with beans, seeds, rice, etc; often used in Latin-American percussion, played by shaking back and forth over the shoulder

Coda a concluding section that is sometimes added to the main part of a composition

Conga drum a single-head drum that is tuned with tension rods; played with the hands

Consort usually, an early music ensemble of vocalists or instrumentalists; also, a set of instruments from the same family, i.e. a consort of viols

Contour usually, the shape of the melody; often, a drawing of a melodic shape

Countermelody a melody added to another, providing contrast or harmonic color

Cowbell a metal bell, used in Latin-American percussion sections, which is bent and fused rather than cast, struck with a beater

Descant a harmony part played or sung at a higher pitch than the melody

Dominant seventh chord the chord built on the fifth scale degree with an added seventh; in the key of C the dominant seventh chord would be g–b–d–f

Drone a repetitive, continuous sound; often used as an accompaniment

Dulcimer (mountain, Appalachian) an American folk instrument whose exact origin has not been traced; having an oval wooden sound box and a narrow fretted fingerboard; the melody string(s) depressed with a noter (dowel) and all the strings strummed with a pick

Fantasia (fantasy) usually, an instrumental composition that takes its form directly from the composer's imagination rather than from a predetermined format

Fine literally "the end"

Form the shape of an entire piece of music in which individual sections may be the same, similar, or different

Gospel a style of American music associated with evangelism and popular devotion; often includes elements of spiritual, jazz, and folk music

Gourd a Latin-American percussion instrument made from either a natural or artificial gourd; the sound produced by shaking or turning the beads inside

Guiro a Latin-American percussion instrument, made from a hollow gourd which has been notched; played by scraping over the notches with a stick

Half step the smallest interval in traditional Western music; equivalent to the distance between any two adjacent keys on a keyboard

Harpsichord a keyboard instrument similar in shape to a small grand piano, its sound produced by thin pieces of crow quills or leather that pluck the strings as the keys are depressed

Ikon a visual image of musical notation

Indefinite pitch usually, a sound or an instrument lacking a precise (or identifiable) pitch

Interlude a section of a musical work that is inserted between two larger sections

Intonation the accurate relationship of pitches to each other; tuning

Introduction a section of music that comes before the main part of the composition

Lute an ancient plucked instrument having a round body shaped like a pear half; produces gentle, finely shaded tones

Maracas a pair of rattles often used in Latin American percussion

Musical a uniquely American form of musical theater that has its roots in vaudeville, light opera, and other stage productions of the early part of this century

Neumes the notational signs that were used to write down music during the Middle Ages

Opera a dramatic musical presentation in which the actors express themselves in song rather than speech, and which also utilizes many other art forms (acting, dancing, etc.)

Orchestration the arrangement of a piece of music for an orchestra; usually refers to instrumentation

Overture usually, the instrumental introduction (prelude) to a music drama; occasionally an independent concert piece for orchestra

Pavane a stately court dance or piece in a slow duple rhythm dating from the 16th century

Percussion an instrument played by striking or shaking; includes the xylophone, celesta, chimes, orchestra bells, timpani and other drums, gongs and cymbals, temple blocks, claves, tambourines, and maracas

Polyrhythm two or more contrasting rhythms that are played simultaneously

Polytonality two or more melodies in different keys that are played simultaneously

Pulse see **beat**

Recorder   an early type of vertical flute that has a soft and slightly reedy tone quality

Recording engineer   someone who manipulates all equipment in a recording studio and is responsible for the quality of the recorded sound

Reverberation   sound continuation; series of echoes

Rhythm section   the rhythmic nucleus or core of a stage, rock, or jazz band, consisting of piano, guitar, bass, and drum set, with other instruments occasionally added: i.e., tambourine, maracas, etc.

Rondo   a classical form that includes two or more episodes (B and C) and a recurring refrain (A), so that the resulting scheme might be ABACA

Scat singing   a style of jazz singing with vocal syllables that often imitate instruments

Score   a notation illustrating the instruments or voices of an ensemble and their particular parts

Semitones   See **half step**

Strings   instruments played by plucking or bowing strings; includes the violin, viola, cello, and double bass

Symphony   usually, a large piece of music of three to four movements in length performed by an orchestra

Synthesizer   an electronic instrument used to produce and organize musical sounds

Temple blocks   a series of hollow, circular blocks played with felt or wooden sticks

Tessitura   the normal range of a melody or a voice part

Tie   a sign used to join two or more notes of the same pitch thus; a single note equal to the length of both notes

Timpani   two or more large hemispherical drums tuned in definite pitches used extensively in orchestral writing; occasionally used as a solo instrument

Transposition   writing or performing a composition in a key other than its original

Tremolo   the rapid reiteration of one pitch or of alternating pitches

Triad   a three-note chord consisting of the root, third, and fifth; the four types of triads including the major (consisting of a major and a minor third), the minor (a minor and a major third), the diminished (two minor thirds), and the augmented (two major thirds)

Trill   the rapid alternation of two consecutive pitches

Waltz   a ballroom dance or instrumental piece in $\frac{3}{4}$ meter with a strong accent on the first beat; dates from the 19th century

Woodwinds   instruments, usually made of wood or metal, in which the sound is produced by vibrations resulting from air blowing into or across a mouthpiece or reed; including the flute, oboe, clarinet, and bassoon

MEDIEVAL AND RENAISSANCE (c. 1000–1600)

ANTHOLOGIES

Vocal & and Instrumental:	*Music of the Gothic Era* (with illustrated 52-page book), Early Music Consort of London, David Munrow	*3 DG ARC-2710019 DG ARC-415292-2AH (excerpts)*
Plainchant:	*Gregorian Chant,* Deller Consort	*Harmoni Mundi 234*

COMPOSERS

Josquin Des Prez:	*Chansons of Josquin Des Prez,* Hilliard Ensemble	*Angel S-38040(D)*
Morley:	*Madrigals of Thomas Morley,* Deller Consort	*Vanguard HM-4*
Palestrina:	*Motets* (with Veni Spousa Christi — Mass, Motet, and Antiphon), St. Johns College Choir of Cambridge, Guest	*Argo ZK-69 PSI*

BAROQUE (1600–1750)

Bach:	*Six Brandenburg Concerti,* English Chamber Orchestra, Leppard	*2-Phil 6747166*
	Cantata 140, "Wachet auf" (with *Cantata 80, "Ein Feste Burg"*), Munich Bach Orchestra and Chorus, Richter	*DG ARC 2533495*
Corelli:	*Christmas Concerto* (with Op. 6, Nos. 5–7), La Petite Bande, Kujiken	*D Har Mon H-99613(Q)*
Handel:	*Water Music* (with *Music for the Royal Fireworks*), Academy of St. Martin's in the Fields, Marriner	*Argo ZRG-697*
Monteverdi:	*Incoronazione di Poppea,* Concentus Musicus, Harnoncourt	*5-Teldec 5635247 Teldec 641974 (excerpts)*
Purcell:	*King Arthur, Dido and Aeneas, Dioclesian, Fairy Queen, Abdelazer,* City of London Chamber Orchestra, McIntosh	*Vox C 9005(D)*
Scarlatti:	*Harpsichord Sonatas,* Kirkpatrick	*DG-ARC-2533072 (Vol. 1)*
Vivaldi:	*Concerto for Two Violins,* St. Paul Chamber Orchestra, Stern, Zuckerman	*CBS IM/MK 37278 (D)*

CLASSICAL (1750–1825)

Haydn:	*Symphony No. 104 in D* (with *Symphony No. 100*), New Philharmonia, Klemperer	*Angel AE-34464*
	String Quartets, Op. 77, Nos. 1 & 2, Guarneri Quartet	*AGL1—4898*
	Piano Trios 14 & 15, Beaux Arts Trio	*Phillips 9500034 PSI*
	Mass in Time of War, Academy of St. Martin's in the Fields, Marriner	*Argo ZRG 0 634 PSI*
Mozart:	*Symphony Nos. 40, 41, & 39,* Israel Philharmonic, Mehta	*Lon 410277-4*
	Magic Flute, K. 620, Vienna Philharmonic, Levine	*CRC4-4586 (D) ARC1-4621 (excerpts)*
	String Quartet in F, K. 590, No. 23 (with Nos. 17 & 19, and Beethoven: Nos. 2, 3, & 10), Budapest Quartet	*3 Odys Y3-35240*
	Piano Concerto No. 21 in C, K. 467, Cleveland Orchestra, Casadesus, Szell	*CBS MY-38523*
	Oboe Quartet, K. 370 (with J. C. Bach, Stamitz, & Vanhal Oboe Quartets), Still, Perlman, Zuckerman, Harrell	*Angel S-37756*
	Mass in C Minor, K. 427, Vienna Singverein, Berlin Philharmonic, Karajan	*DG 2532028 (D)*

ROMANTIC (1825–1900)

Beethoven: *Symphony No. 5*, NBC Symphony Orchestra, Toscanini — RCA-VICS-1648E

String Quartet Op. 59, No. 1 in F, "Rasumovsky" (with *Op. 59, Nos. 2 & 3; Ops. 74 & 95*), Guarneri Quartet — 4 RCA VCS 6415

Berlioz: *Symphonie Fantastique*, Boston Symphony Orchestra, Munch — RCA-AGL1-5203

Brahms: *Clarinet Quintet in B Minor, Op. 115*, Leister, Vermeer Quartet — S 068831

Symphony No. 3, Cleveland Orchestra, Szell — CBS-MY-37777

Mahler: *Symphony No. 5* (with *Kindertotenlieder*) New York Philharmonic, Walter — 2 Odys 32260016 E

Mendelssohn: *Violin Concerto, Op. 64* (with Bruch: *Violin Concerto*), Perlman, Concertgebouw Orchestra, Haitink — Angel DS 38150 (D)

Schubert: *Die Schöne Müllerin*, Fischer-Diskau, Gerald Moore — DG 415186-2GH

Symphony No. 8, "Unfinished," Concertgebouw Orchestra, Haitink — Phil. Seq. 412370-1PS

Strauss: *Don Quixote, Op. 35* (with Schönberg: *Cello Concerto*), Yo-yo Ma, Boston Symphony Orchestra, Ozawa, — IM 39863 (D)

Tchaikovsky: *Symphony No. 5*, Cleveland Orchestra, Szell — CBS MY 37767

Verdi: *La Traviata*, National Philharmonic, Bonynge — Lon LDR 73002 (D) / Lon LDR 71062 (D) (excerpts)

Wagner: *Tristan and Isolde*, Dresden State Opera, Kleiber — 5 DG 2741006 (D)

Die Meistersinger von Nürnburg (excerpts), New York Philharmonic, Bernstein — CBS MS–7141

TWENTIETH CENTURY (1900–PRESENT)

Armstrong: *The Genius of Louis Armstrong* (Vol. 1) — Col CG 30416

Bartók: *Concerto for Orchestra*, Chicago Symphony, Reiner — RCA AGL1-2909

Music for Strings, Percussion, and Celesta (with Berio: *Sinfonia*), New York Philharmonic Orchestra, Bernstein — CBS MP 38779

Beatles, The: *Sgt. Pepper's Lonely Hearts Club Band* — Cap SMAS 02653

Berg: *Violin Concerto*, London Symphony Orchestra, Zuckerman, Boulez — IM 39741

Davis: *Kind of Blue* — PC 8163

Debussy: *Le Mer* (with Ravel: *Daphnis et Chloé* & *Pavane*), Cleveland Orchestra, Szell — Odys YT 31928

Dylan: *Times They Are A-Changin'* — Col PC 8905

Ives: *The Unanswered Question* (with *Central Park in the Dark*), New York Philharmonic, Bernstein — MP 38777

Schönberg: *Serenade, Op. 24* (with "Song of the Wood Dove" from *Gurrelieder; Ode to Napoleon Bonaparte*), Ensemble InterContemporain, Boulez — M-36735

Stravinsky: *The Rite of Spring*, London Symphony Orchestra, Bernstein — CBS M-31520

Petrouchka (with *Firebird Suite*), New York Philharmonic, Bernstein — CBS MY-37221

Varèse: *Poème Electronique* (with *Density 21.5, Hyperprism, Intégrales, Ionisation, Octandre*), Columbia Symphony, Craft — MP 38873

Webern: *Complete Works* (Volume 1), Boulez (Op. 1–31) — MA 35193

ACKNOWLEDGMENTS

Grateful acknowledgment is made to the following copyright owners and agents for their permission to reprint the following copyrighted material. Every effort has been made to locate all copyright owners; any errors or omissions in copyright notice are inadvertent and will be corrected as they are discovered.

"Amen," arranged by Marion Downs, from *Junior High Sings.* Adapted, reprinted and recorded by permission of World Around Songs.

"Aura Lee," American folk song, arranged by Buryl Red. Copyright © 1980 Generic Music. Reprinted and recorded by permission.

"Bells and Pachelbels," music by Buryl Red. Copyright © 1986 by Generic Music. Reprinted and recorded by permission.

"By the Light of the Silvery Moon," words by Ed Madden, music by Gus Edwards. Copyright © 1909 (Renewed) WARNER BROS. INC. All Rights Reserved. Reprinted by Permission. Recording licensed through the Harry Fox Agency.

"Bye, Bye Blues," by Fred Hamm, Dave Bennett, Bert Lown and Chauncey Gray. © Copyright 1925, 1930, 1962 by Bourne Co., Music Publishers. Copyright renewed. Reprinted by permission. Recording licensed through the Harry Fox Agency.

"Can the Circle Be Unbroken," adapted and arranged by Dan Fox. This Arrangement Copyright © 1978 Cherry Lane Music Co., Inc. International Copyright Secured. All Rights Reserved. Reprinted by Permission. Recording licensed through the Harry Fox Agency.

"Carry It On," words and music by Gil Turner. TRO - © Copyright 1964 and 1965 Melody Trails, Inc., New York, NY. Reprinted by Permission of The Richmond Organization. Recording licensed through the Harry Fox Agency.

"A Christmas Happening," by Buryl Red, copyright © 1970 by Generic Music. Reprinted and recorded by permission.

"Come Join in the Chorus," music from "The Magic Flute" by Mozart, words from *The Three-Way Chorister* by Maurice Gardner, copyright © 1957 by Staff Music Publishing Company. Reprinted by permission. Recording licensed through the Harry Fox Agency.

"The Cruel War," by Paul Stookey and Peter Yarrow. © 1962 PEPAMAR MUSIC CORP. All Rights Reserved. Reprinted by Permission of Warner Bros. Music Corp. Recording licensed through the Harry Fox Agency.

"El Cumbanchero," Spanish words and music by Rafael Hernandez. Copyright © 1943 (Renewed) by Peer International Corporation. Reprinted by permission of Columbia Pictures Publications. Recording licensed through the Harry Fox Agency.

"Factory Fantasia," by Jay W. Gilbert, copyright by Jay W. Gilbert. Reprinted and recorded by permission.

"Fame," lyrics by Dean Pitchford, music by Michael Gore. Copyright ©1980 Metro-Goldwyn-Mayer Inc. All rights assigned to CBS Catalogue Partnership. All rights administered by CBS Affiliated Catalog Inc. Reprinted by permission of Columbia Pictures Publications. Recording rights licensed through the Harry Fox Agency.

"Finding the Fifth," from *Learning Unlimited Jazz Improvisation Series, Level 1: Blues and the Basics* by Dominic Spera. Copyright © 1975 by Hal Leonard Publishing Corporation. International Copyright Secured. ALL RIGHTS RESERVED. Reprinted by Permission. Recording licensed through the Harry Fox Agency.

"Follow," by Jack Noble White, arranged by Buryl Red. Copyright © 1985 by Hinshaw Music, Inc. Reprinted and recorded by permission.

"Freedom," lyric by Peter Udell, music by Gary Geld, from "Shenandoah." © 1974, 1975 GARY GELD and PETER UDELL. All Rights Controlled by EDWIN H. MORRIS & COMPANY, A Division of MPL Communications, Inc. International Copyright Secured. All Rights Reserved. Reprinted By Permission. Recording licensed through the Harry Fox Agency.

"The Gift of Song," words and music by Patti Ingalls, arranged by Buryl Red. Copyright © 1963 by Irving Music, Inc. (BMI). International Copyright Secured. Reprinted and recorded by permission.

"Gotta Travel On," words and music by Paul Clayton, copyright © 1958 by Sanga Music Inc. Reprinted by permission. Recording licensed through the Harry Fox Agency.

"Hodie Christus Natus Est," from A CEREMONY OF CAROLS by Benjamin Britten. © Copyright 1943 by Boosey & Co. Ltd.; Renewed 1970. Reprinted by permission of Boosey & Hawkes, Inc.

"Hyda," Israeli round, from *New Dimensions in Music, Grade 4,* copyright © 1980 by D. C. Heath and Company. Reprinted and recorded by permission.

"Joan's Blues," by Joan Wildman. Copyright by Joan Wildman. Reprinted and recorded by permission.

"Leavin's Not the Only Way to Go," words and music by Roger Miller. Copyright © 1985 by Tree Publishing Co., Inc. and Roger Miller Music, 8 Music Square West, Nashville, TN 37203. International Copyright Secured. ALL RIGHTS RESERVED. Reprinted by Permission of Hal Leonard Publishing Corporation. Recording licensed through the Harry Fox Agency.

"The Lesson Cycle," from *Model for Effective Teaching and Supervision* by Jim Boyd, copyright © 1985 by Jim Boyd. Reprinted by permission.

"Let the Rafters Ring," by Dick Smith. Copyright © 1966 by Up With People, Inc. Reprinted by permission. Recording licensed through the Harry Fox Agency.

"Let the Sun Shine In," words by James Rado and Gerome Ragni, music by Galt MacDermot. Copyright © 1966, 1967, 1968 James Rado, Gerome Ragni, Galt MacDermot, Nat Shapiro and United Artists Music Co., Inc. All rights controlled and administered by United Artists Music Co., Inc. Reprinted by permission of Columbia Pictures Publications. Recording licensed through the Harry Fox Agency.

"Looky, Looky Yonder," copyright © 1975 by Chappell & Co., Inc. International Copyright Secured. ALL RIGHTS RESERVED. Reprinted by Permission of Hal Leonard Publishing Corporation. Recording licensed through the Harry Fox Agency.

"The Lowered 'Blues' Seventh," from *Learning Unlimited Jazz Improvisation Series, Level 1: Blues and the Basics* by Dominic Spera. Copyright © 1975 by Hal Leonard Publishing Corporation. International Copyright Secured. ALL RIGHTS RESERVED. Reprinted by Permission. Recording licensed through the Harry Fox Agency.

"The Lowered 'Blues' Third," from *Learning Unlimited Jazz Improvisation Series, Level 1: Blues and the Basics* by Dominic Spera. Copyright © 1975 by Hal Leonard Publishing Corporation. International Copyright Secured. ALL RIGHTS RESERVED. Reprinted by Permission. Recording licensed through the Harry Fox Agency.

"Matilda," originally "Matilda Run Venezuela," new words and new music adaptation by Massie Peterson and Sammy Heyward, based on a traditional song. Copyright © 1963 by Ludlow Music, Inc. Copyright assigned to Samuel Patterson and Sammy Heyward. Reprinted and recorded by permission.

"Missa," words and music by Neil Diamond, © 1970 PROPHET MUSIC, INC. This arrangement © 1987 PROPHET

Classified Index of Music, Art, and Poetry

*Topics of special interest to teachers who use the Kodaly and Orff methods are indicated with a **K** and an **O**.*

Classified Index of Activities and Skills

*Topics of special interest to teachers who use the Kodaly and Orff methods are indicated with a **K** and an **O**.*

TEACHER'S NOTES

TEACHER'S NOTES

TEACHER'S NOTES

TEACHER'S NOTES